Practice Tests Plus

PTE ACADEMIC™

PEARSON TEST OF ENGLISH ACADEMIC

FROM THE TEST DEVELOPERS

TEACHING, NOT JUST TESTING

Pearson Education Limited
Edinburgh Gate
Harlow
Essex CM20 2JE
England
and Associated Companies throughout the world.

www.pearsonELT.com

First published 2013
Eighth impression 2017

ISBN: 978-1-4479-3794-4 (PTE Academic Practice Tests Plus with Key)

Set in Gill Sans
Printed in Slovakia by Neografia

Acknowledgements

We are grateful to the following for permission to reproduce copyright material:

Text

Article Test 1.2 adapted from Dark earth: How humans enriched the rainforests *New Scientist Magazine* (Fred Pearce); Extract Test 1.3 from Lecture: The University of Western Australia, Prof Richard Hobbs 26 March 2012; Extract Test 2.4 from http://www.cosmosmagazine.com/features/print/98/oceans-noise; Extract Test 2.5 from *Australian Geographic* (Gamble B), http://www.australiangeographic.com.au/journal/why-chillies-are-hot-the-science-behind-the-heat.htm; Extract Test 3.6 adapted from http://www2.lse.ac.uk/newsAndMedia/news/archives/2012/05/GlobalPolicy.aspx, London School of Economics and Political Science press office; Article Test 3.7 adapted from 'Oh, to be bilingual in the Anglosphere', *New Scientist*, 2863; Article Test 3.8 adapted from http://www.metoffice.gov.uk/learning/snow/how-is-snow-formed; Extract Test 3.9 adapted from http://openlearn.open.ac.uk/mod/oucontent/view.php?id=399252§ion=4.1; Extract Test 4.10 adapted from 'Expand your mindfulness', *Management Today* (Morrish J), http://www.managementtoday.co.uk/features/1133191/expand-mindfulness; Extract Test 4.11 adapted from http://politicalprof.tumblr.com/post/6352559015/in-defense-of-pointless-research; Article Test 4.12 adapted from http://www.google.co.uk/url?sa=t&rct=j&q=&esrc=s&source=web&cd=2&ved=0CC8QFjAB&url=http%3A%2F%2Fwww.sportengland.org%2Fresearch%2Fidoc.ashx%3Fdocid%3D9c94715d-c5e0-4479-9e7b-c67d8e8d4381%26version%3D-1&ei=6-ZFUJLhBsel0QWk7oDoBw&usg=AFQjCNFl-abzm_sV2n9MAgaRKfHoZgnDkQ, Professor Fred Coalter, Sport England and Professor Fred Coalter / Sport England /; Extract Test 4.13 adapted from *Nigeria's Traditional Crafts* ISBN 0905788 125, Ethnographica (Hodge A 1982) p.7; Extract Test 4.14 adapted from *Syllabus Design* ISBN194371395, OUP (Nunan D 1988) p.4; Extract Test 4.15 adapted from *America Observed* ISBN 0 14 011509 9, Penguin (Cooke A 1988) pp.1-2, © Cooke Americas, RLLP

In some instances we have been unable to trace the owners of copyright material, and we would appreciate any information that would enable us to do so.

Photographs

(Key: b-bottom; c-centre; l-left; r-right; t-top)
Alamy Images: Michael Kemp 67t; **Digital Vision**: 21t; **Fotolia.com**: Aaron Amat 122t; **Pearson Education Ltd**: Jules Selmes 122c; **PhotoDisc**: Keith Brofsky 21c; **Shutterstock.com**: Chad Kawalec Studios 21b, zhu difeng 95, Paul Fleet 67c, GuoZhongHua 122b

All other images © Pearson Education

In some instances we have been unable to trace the owners of copyright material, and we would appreciate any information that would enable us to do so.

Every effort has been made to chase the copyright holders and we apologise in advance for any unintentional omissions. We would be pleased to insert the appropriate acknowledgement in any subsequent edition of this publication.

Illustrations

Vladimir Dimitrov pp 19b, 66b, 67b, 92b, 94b, 95, 120t; **Svetlana Koeva** pp 17, 18, 19t, 64, 65, 66t, 92t, 93, 94t, 119, 120b, 121.

CONTENTS

INTRODUCTION

Test overview

PTE Academic (Pearson Test of English Academic) is an international computer-based English language test. It accurately measures English language ability and can be used to apply to educational institutions, and professional and government organizations. The test uses task-based questions to represent the kinds of functions and situations students will find themselves in during academic study.

Most real-life tasks in an academic setting involve using more than one language skill together, for example listening to a lecture and writing notes. PTE Academic reflects this through its 20 task types, each of which tests a combination of skills. For example, one task type asks you to demonstrate your understanding of a passage by providing a written summary, while another tests your understanding of a lecture by asking you to re-tell the lecture.

The test is divided into three main parts and lasts for approximately three hours with an optional break of ten minutes:

Part 1: Speaking and writing (77–93 minutes)

Part 2: Reading (32–41 minutes)

Part 3: Listening (45–57 minutes)

Part 1: Speaking and writing

Section	Task type	Task description	Time allowed
Section 1	Personal introduction	After reading the instructions, you have 30 seconds to give a recorded introduction about yourself. This part is not assessed, but is sent to institutions you choose along with your Score Report.	1 minute
Section 2	Read aloud	A text appears on screen. Read the text aloud.	30–35 minutes
	Repeat sentence	After listening to a sentence, repeat the sentence.	
	Describe image	An image appears on screen. Describe the image in detail.	
	Re-tell lecture	After listening to or watching a video of a lecture, re-tell the lecture in your own words.	
	Answer short question	After listening to a question, answer with a single word or a few words.	
Section 3–4	Summarize written text	After reading a passage, write a one-sentence summary of the passage of between 5 and 75 words.	20 minutes
Section 5	Summarize written text or Write essay	Either a *Summarize written text* task or a *Write essay* task, depending on the combination of tasks in your test.	10 or 20 minutes
Section 6	Write essay	Write an essay of 200–300 words on a given topic.	20 minutes

For more detail, see the Speaking and writing overview on page 11.

Part 2: Reading

Section	Task type	Task description	Time allowed
	Multiple-choice, choose single answer	After reading a text, answer a multiple-choice question on the content or tone of the text by selecting one response.	32–41 minutes
	Multiple-choice, choose multiple answers	After reading a text, answer a multiple-choice question on the content or tone of the text by selecting more than one response.	
	Re-order paragraphs	Several text boxes appear on screen in random order. Put the text boxes in the correct order.	
	Reading: Fill in the blanks	A text appears on screen with several blanks. Drag words or phrases from the blue box to fill in the blanks.	
	Reading & writing: Fill in the blanks	A text appears on screen with several blanks. Fill in the blanks by selecting words from several drop-down lists of response options.	

For more detail, see the Reading overview on page 29.

Part 3: Listening

Section	Task type	Task description	Time allowed
Section 1	Summarize spoken text	After listening to a recording, write a summary of 50–70 words.	20 or 30 minutes
Section 2	Multiple-choice, choose multiple answers	After listening to a recording, answer a multiple-choice question on the content or tone of the recording by selecting more than one response.	23–28 minutes
	Fill in the blanks	The transcription of a recording appears on screen with several blanks. While listening to the recording, type the missing words into the blanks.	
	Highlight correct summary	After listening to a recording, select the paragraph that best summarizes the recording.	
	Multiple-choice, choose single answer	After listening to a recording, answer a multiple-choice question on the content or tone of the recording by selecting one response.	
	Select missing word	After listening to a recording, select the missing word or group of words that completes the recording.	
	Highlight incorrect words	The transcription of a recording appears on screen. While listening to the recording, identify the words in the transcription that differ from what is said.	
	Write from dictation	After listening to a recording of a sentence, type the sentence.	

For more detail, see the Listening overview on page 44.

Introduction to PTE Academic Practice Tests Plus

PTE Academic Practice Tests Plus includes three main sections

First, there is an introduction to the test and to the *Practice Tests Plus* book. This gives you information about the test itself, about taking the test, and about how you can use this book to help you prepare.

The main section of the book is the practice tests. There are four complete tests, all written by people who write the actual test. Test 1 provides a full page of information and strategies for each of the 20 task types. There is a tip for each question in Test 1 to help you get used to the task and how to approach it. Some tips refer directly to the content of the question and some give general guidance. In Test 2, there is one tip for each task type with a useful reminder of how to do the task. Then, in Tests 3 and 4, you're on your own!

Finally, the *with key* version of the book includes the detailed answer key, audio scripts and sample answers from PTE Academic students along with explanations to help you see how your answers might score.

Paper-based practice – computer-based test

You will do the actual test on a computer at a Pearson test centre and when you complete a task, the next one will appear on the screen. You will hear the audio through your headphones and speak into the microphone on your headset. You will be able to take notes on an Erasable Noteboard Booklet, but you will type your answers into the computer.

The practice tests in this book are paper-based and are designed to be used in class or for self study. The instructions on the page are exactly the same as those you will get in the actual test. This means you won't have any surprises when you get to the test centre! However, because the instructions are for a digital format, they don't tell you exactly what to do on paper. You will find some advice on this below.

You can see what the task will look like on screen in Test 1, where you will find a screenshot for each task type in the *About the task type* section before the actual tasks. You will also find a grey 'In the test' box with a mouse cursor at the beginning of each task type in all four tests. This gives you a short description of the on-screen task.

In the test, there are 6–7 tasks. For each task, you read the text aloud into the microphone. The wording in the instructions below is the same as you will see in the actual test. See page 12 for help.

Timings

In the test, some tasks are automatically timed by the length of the audio and some tasks have a timer. When you use the *Practice Tests Plus* book, you can choose to time yourself or to take as long as you need. You could time yourself using your watch, mobile phone or computer.

If there is a time limit for a task, you will find this information in the timer icon next to the instructions.

Listening tasks

For some tasks, you have to listen to an audio extract and then complete the task. In the test, the audio will begin automatically after you have had time to read the instructions. Using the practice tests, you will have to play the relevant audio track yourself. You will find the relevant track number next to the task. ❶ ▸31

Each task is on a separate track. This means you can work on tasks individually, or keep the audio running to try a complete set of tasks for a task type.

Giving answers

You will have to give one of three kinds of answers: spoken, written or computer-based interaction (choosing answers from those presented on screen).

Spoken answers

In the test, you will speak into the microphone on your headset. There will be a message on screen telling you when you will begin speaking, and then how long you have been speaking for.

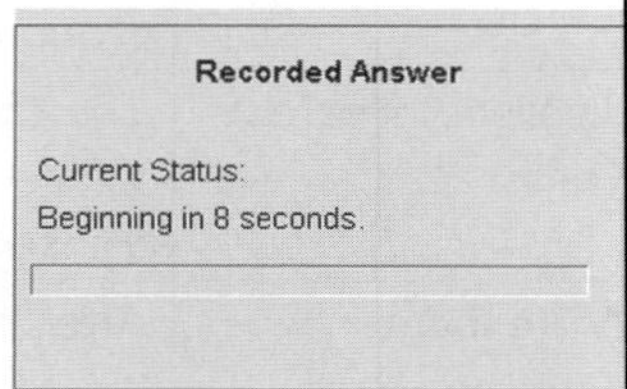

When using the practice tests, it is a good idea to record your answers so that you can listen back and think about how to improve. You could record your answers on your computer or mobile phone. Alternatively, you can work with a partner and take turns to answer the tasks and listen to each other.

Written answers

When you sit the actual test, you will type your answers into the computer. Here, there is space for you to write most of your answers directly into the practice tests book. If you prefer, you could write your answers in a notebook. For the *Write essay* task, it is a good idea to practise typing your answer on the computer. In the test, you will be able to cut, copy and paste text.

Computer-based interaction

For some tasks in the Reading and Listening parts, you have to use tools on the computer screen, for example click the correct answer from a drop-down list, select the correct button or drag and drop the correct word into the box. Although this book has paper-based practice tests, the instructions are exactly the same as you will see on the computer in the actual test. When practising, simply write your answer in the relevant box, or tick the button next to the correct answer.

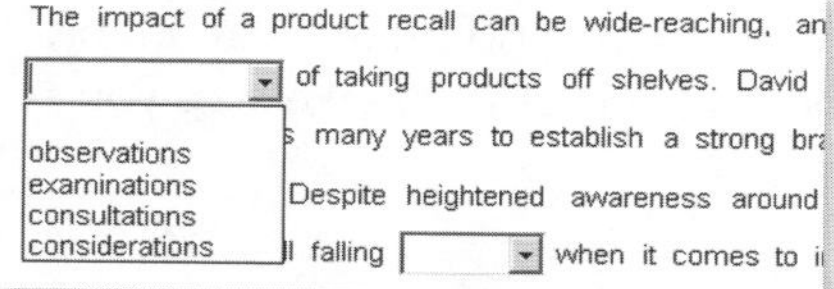

On screen, click the correct answer.

adults' and 'established adults'. [4] ______ markets no longer talk about 'children', but tend to refer to a fuller range of categories that includes 'kids', 'tweens', 'pre-teens' and 'teenagers'. We now have a very diverse population in terms of age, and that can only be a [5] *bonus* for business.

1	A usual	B precise	C right	D honest
2	A linked	B mixed	C concerned	D involved
3	A rather than	B by	C even when	D while
4	A While	B Similarly	C Even	D Really
5	A desire	B favour	C bonus	D promise

On the page, write the correct answer in the box.

Scoring the practice tests

Some tasks in PTE Academic have clear right answers, for example the *Multiple-choice* and *Fill in the blanks* tasks. For these tasks, there are clear answers in the *with key* version of the book.

For most tasks with spoken or written answers, you will score within a range because the task tests a number of language areas, for example content, grammar, etc. For these tasks, you will find three sample responses in the *with key* version of the book, at B1, B2 and C1 level, all with brief explanations. To get an idea of your score on these tasks, look at all of the sample answers. Which is closest to your answer? What did you do better or less well than this student? For the *Write essay* questions, there is also a model essay outline for each task.

Task type	Skills assessed	Type of answer
Part 1: Speaking and writing		
Personal introduction	not assessed	no answer
Read aloud	reading and speaking	sample response
Repeat sentence	listening and speaking	sample response
Describe image	speaking	sample response
Re-tell lecture	listening and speaking	sample response
Answer short question	listening and speaking	right answer
Summarize written text	reading and writing	sample response
Write essay	writing	sample response
Part 2: Reading		
Multiple-choice, choose single answer	reading	right answer
Multiple-choice, choose multiple answers	reading	right answer
Re-order paragraphs	reading	right answer
Reading: Fill in the blanks	reading	right answer
Reading & writing: Fill in the blanks	reading and writing	right answer
Part 3: Listening		
Summarize spoken text	listening and writing	sample response
Multiple-choice, choose multiple answers	listening	right answer
Fill in the blanks	listening and writing	right answer
Highlight correct summary	listening and reading	right answer
Multiple-choice, choose single answer	listening	right answer
Select missing word	listening	right answer
Highlight incorrect words	listening and reading	right answer
Write from dictation	listening and writing	right answer

Preparing for PTE Academic

If you know exactly what to expect before you sit the test, you will feel more confident on the day and increase your chances of doing well. Try to familiarize yourself with the test as much as possible, for example:

- how long the test lasts, and how this is divided into the different test parts and tasks
- how many tasks there are in each part and in the test as a whole
- what the different task types are
- what you will be asked to do for each task type
- what the tasks will look like on screen
- what skills are assessed in each task type and how they will be scored

Don't forget to think about your personal introduction. See page 10 for more information.

There are many different ways to use the practice tests in this book. You may use them in class or for self study. If you use them in class, your teacher will tell you which sections to complete when and advise you on how to give your answers.

Below you will find some ideas for using the tests for self study.

Get to know the task types

Use Test 1 to focus on the task types, one task type at a time.

- First, read the strategy page to find out what the task involves and what is expected of you. This will also give you some ideas of the kinds of study you need to do to be successful in this task type.
- Next, look at the first task and make sure you understand exactly what you have to do. Use the tip to help you.
- Complete the task as well as you can.
- If you have the *with key* version of the book, look at the score guide at the back of the book and think about what the purpose of the task is. Then look at the key or the sample student answers to get an idea of how you did.
- Work through the rest of the questions for that task type in Test 1.

Think about timing

You could use one of the practice tests to work on timing.

- Look at the instructions or the overview in Test 1 to find out how long you have to answer each task for that task type.
- Think about how you will spend that time. For example, in the *Write essay* task, how much of that time will you spend planning, writing and checking? In the *Describe image* task, how long should you spend on an introductory description, how long on detail and how long on conclusions?
- Set a countdown on your mobile phone or computer, then try one task and get a feel for how long you have to speak, read or write.
- Time yourself, moving immediately on to the next task, and work through all of the tasks for that task type.

Take a mock test

Before you take the actual test, you could work through a whole practice test, timing yourself for each section to get an idea of how you would do on test day. In this case, try to find somewhere quiet and make sure you will not be interrupted.

Analyze your answers

However you have answered the tasks, it is very useful to spend time looking at your answers.

For questions with a spoken response, record yourself completing the tasks. Then think about what you think a good answer would include. If you have the *with key* version, listen to the sample student answers and look at the examiner comments. Then listen to your answer and think about how you did on that task, and how you could improve in the future. Use the score guide to help you.

Similarly, if you need to give a written answer, complete the task. Then look at the answer key, where you will see a model answer with an explanation, where relevant. Look at the sample student answers with comments, and compare them to the model answer and your own. How did you do, and how could you improve in the future?

Taking the test

When you take the actual test, you'll go to one of Pearson's secure test centres. You can find your nearest centre on the Pearson website at www.pearsonpte.com. This is also where you can register and book a test for a time that suits you.

On the day, make sure you arrive early so that you have time to register and go through the security procedure. Then you'll be taken to a computer and the test will begin. All parts of the test are done at a computer and the whole test takes around three hours. This includes an untimed introduction and one optional break of up to ten minutes.

After the test, you'll get an email to tell you that your PTE Academic scores are ready. This is normally within five working days from your test date. You can then log in to your account to view and print your scores, and send them to the institutions that you choose. Your scores are valid for two years from your test date.

Your Score Report

Your Score Report will give you an overall score on the Pearson Scale of English. This will then be broken down into the four communicative skills: listening, reading, speaking and writing. You will also get a score for enabling skills: grammar, oral fluency, pronunciation, spelling, vocabulary and written discourse. Please see page 145 for more detail on scores.

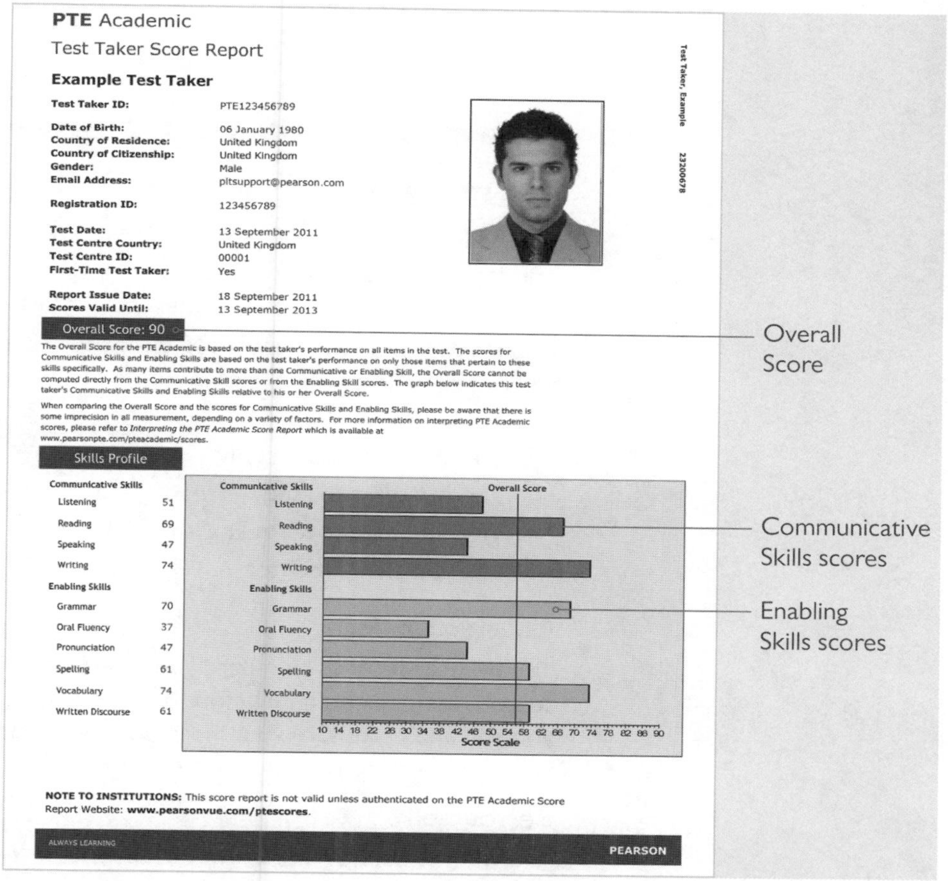

PTE Academic

Test Taker Score Report

Example Test Taker

Test Taker, Example 23200678

Test Taker ID:	PTE123456789
Date of Birth:	06 January 1980
Country of Residence:	United Kingdom
Country of Citizenship:	United Kingdom
Gender:	Male
Email Address:	pitsupport@pearson.com
Registration ID:	123456789
Test Date:	13 September 2011
Test Centre Country:	United Kingdom
Test Centre ID:	00001
First-Time Test Taker:	Yes
Report Issue Date:	18 September 2011
Scores Valid Until:	13 September 2013

Overall Score: 90

The Overall Score for the PTE Academic is based on the test taker's performance on all items in the test. The scores for Communicative Skills and Enabling Skills are based on the test taker's performance on only those items that pertain to these skills specifically. As many items contribute to more than one Communicative or Enabling Skill, the Overall Score cannot be computed directly from the Communicative Skill scores or from the Enabling Skill scores. The graph below indicates this test taker's Communicative Skills and Enabling Skills relative to his or her Overall Score.

When comparing the Overall Score and the scores for Communicative Skills and Enabling Skills, please be aware that there is some imprecision in all measurement, depending on a variety of factors. For more information on interpreting PTE Academic scores, please refer to *Interpreting the PTE Academic Score Report* which is available at www.pearsonpte.com/pteacademic/scores.

Skills Profile

Communicative Skills	
Listening	51
Reading	69
Speaking	47
Writing	74
Enabling Skills	
Grammar	70
Oral Fluency	37
Pronunciation	47
Spelling	61
Vocabulary	74
Written Discourse	61

NOTE TO INSTITUTIONS: This score report is not valid unless authenticated on the PTE Academic Score Report Website: **www.pearsonvue.com/ptescores**.

ALWAYS LEARNING PEARSON

Your Score Report will be ready within five working days.

Personal introduction

About the task type

At the beginning of the test you will be asked to introduce yourself, speaking into the microphone for 30 seconds. This *Personal introduction* is not scored. The purpose is to give university admissions officers an impression of you as a person. Institutions also use the recorded introduction as an additional identity check. Your introduction will be sent along with your Score Report to the institutions that you choose.

You will have 25 seconds to read the instructions, then 30 seconds to record your introduction. There is a Recording Status box which will tell you when to start recording and how much time you have left. You cannot re-record your introduction.

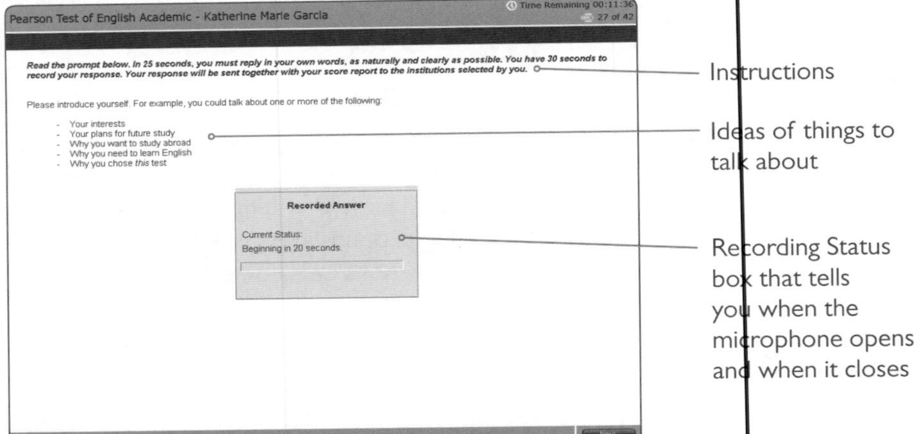

Task strategies

Be prepared!

This is your opportunity to give the admissions officers a first impression of who you are – so make it a positive one! For this task, you can be completely prepared.

Plan in advance what you want to talk about. Start by giving your name, and saying where you're from. Then, include some of the ideas from the instructions:

- Your interests
- Your plans for future study
- Why you want to study abroad
- Why you need to learn English
- Why you chose *this* test

Check your timing

You have 30 seconds to record your message, and you only have one opportunity to get it right! Spend time before the test practising your introduction. Time yourself and make sure your message takes as close to 30 seconds as possible – you don't want to run out of time!

Be yourself

You want to sound natural. Try not to write a speech and memorize it – this can often sound very unnatural and nerves on the day might make you forget the exact words you rehearsed. Instead, practise the kinds of things you want to say. Record yourself speaking, then listen to your introduction. If you were an admissions officer, would your message make a positive impression?

TEST 1

Overview: Speaking and writing

Part 1 of the PTE Academic test is Speaking and writing. This part tests your ability to produce spoken and written English in an academic environment.

The table shows what you will see in the test, which you will take on a computer. When practising with this book, you will have to write your written answers in the book, your notebook or on your own computer, and you could record your spoken answers on your own computer or mobile phone.

Part 1: Speaking and writing					
Speaking (total time 30–35 minutes)					
Task type	**Number of tasks**	**Task description**	**Skills assessed**	**Text/ Recording length**	**Time to answer**
Read aloud	6–7	A text appears on screen. Read the text aloud into your microphone.	reading and speaking	text up to 60 words	varies by task, depending on the length of text
Repeat sentence	10–12	After listening to a sentence, repeat the sentence into your microphone.	listening and speaking	3–9 seconds	15 seconds
Describe image	6–7	An image appears on screen. Describe the image in detail into your microphone.	speaking	n/a	40 seconds
Re-tell lecture	3–4	After listening to or watching a lecture, re-tell the lecture in your own words into your microphone.	listening and speaking	up to 90 seconds	40 seconds
Answer short question	10–12	After listening to a question, answer with a single word or a few words into your microphone.	listening and speaking	3–9 seconds	10 seconds
Writing (total time 50–60 minutes)					
Task type	**Number of tasks**	**Task description**	**Skills assessed**	**Text/ Recording length**	**Time to answer**
Summarize written text	2–3	After reading a passage, write a one-sentence summary of the passage.	reading and writing	text up to 300 words	10 minutes
Write essay	1–2	Write an essay of 200–300 words on a given topic.	writing	up to 4 sentences	20 minutes

Each recording is played only once. You may take notes using the Erasable Noteboard Booklet and pen, and use these notes as a guide when answering the tasks.

Speaking task types are not timed individually, but writing task types are. In both sections you can refer to the timer in the upper right-hand corner of the computer screen, *Time Remaining*, which counts down the time remaining for the Speaking section.

Read aloud

About the task type

This is a long-answer speaking task type that tests reading and speaking skills. You have to read aloud a short text, with correct pronunciation and intonation. You will do 6–7 *Read aloud* tasks.

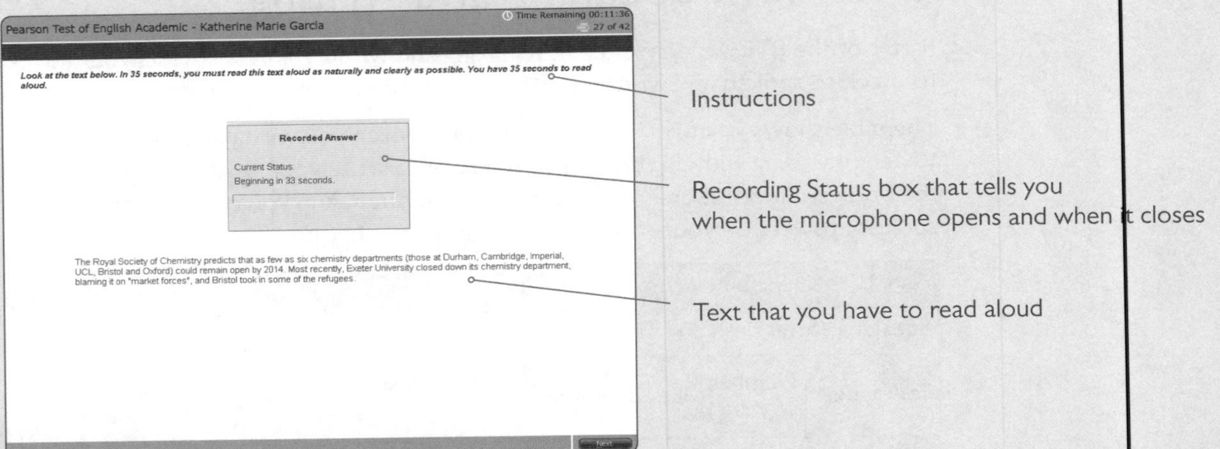

STRATEGIES

Strategies

Read the text through first

- Use the 30–40 seconds before the microphone opens to skim the text and understand the topic.
- Use the punctuation and grammar to identify where pauses will be needed between meaning groups.
- Identify any words that may be less familiar to you and think how they might be pronounced.
- Read the first part aloud before the microphone opens. This will help you to begin speaking when you hear the tone.

While you read

- Begin reading as soon as the tone sounds and the recording status changes to a blue bar. As you read, stress the words that carry important information. Use pausing to group the text into meaningful chunks.
- Use rising intonation to show a contrast, and falling intonation to show that you have finished a point or sentence, or come to the end of what you are saying.

Take your time

- You have plenty of time so do not rush. Read with meaning, at a normal volume. Do not leave out any words.
- If you make a mistake, correct it and continue. Do not stop reading, and do not begin again at the beginning. Click 'Next' when you are ready to go on to the next task.

Testing focus Scoring ➤ page 147

Subskills tested

Reading: identifying a writer's purpose, style, tone or attitude; understanding academic vocabulary; reading a text under timed conditions.

Speaking: speaking for a purpose (to repeat, to inform, to explain); reading a text aloud; speaking at a natural rate; producing fluent speech; using correct intonation; using correct pronunciation; using correct stress; speaking under timed conditions.

Preparation

- Practise reading sentences out loud, grouping the words into meaningful chunks. Practise putting short pauses at commas and between meaning groups, and longer pauses at full stops.
- Select 6 or 7 short texts of 2 or 3 sentences (up to 60 words) from a magazine or online. Look at the punctuation and grammar and mark the chunks with a slash /. Time yourself reading each one. After 40 seconds, go on to the next text.
- Listen to the way the final sound in one word links to the first sound in the next when people speak. Try to do this when you read aloud.
- You will score higher if your fluency shows a natural rhythm, which is given by chunking and stress. Read a sentence and clap your hands on each stressed word. Be aware of the weak forms between stressed words.
- When practising reading aloud, read on smoothly even if you make a mistake as hesitations, false starts and repetitions can lower your score.
- Practise using rising intonation in lists and falling intonation at the end of sentences.
- When you learn a new word, use a dictionary that has the words recorded so you can check both the pronunciation of the sounds and where the word stress falls.
- You will read more fluently if you understand what you are reading, so work on your reading and vocabulary skills as well as your speaking skills.

Read aloud

TIP STRIP

1. Break the text up into chunks and pause slightly between each one as you read. Before the recording begins, use the punctuation to help you decide where to pause and where each new chunk will begin.
2. As you read, stress the words that carry important information. This makes it easier to understand what you are saying.
3. Use rising intonation patterns to show a contrast. For example, here you need to contrast the *buildings* with *trees*.
4. Try to get the word stress right on multi-syllable words. In Text 4, there are words that end in '*ion*'. Usually, the stress falls on the syllable before this – *pollution*, *combustion*, *stations*.
5. Look for sense groups, as well as the grammatical structure, to notice which groups of words should be said in one chunk: */ to provide individuals with an income / once they stop working /*.
6. Use falling intonation patterns to show that you have finished a point, or come to the end of what you are saying: *on our moods, about our lives*.

In the test, there are 6–7 tasks. For each task, you read the text aloud into the microphone. The wording in the instructions below is the same as you will see in the actual test. See page 12 for help.

40 sec. **Look at the text below. In 40 seconds, you must read this text aloud as naturally and as clearly as possible. You have 40 seconds to read aloud.**

1. Market research is a vital part of the planning of any business. However experienced you or your staff may be in a particular field, if you are thinking of introducing a service to a new area, it is important to find out what the local population thinks about it first.

2. Not a lot is known about how the transportation of goods by water first began. Large cargo boats were being used in some parts of the world up to five thousand years ago. However, sea trade became more widespread when large sailing boats travelled between ports, carrying spices, perfumes and objects made by hand.

3. When the young artist was asked about his drawing, he explained that he had started by taking a photograph of himself sitting by a window at home. He then drew his face from the photograph and replaced the buildings which were outside the window with trees. This gave the picture a softer, more artistic background.

4. Humans need to use energy in order to exist. So it is unsurprising that the way people have been producing energy is largely responsible for current environmental problems. Pollution comes in many forms, but those that are most concerning, because of their impact on health, result from the combustion of fuels in power stations and cars.

5. Clearly, times are changing and while many people are saving for their retirement, many more still need to do so. Most countries have a range of pension schemes that are designed to provide individuals with an income once they stop working. People need to take advantage of these if they are to have sufficient money throughout their retirement years.

6. According to recent research, sunshine and warm weather have a positive effect on our moods. The British Journal of Psychology has published a report in which it claims that anxiety levels fall when temperatures rise, while increased exposure to sunshine makes us think more positively about our lives.

Repeat sentence

About the task type

This is a short-answer speaking task type that tests listening and speaking skills. You have to repeat a sentence that you hear, with correct pronunciation. You will do 10–12 *Repeat sentence* tasks.

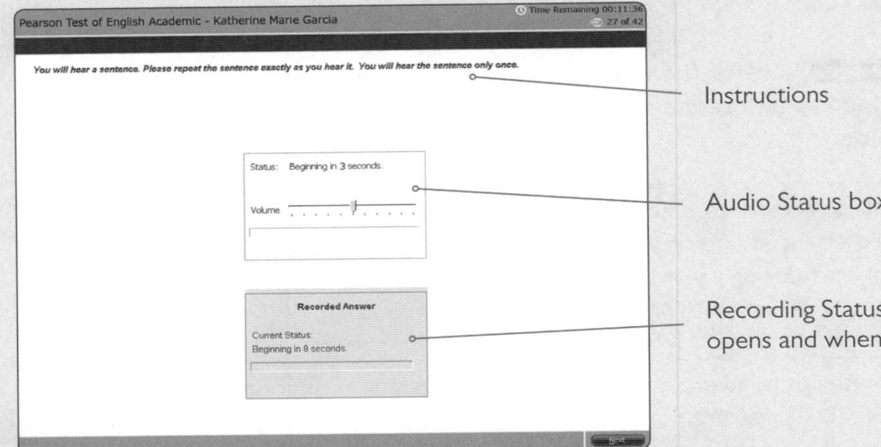

STRATEGIES

Strategies

Be ready

- The Audio Status box will count down from 3 seconds and then the recording will play.
- Be ready to hear, understand and repeat the short sentence (3 to 9 seconds). Stay focused.

Focus on the meaning

- Listen to the way the speaker groups words into meaningful phrases, and copy this phrasing.
- Listen for the speaker's intonation and try to copy it.
- Listen for the grammatical structure to help you to reconstruct what you have heard.
- There isn't time to write the words.

Speak clearly

- Wait until the blue bar that shows the microphone is open, then speak; there is no tone. Remember, the microphone will close after 3 seconds of silence.
- Take a breath before you speak; this will help you speak clearly.
- Say every word you hear, but if you don't know a word, say what you think you heard.
- Pronounce the vowels and consonants clearly, and link words together as the speaker did.
- Speak at a normal speed and volume, and don't rush – you have plenty of time.
- Don't try to copy the speaker's accent; just speak normally.
- Click 'Next' to move on.

Testing focus Scoring ➤ page 147

Subskills tested

Listening: understanding academic vocabulary; inferring the meaning of unfamiliar words; comprehending variations in tone, speed and accent.

Speaking: speaking for a purpose (to repeat, to inform, to explain); speaking at a natural rate; producing fluent speech; using correct intonation; using correct pronunciation; using correct stress; speaking under timed conditions.

Preparation

- Train your short-term memory by repeating short announcements or advertisements that you hear; ask a friend to read aloud 10–12 short sentences from a magazine for you to repeat each one.
- Develop your understanding of English grammar so that you recognize verb phrases and clause structure. When you hear someone speaking, repeat the words to yourself and think of the structures they used.
- Your score will be higher if you say the correct words in the right sequence, so practise saying phrases with correct word order.
- Use a dictionary where you can listen to the words pronounced in different accents so that when you learn a new word you also know what it sounds like.
- Practise saying new words with the correct syllable stress. Check the dictionary if you are not sure.
- Notice where people put the stress in sentences – the important words are stressed and the other words are weak or unstressed. Try to do this when you speak; your score will be higher if your rhythm, phrasing and stress are smooth and effective.
- Listen to someone giving a talk in a podcast and stop the recording regularly so you can repeat the words you heard. Begin by stopping after 3 or 4 words, then gradually expand until you stop about every 7–9 seconds.
- Listen to podcasts by speakers with different English accents to become familiar with them.

Repeat sentence

TIP STRIP

1. Listen to the way the speaker groups the words into meaningful phrases, e.g. *such as cost and function*, *the design of a bridge*.
2. Speak as clearly as you can. If you mumble, your words may not be recognized.
3. Listen to the speaker's intonation and aim to copy this.
4. Listen to the syllable stress on long words, such as *financial* and *available* and say the words the same way.
5. Note how the speaker uses word stress to highlight the important information, for example, *Extra seminars*. Try to do the same.
6. Your score will be improved if you produce correct word sequences including phrasal verbs such as *switch off* and noun phrases such as *electronic devices*.
7. Many words in a sentence are unstressed or 'weak forms', for example in the phrase *as a team*, *as a* is unstressed. You will not hear weak forms clearly but the grammar tells you they are present.
8. Remember there is no tone before the microphone opens in this task, so start to speak as soon as the Status box changes to 'Recording'.
9. Be prepared for long noun phrases before the verb in some tasks, as in *Detailed analysis of population growth*.
10. You will hear a range of accents in this task, but don't try to copy the accent. Just speak naturally.

In the test, there are 10–12 tasks. For each task, you listen and repeat the sentence you hear into the microphone. The wording in the instructions below is the same as you will see in the actual test. See page 14 for help.

▶ 2–11 15 sec. You will hear a sentence. Please repeat the sentence exactly as you hear it. You will hear the sentence only once.

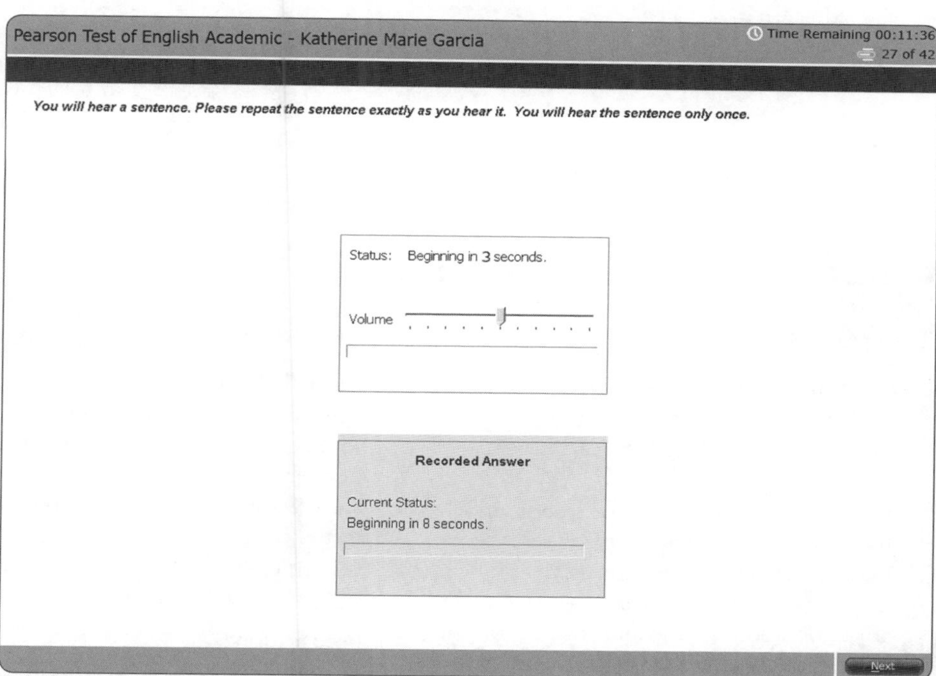

Repeat sentence: Each question is displayed on a new screen.

TEST 1 SPEAKING

Describe image

About the task type

This is a long-answer speaking task type that tests speaking skills. You have 40 seconds to describe the information in a graph, chart, map, picture or table. You will do 6–7 *Describe image* tasks.

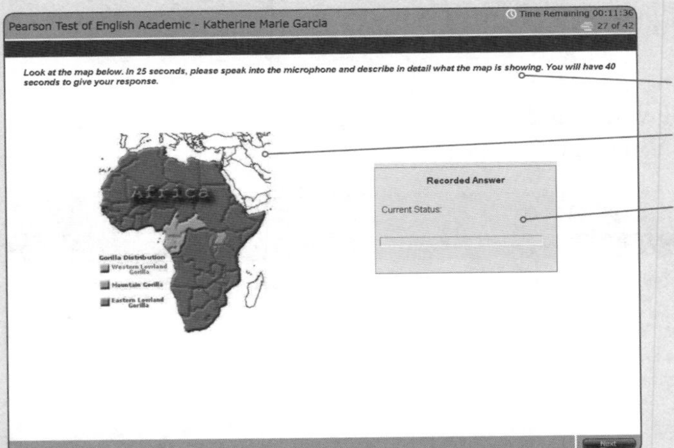

Strategies

Look carefully at the image

- You have 25 seconds before the microphone opens to look carefully at the image.
- Identify the main features or trends, and the names of features or variables in labels. Identify the significant features, major contrasts or changes over time. Think of any implications of the information, or any conclusions that can be drawn.
- Make notes of the main points on your Erasable Noteboard Booklet, and decide the order in which you will describe the information.

Focus on the main points

- After the tone, start with a general statement of what the image is about. Then describe the most important features or trends or contrasts.
- Don't try to describe every detail; use relevant data to illustrate the main points of the information.
- Use your notes to make sure your description is clearly organized.
- Conclude with a comment on any implications or conclusions.

Keep speaking

- Keep speaking. The more you say, the more thorough your description will be.
- If you make an error in the information, don't worry; correct yourself and move on. When the microphone closes, click 'Next'.

Testing focus Scoring ➤ page 148

Subskills tested

Speaking: speaking for a purpose (to repeat, to inform, to explain); supporting an opinion with details, examples and explanations; organizing an oral presentation in a logical way; developing complex ideas within a spoken discourse; using words and phrases appropriate to the context; using correct grammar; speaking at a natural rate; producing fluent speech; using correct intonation; using correct pronunciation; using correct stress; speaking under timed conditions.

Preparation

- Practise interpreting different types of image, including line, bar and pie graphs, process diagrams and maps, that you see in news stories.
- Find an image that interests you. Take brief notes of the main points using key words, with arrows to indicate the order of what you will say. Practise using your notes to organize your description.
- Practise giving an overview by summarizing the information in an image in one sentence. Set a timer so that you are ready to give the overview after 25 seconds.
- You will score higher if you include, as well as all the main points, any developments or implications, or any conclusions that can be drawn.
- Set a timer for 40 seconds and practise describing a picture or graph so you are familiar with the time you have to speak in this task. Then find 6 or 7 images to describe, and practise describing all of them, with 25 seconds to look at each image and 40 seconds to describe it.
- Record yourself describing an image then compare your response with the image to check how complete your description was.
- Practise using words and phrases used to describe amounts (*more than, less than, approximately*) and trends (*rose, fell, fluctuated, remained stable*), as well as comparatives and superlatives (*greatest, highest, lowest, higher than, lower than*).

STRATEGIES

Describe image

TIP STRIP

1. Look at the image carefully and make sure you understand what it shows. If you have a graph, look closely at both axes. In this graph, the vertical axis shows the percentage of the world population NOT the population figures.
2. If there are two graphs or charts, this means you have to make comparisons. Look for the most significant similarities and differences.

In the test, there are 6–7 tasks. For each task, you look at the image and describe it into the microphone. The wording in the instructions below is the same as you will see in the actual test. See page 16 for help.

1 40 sec. Look at the graph below. In 25 seconds, please speak into the microphone and describe in detail what the graph is showing. You will have 40 seconds to give your response.

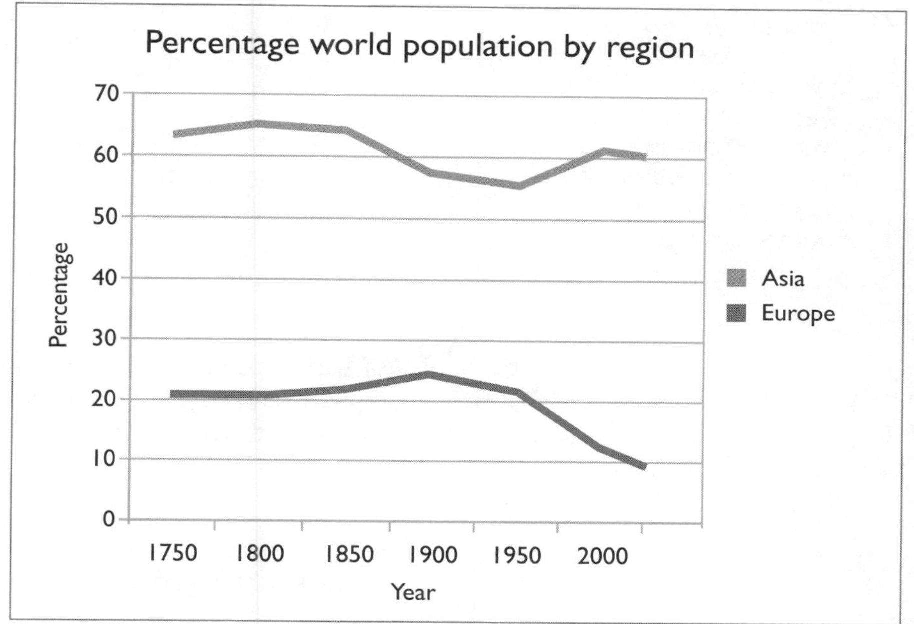

2 40 sec. Look at the charts below. In 25 seconds, please speak into the microphone and describe in detail what the charts are showing. You will have 40 seconds to give your response.

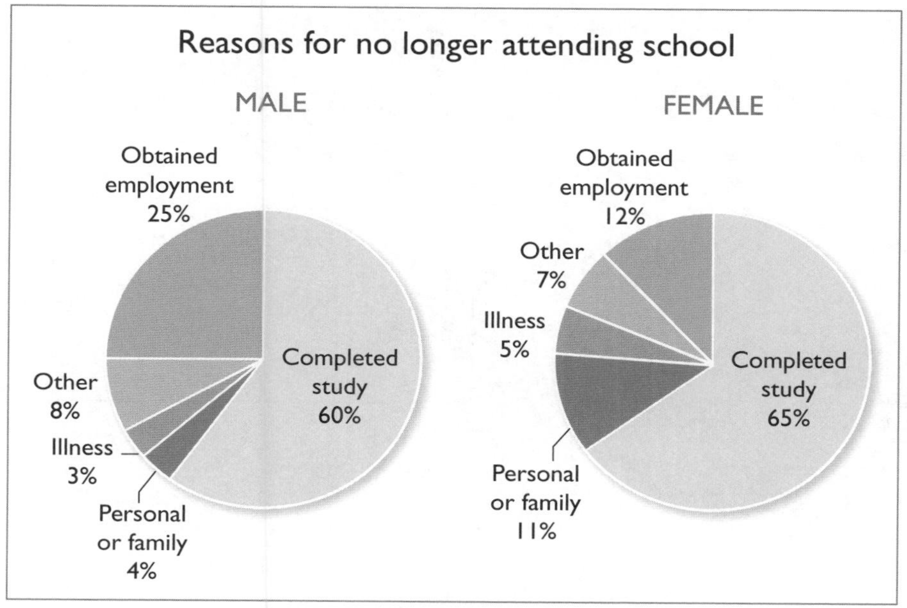

TEST 1

SPEAKING

3 40 sec. Look at the chart below. In 25 seconds, please speak into the microphone and describe in detail what the chart is showing. You will have 40 seconds to give your response.

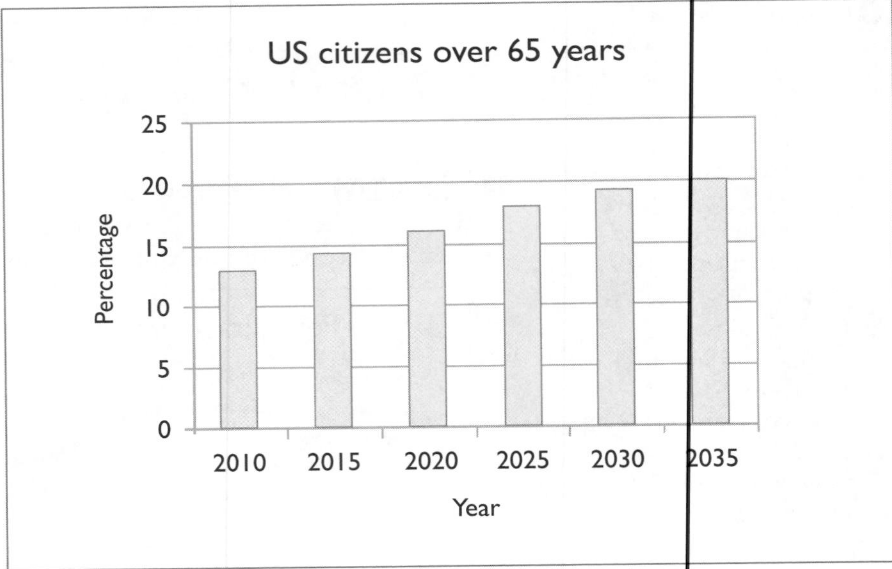

4 40 sec. Look at the graph below. In 25 seconds, please speak into the microphone and describe in detail what the graph is showing. You will have 40 seconds to give your response.

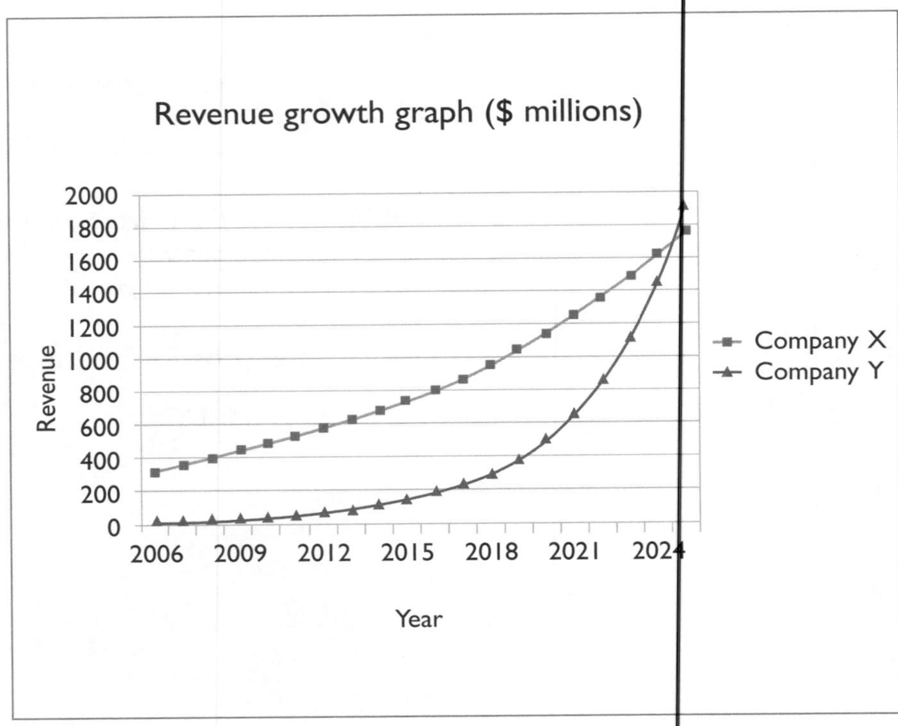

TIP STRIP

3 Look at the overall idea or pattern and make sure you describe that. Don't just focus on the details. You will score higher if you include possible developments, conclusions or implications.

4 When a graph gives information on large numbers or quantities, make sure you say these correctly. In this case, the graph title tells you that it shows figures in millions of dollars, not hundreds.

TIP STRIP

5 You cannot always describe every point on a graph. Look at the trend. If it is quite steady, describe what it shows overall and only highlight significant differences.

6 If you have a diagram of a process, start by describing the different parts or elements of the process and then move on to describing the process itself.

5 40 sec. Look at the graph below. In 25 seconds, please speak into the microphone and describe in detail what the graph is showing. You will have 40 seconds to give your response.

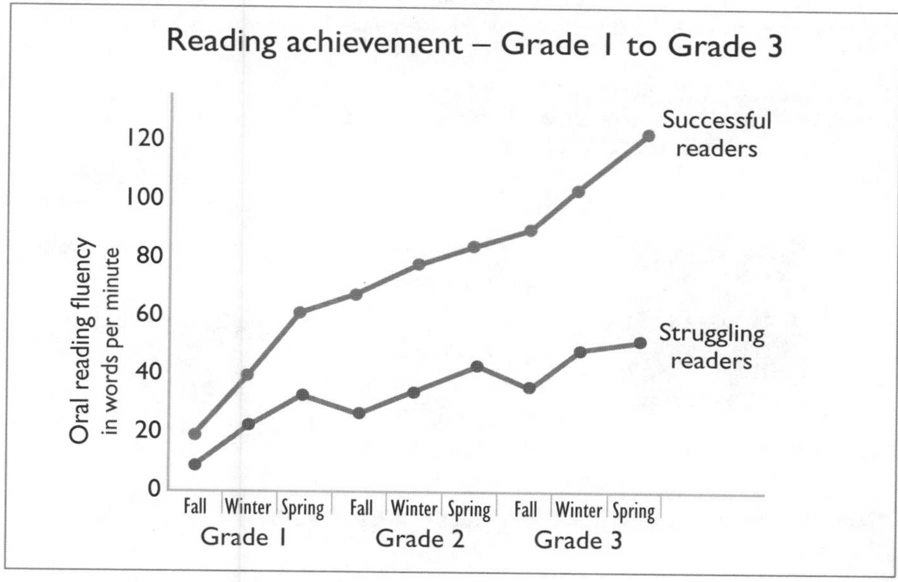

6 40 sec. Look at the diagram below. In 25 seconds, please speak into the microphone and describe in detail what the diagram is showing. You will have 40 seconds to give your response.

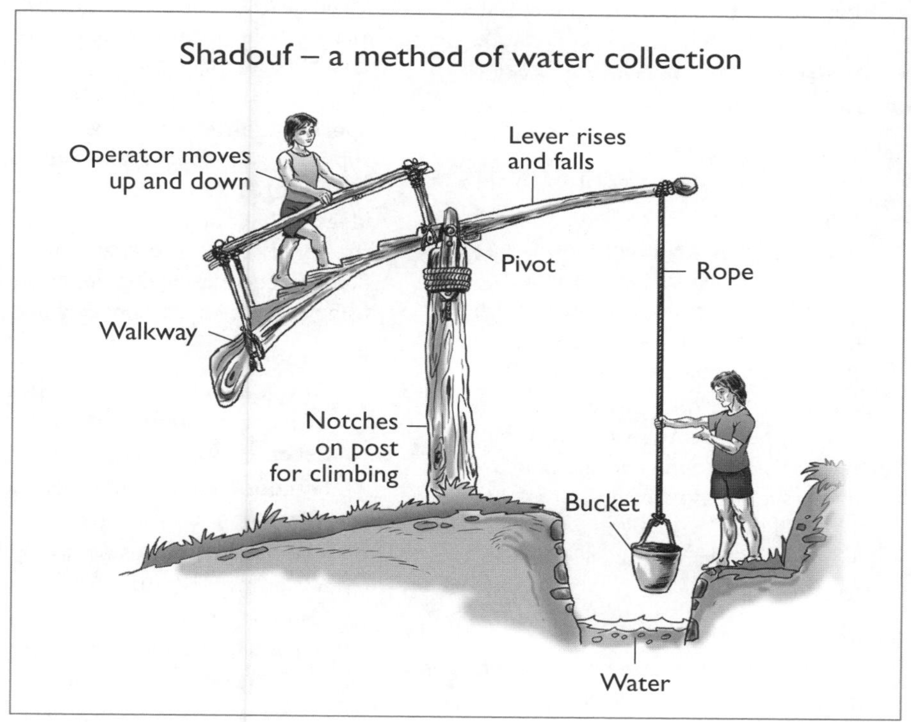

TEST 1 SPEAKING

Re-tell lecture

About the task type

This is a long-answer speaking task type that tests both listening and speaking skills. You have to re-tell in your own words the information in a 60–90 second lecture. You will do 3–4 *Re-tell lecture* tasks.

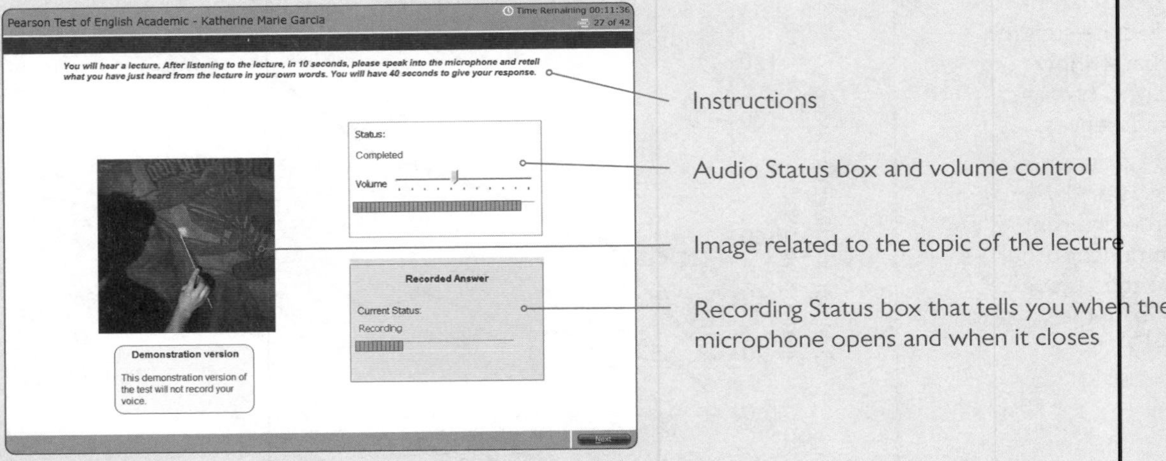

STRATEGIES

Strategies

Be ready

- Before the recording begins, look at the image to help you to anticipate the topic of the lecture.
- Be ready to take notes on the Erasable Noteboard Booklet.
- Remember you can change the volume using the slider in the Audio Status box.

Take notes as you listen

- As you listen, take notes of the main and supporting ideas.
- Don't try to write down everything you hear. Use key words, abbreviations, symbols and arrows to capture the most important ideas and organize them so you can use your notes to speak.
- When the recording stops, you have 10 seconds before a tone indicates that the microphone is open and the blue bar appears in the Recording Status box. Use this time to plan how you will begin, and the order in which you will present the information.

Summarize

- Use your notes to summarize all the main points and add as many supporting details or examples as you can, as well as any implications or conclusions.
- Speak clearly and at a natural pace. You have 40 seconds to re-tell the information so you do not need to rush. When the microphone closes, click 'Next'.

Testing focus Scoring ➤ page 148

Subskills tested

Listening: identifying the topic, theme or main ideas; identifying supporting points or examples; identifying a speaker's purpose, style, tone or attitude; understanding academic vocabulary; inferring the meaning of unfamiliar words; comprehending explicit and implicit information; comprehending concrete and abstract information; classifying and categorizing information; following an oral sequencing of information; comprehending variations in tone, speed and accent.

Speaking: speaking for a purpose (to repeat, to inform, to explain); supporting an opinion with details, examples and explanations; organizing an oral presentation in a logical way; developing complex ideas within a spoken discourse; using words and phrases appropriate to the context; using correct grammar; speaking at a natural rate; producing fluent speech; using correct intonation; using correct pronunciation; using correct stress; speaking under timed conditions.

Preparation

- Develop your own techniques for rapid note-taking. Decide on your own abbreviations and symbols and practise using them so they become automatic.
- Practise starting your response with a topic sentence that introduces the topic and main idea.
- The best responses will include any conclusions or implications, so always consider the significance of the information.
- Listen to 30 seconds of a lecture, noting the key words, then stop the audio and state the main point. Repeat this, extending the time to 90 seconds.
- Find podcasts of lectures with a transcript. Highlight the signal words that indicate the main points and the examples, or evidence, or opposing arguments, then listen for them in the audio. Use the signal words in your own re-telling of the lecture.
- Find 3 or 4 podcasts of lectures and listen to the first 90 seconds, taking notes. Time yourself for 40 seconds re-telling the extract from the lecture using your notes, then move on to the next one.

Re-tell lecture

TIP STRIP

1 Use the image to anticipate the vocabulary you might hear. For example, the picture of a polluted city means you are likely to hear *air pollution, industrial pollution, smog, source of pollution, health problems, motor vehicles*, and so on.

2 Be ready to take notes. Don't try to write every word. Use key words, symbols and arrows to note the main and supporting ideas. Stay focused and keep taking notes until the lecture stops. You will improve your score if you include relevant detail with the main points.

3 Listen and take note of any signposts to help you recognize the main points. Phrases such as *There are three main areas* can guide your note taking. If your notes follow the speaker's sequencing, you can use this to organize your own response. Remember, after the audio stops you only have ten seconds before the tone sounds to tell you to begin speaking, so well-organized notes are important.

In the test, there are 3–4 tasks. For each task, you see an image on the screen. Listen to the lecture and then speak into the microphone. The wording in the instructions below is the same as you will see in the actual test. See page 20 for help.

40 sec. You will hear a lecture. After listening to the lecture, in 10 seconds, please speak into the microphone and retell what you have just heard from the lecture in your own words. You will have 40 seconds to give your response.

1 ▶ 12

2 ▶ 13

3 ▶ 14

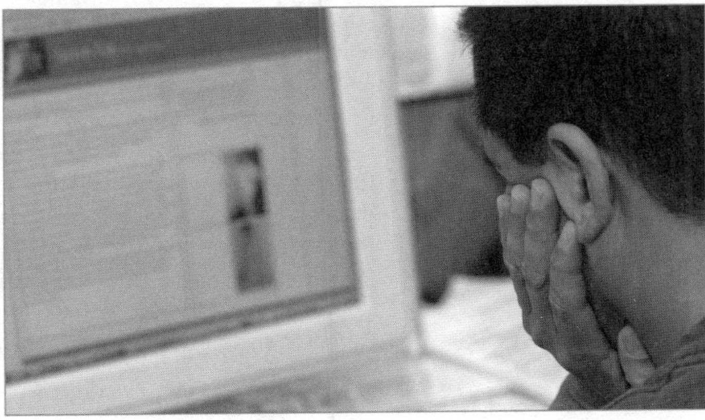

TEST 1

SPEAKING

Answer short question

About the task type

This is a short-answer speaking task type that tests listening and speaking skills. You have to respond to a short question, in one or a few words. You will do 10–12 *Answer short question* tasks.

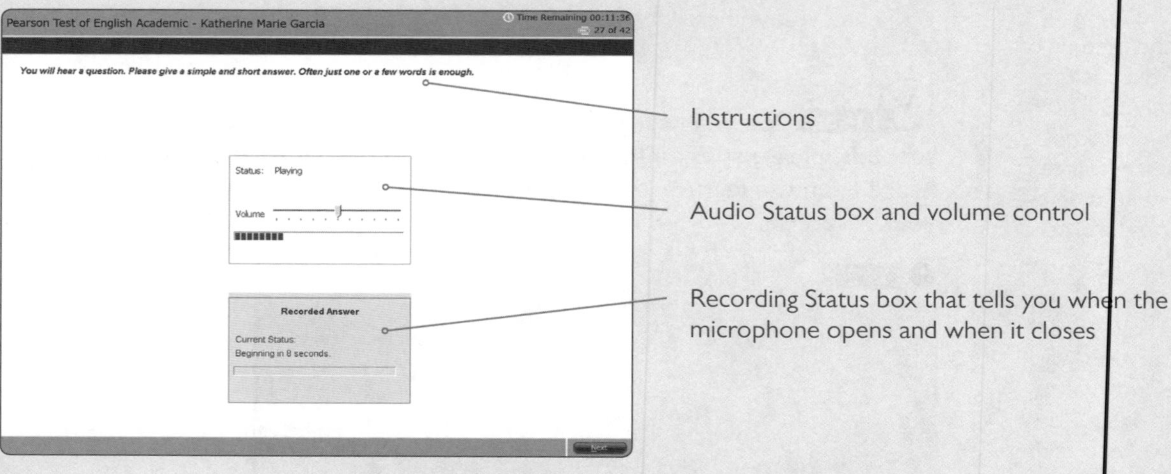

STRATEGIES

Strategies

Stay focused

- In the 3 seconds before the audio begins for each task, focus on the task so you are ready to understand the question.
- The questions are short, and you must answer as soon as the microphone opens, so keep your concentration through all the tasks.
- Don't let your mind wander as there is no time to 'tune in' to what you will hear.

Understand the question

- Listen for the question word (*who, what, when, how, why*) that will help you to understand the question.
- Do not be afraid that you will not have the specific knowledge needed; all the questions are about topics that every educated person knows.
- There is one correct answer that is usually one word or a short phrase.

Speak clearly

- Speak when the blue recording bar appears in the Recording Status box (there is no tone). The microphone will close if there is silence for more than 3 seconds.
- If you realize you have made a mistake, correct yourself, as the score depends on the correct word or words only. Once you have answered, click 'Next'.

Testing focus Scoring ➤ page 149

Subskills tested

Listening: identifying the topic, theme or main ideas; understanding academic vocabulary; inferring the meaning of unfamiliar words.

Speaking: speaking for a purpose (to repeat, to inform, to explain); using words and phrases appropriate to the context; speaking under timed conditions.

Preparation

- To practise giving quick responses to short questions, work with a friend to write a set of short questions on cards on general knowledge topics you know well, then exchange cards and ask each other the questions (*What satellite of the earth lights the sky at night? Where would you find whales? What part of their body do birds use to fly?* etc.). Answer with one or a few words only.
- Expand your vocabulary by developing association balloons: take a common word, put it inside a circle, then add any words you associate with that word. Use a dictionary and a thesaurus to add to the words in your circle, for example, for *medicine*, you might put *hospital, doctor, nurse, disease, illness, x-ray, health, exercise, bones, veins, surgery*.
- Practise understanding question forms by writing a series of short statements about a topic you know well, then converting them all to questions. Ask a friend to ask you the questions in random order, and you answer them.
- Practise using question forms across as many tenses as you can, e.g. *What does …, What did …, What will …, What would …* .
- Check the pronunciation of any new words you learn by using a dictionary with the words recorded. Make sure you know where the stress falls within the word.
- Practise listening for the stressed words in questions you hear. Repeat the question to yourself and clap on the stressed words. Remember that the stressed words carry the main meaning in a question.

Answer short question

In the test, there are 10–12 tasks. For each task, you hear a question and speak your answer into the microphone. The wording in the instructions below is the same as you will see in the actual test. See page 22 for help.

▶ 15-24  10 sec. You will hear a question. Please give a simple and short answer. Often just one or a few words is enough.

TIP STRIP

1. Start your answer as soon as the Recording Status box changes to 'Recording'. If you wait longer than three seconds, you will lose your opportunity to answer and the recording will move on to the next question.
2. This task type is not individually timed. You must click 'Next' to move to the next task after you have given your response. The timer for the Speaking section will continue running, so once the microphone closes, click 'Next' and move on.
3. Follow the instructions and only give a short answer. For example, if the answer is *stage*, then *stage*, *a stage*, *the stage*, *it's called a stage*, *It's a stage* will all be correct and will score the same marks. The important word is *stage*.
4. Sometimes you can use words in the question to help you answer, e.g. the word *desk* is often used with the answer to form a well-known phrase.
5. The answer will usually not include words in the question. For example, *designer* or *building designer* is not the correct answer for this question because it's too general; it's not the specific job title.
6. Listen carefully to the whole question. For this question, you might pay a cheque or cash to a landlord; but these are ways of paying for something, not the term used for the amount of money you pay.
7. Listen for the question word, e.g. *who*, *what*, *how*. In this question, *What do we call* tells you the answer is the name of something, and *meal* tells you the 'something' is to do with food.
8. Remember that you will do 10–12 tasks of this type. Keep your concentration as you move through the questions.
9. Once the microphone closes, you cannot change your answer. If you realize your first answer was not correct, keep speaking and give the correct answer. You have ten seconds to give your response, but the microphone will close if there are more than three seconds of silence.
10. Don't pause in the middle of your answer for more than three seconds. If you do so, the recording will move on to the next question and your answer will be incomplete.

Summarize written text

About the task type

This is a short-answer writing task type that tests reading and writing skills. You have 10 minutes to write a one-sentence summary of a reading passage. You will do 2–3 *Summarize written text* tasks.

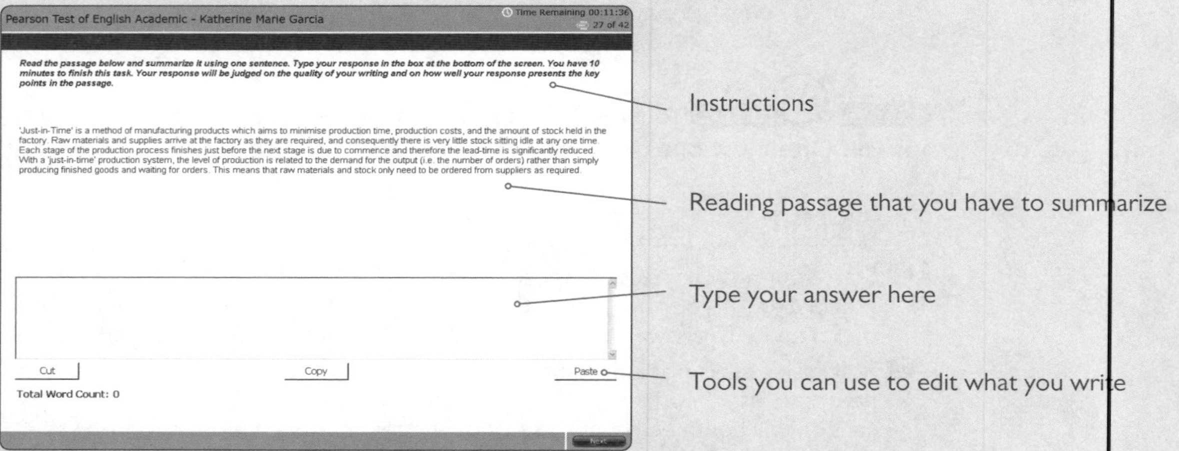

STRATEGIES

Strategies

Use your reading skills

- Take the time to read the passage calmly. First, skim for the general topic, then read carefully for the main ideas.
- Note the main idea and supporting ideas using key words, and arrows and symbols to indicate how the ideas are organized. Effective note-taking will ensure that your summary has all the main points.

Construct your summary

- Type the main point of the passage in the box, then add the supporting or other details.
- Remember, your response must be one sentence only, between 5 and 75 words, so you must use grammatical structures and punctuation that allow you to include all your points within one sentence.
- Use the 'Cut', 'Copy', and 'Paste' buttons to move text around. There is a word counter below the writing box, and a timer running at the top of the screen.

Check your writing

- Take a few minutes to check your grammar and vocabulary. Does your sentence begin with a capital letter and end with a full stop?
- Your response will not be scored if it is more than one sentence, or if it is written all in capital letters.
- At the end of 10 minutes, the screen will stop responding.

Testing focus Scoring ➤ page 149

Subskills tested

Reading: reading a passage under timed conditions; identifying a writer's purpose, style, tone or attitude; comprehending explicit and implicit information; comprehending concrete and abstract information.

Writing: writing a summary; writing under timed conditions; taking notes while reading a text; synthesizing information; writing to meet strict length requirements; communicating the main points of a reading passage in writing; using words and phrases appropriate to the context; using correct grammar and spelling.

Preparation

- Practise skimming short texts quickly (up to 300 words) to identify the main points. In a longer article, stop reading after each paragraph and summarize the main point in one sentence.
- Work with a friend to agree on what are the main ideas and supporting ideas in texts.
- Develop your own techniques for rapid note-taking. Decide on your own abbreviations and symbols and practise using them so they become automatic.
- Revise complex structures such as subordinate clauses and the use of conjunctions that will allow you to include more ideas within one sentence. Analyze long sentences in texts to identify how the writer has constructed each one.
- Find a short text (up to 300 words) and time yourself reading and summarizing it. Take one minute to skim for the main idea, then 2 minutes to read carefully and take notes. Spend 5 minutes writing a one sentence summary, and 2 minutes checking your work.
- Compare your summary to the original text. The best response will clearly summarize the main idea and condense essential supporting ideas.
- Find a set of 2 or 3 short texts and time yourself summarizing them, one after the other. Make sure you only spend 10 minutes on each text.

Summarize written text

TIP STRIP

In order to get the main points into one sentence, you will need to use grammatical features, such as conjunctions (*and, but,* etc.), conditional clauses (*if, when*, etc.) and relative clauses (*who, which, that*, etc.).

In the test, there are 2–3 tasks. Each task has a text on the screen. You type your summary of the text into the box at the bottom of the screen. The wording in the instructions below is the same as you will see in the actual test. See page 24 for help.

1 **10 min.** **Read the passage below and summarize it using one sentence. Type your response in the box at the bottom of the screen. You have 10 minutes to finish this task. Your response will be judged on the quality of your writing and on how well your response presents the key points in the passage.**

By far the most popular and most consumed drink in the world is water, but it may come as no surprise that the second most popular beverage is tea. Although tea was originally grown only in certain parts of Asia – in countries such as China, Burma and India – it is now a key export product in more than 50 countries around the globe. Countries that grow tea, however, need to have the right tropical climate, which includes up to 200 centimetres of rainfall per year to encourage fast growth, and temperatures that range from ten to 35 degrees centigrade. They also need to have quite specific geographical features, such as high altitudes to promote the flavour and taste of the tea, and land that can offer plenty of shade in the form of other trees and vegetation to keep the plants cool and fresh. Together these conditions contribute to the production of the wide range of high-quality teas that are in such huge demand among the world's consumers. There is green tea, jasmine tea, earl grey tea, peppermint tea, tea to help you sleep, tea to promote healing and tea to relieve stress; but above all, tea is a social drink that seems to suit the palates and consumption habits of human beings in general.

....

....

....

....

....

TIP STRIP

Remember to only write one sentence. Make sure your answer has a capital letter at the start and ends with a full stop. Also, check that you have used commas appropriately within your sentence.

TEST 1

WRITING

2 **10 min.** Read the passage below and summarize it using one sentence. Type your response in the box at the bottom of the screen. You have 10 minutes to finish this task. Your response will be judged on the quality of your writing and on how well your response presents the key points in the passage.

> With all the discussions about protecting the earth and saving the planet, it is easy to forget that we also need to preserve the many species of fish that live in the oceans. In developed countries, much larger quantities of fish are consumed than was the case a century ago when fish only featured on the menu once a week. These days, fish has become a popular healthy alternative to meat and this has created a demand for species such as cod, mackerel and tuna that far outstrips the demands of the previous generation. Throughout the world too, increasing consumption during the past 30 years has meant that the shallow parts of the ocean have been overfished in an effort to supply homes, shops and restaurants with the quantities of fish that they require. Yet despite the sophisticated fishing techniques of today, catches are smaller than they were a century or more ago. What is more, boats are having to drop their nets much deeper into the oceans and the fish they are coming up with are smaller and weigh less than they used to. While government controls have had some effect on fish stocks, the future does not offer a promising picture. Experts predict large-scale extinctions and an irreversibly damaging effect on entire ecosystems, unless greater efforts are made to conserve fish stocks and prevent overfishing in the world's waters.

....

....

....

....

....

Write essay

About the task type

This is a long-answer writing task type that tests writing skills. You have 20 minutes to write a 200–300 word persuasive or argumentative essay on a given topic. You will do 1–2 *Write essay* tasks.

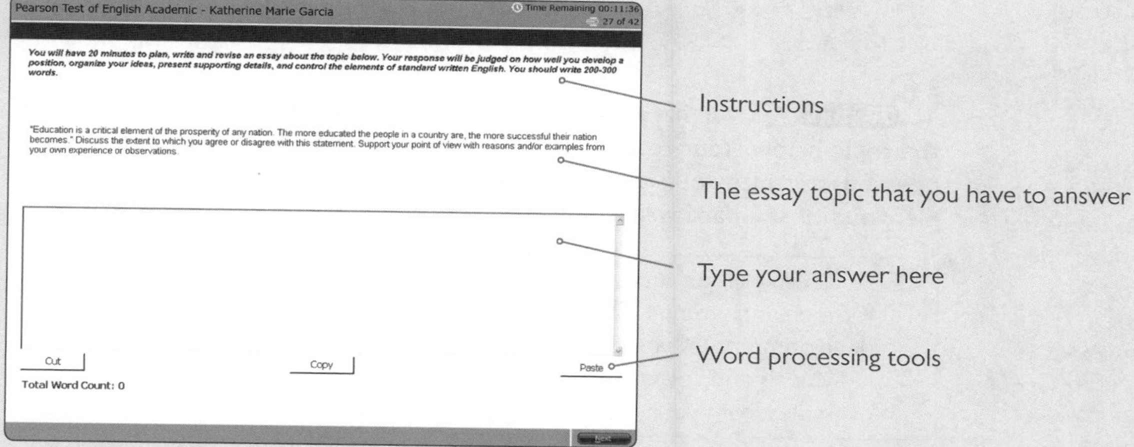

Strategies

Analyze and plan

- First, analyze the essay task. Identify the key words that tell you the general topic, then look for the particular aspect of the topic you are being asked about (often in the form of a statement of a position).
- Look closely at the task to see exactly what you have to do – agree/disagree, answer specific questions, etc.
- Use your Erasable Noteboard Booklet to plan your essay. Note the ideas you want to include, and decide how you will order them.

Write your essay

- Use your outline notes to present your position on the task, and support your opinion with evidence and examples. Remember that it doesn't matter what your opinion is as long as you argue it clearly and with support.
- Make sure you cover all the required aspects of the question.
- Make sure your essay is well organized, with a new paragraph for each new idea, to develop your argument.

Check your writing

- Save a few minutes to check your writing. You will lose marks for poor grammar and for spelling mistakes.
- After 20 minutes the screen will stop responding, so click 'Next' and move on.

Testing focus Scoring ➤ page 150

Subskills tested

Writing: writing for a purpose (to learn, to inform, to persuade); supporting an opinion with details, examples and explanations; organizing sentences and paragraphs in a logical way; developing complex ideas within a complete essay; using words and phrases appropriate to the context; using correct grammar; using correct spelling; using correct mechanics; writing under timed conditions.

Preparation

- Look at the *Write essay* tasks in this book and in *The Official Guide to PTE Academic*. Circle the topic in each one, then underline the particular aspect of the topic you must write about. Identify the instruction that tells you exactly what you must do – agree/disagree, answer specific questions, etc.
- Practise developing outlines for essay topics. Look again at the essay topics in this book and in *The Official Guide to PTE Academic*, and prepare quick outlines for each one. Remember that a response that does not address the topic will be scored zero.
- Practise writing introductory paragraphs, with one sentence that makes a general statement on the topic and a second sentence that introduces your opinion.
- Practise writing conclusions that re-state or summarize your argument in one sentence.
- Make a list of signpost words you can use to show how an argument is organized, such as *Firstly, Secondly, However, In addition, On the other hand*, etc. Write paragraphs that use these signpost words.
- Write 250 words on one essay topic on your computer and time how long it takes you to do this. Decide how much time you can spend planning your essay, how much time writing, and how much time checking.
- Practise writing without using the spell-checker and grammar checker on your computer so that you learn to recognize wrong spellings. You cannot use a spell-checker or grammar checker in the actual test.

TEST 1

WRITING

Write essay

TIP STRIP

❶ In this type of essay, you need to write about the questions you are asked. In Topic 1, there are two questions, so you must answer both of them. Read the questions carefully. Make sure you know what any pronouns refer to. For example, in Topic 1 what does *this* refer to in the second sentence?

❷ Think carefully about the question before you start. Sometimes it helps to re-word a statement as a question, e.g. for Topic 2: *Should schools prepare students for university, rather than work?*

In the test, there are 1–2 tasks. For each task, the essay question is on the screen. You type your essay into the box on the screen. The wording in the instructions below is the same as you will see in the actual test. See page 27 for help.

20 min. **You will have 20 minutes to plan, write and revise an essay about the topic below. Your response will be judged on how well you develop a position, organize your ideas, present supporting details, and control the elements of standard written English. You should write 200–300 words.**

❶ As a result of advances in medical care, average life expectancy is increasing for men and women. Do you think most people will see this as a positive development? What are the disadvantages of an ageing population for individuals and society? Support your point of view with reasons and/or examples from your own experience or observations.

❷ 'Schools should prepare students for university, rather than for work.' How far do you agree with this statement? Support your point of view with reasons and/or examples from your own experience or observations.

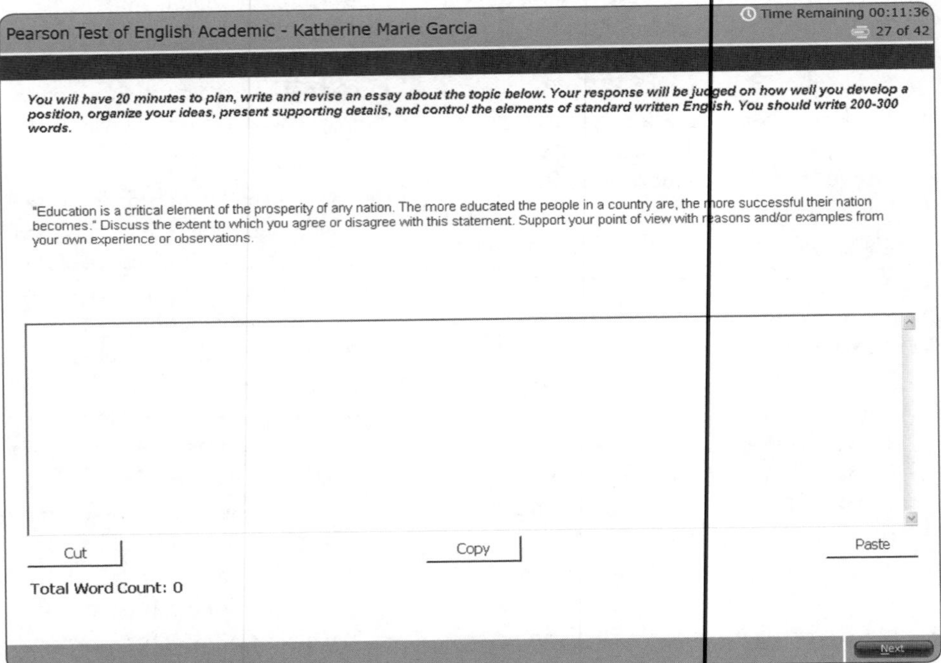

Write essay: Each question is displayed on a new screen.

Overview: Reading

Part 2 of the PTE Academic test is Reading. This part tests your ability to understand written English in an academic environment.

The table shows what you will see in the test, which you will take on a computer. When practising with this book, you will have to write your written answers in the book, your notebook or on your own computer.

Part 2: Reading				
Reading (total time 32–41 minutes)				
Task type	**Number of tasks**	**Task description**	**Skills assessed**	**Text/ Recording length**
Multiple-choice, choose single answer	2–3	After reading a text, answer a multiple-choice question on the content or tone of the text by selecting one response.	reading	text up to 300 words
Multiple-choice, choose multiple answers	2–3	After reading a text, answer a multiple-choice question on the content or tone of the text by selecting more than one response.	reading	text up to 300 words
Re-order paragraphs	2–3	Several text boxes appear on screen in random order. Put the text boxes in the correct order.	reading	text up to 150 words
Reading: Fill in the blanks	4–5	A text appears on screen with several blanks. Drag words or phrases from the blue box to fill in the blanks.	reading	text up to 80 words
Reading & writing: Fill in the blanks	5–6	A text appears on screen with several blanks. Fill in the blanks by selecting words from several drop-down lists of response options.	reading and writing	text up to 300 words

You may take notes using the Erasable Noteboard Booklet and pen, and use these notes as a guide when answering the tasks.

Authentic texts about academic subjects in the humanities, natural sciences or social sciences are presented. Although you may not be familiar with the topics presented, all the information you need to answer the tasks is contained in the texts.

Reading task types are not timed individually. You can refer to the timer in the upper right-hand corner of the computer screen, *Time Remaining*, which counts down the time remaining for the Reading part.

Multiple-choice, choose single answer

About the task type

This is a multiple-choice reading task type that tests reading skills. You have to select a single answer to a question about information in a text. You will do 2–3 *Multiple-choice, choose single answer* tasks.

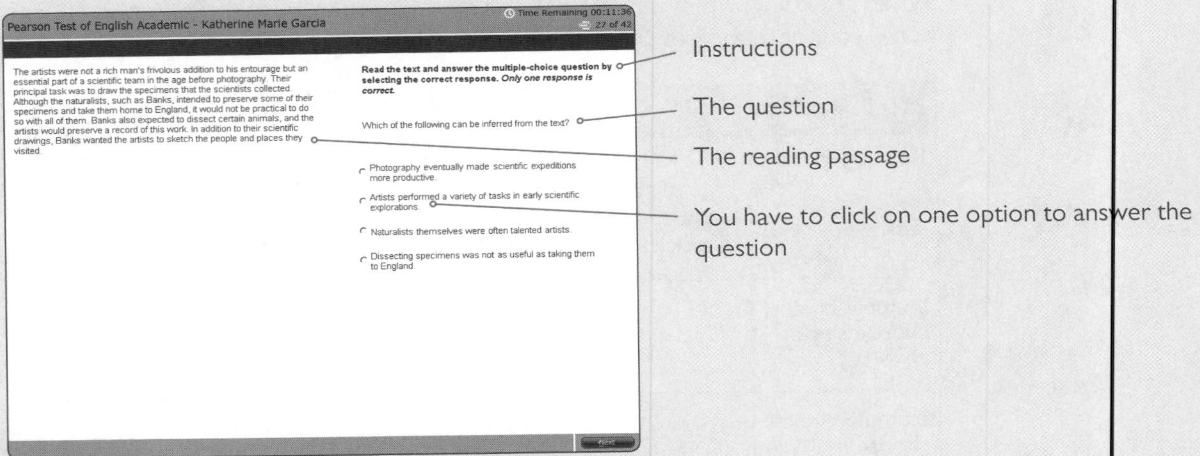

Strategies

Read with purpose

- Read the question before you read the passage. This will tell you what information you are looking for in the text. It could be the main idea, the writer's purpose or attitude, some detailed information, or inferences.
- Next, skim the text to get an idea of the general content and the development of the ideas. Don't worry if you don't understand every word.

Select the option

- From the prompt, identify whether the answer you need is located in the whole text or in part of it, then read carefully the whole text or the relevant part.
- Remember, the options may use synonyms for words in the passage, not the exact words.
- If you don't know an important word in the text, try to guess its meaning from the context.
- Answer the question by clicking on one option or on its radio button ○ .

Confirm your choice

- After you have chosen an option, compare each of the other options to the text to eliminate each one. If you change your mind, click on the option again to de-select it, then click on the correct option.
- Be aware of the time and don't spend too much time on one task. Click 'Next' and move on.

Testing focus Scoring ➤ page 152

Subskills tested

Reading: any of the following depending on the task: identifying the topic, theme or main ideas; identifying the relationships between sentences and paragraphs; evaluating the quality and usefulness of texts; identifying a writer's purpose, style, tone or attitude; identifying supporting points or examples; reading for overall organization and connections between pieces of information; reading for information to infer meanings or find relationships; identifying specific details, facts, opinions, definitions or sequences of events; inferring the meaning of unfamiliar words.

Preparation

- Practise skimming short texts of about one paragraph to answer this question: *What is the writer's main point?* Summarize the main point in a short sentence.
- Practise skimming short texts to answer this question: *What is the writer's purpose in this passage?* (to criticize, to argue, to persuade the reader, to describe, to explain, etc.).
- Practise identifying the topic sentences in paragraphs; this helps to identify the main theme.
- Take notes of the information in a text and use arrows to show how the writer's ideas develop.
- Highlight the cohesive devices used in a text, such as pronoun use, article use, substitution, etc.
- Highlight any words you don't know in a text and practise guessing what they mean from the context. Check your guess in a dictionary.
- Work with a friend to see if you agree on what is the main point and what are the supporting points in a text. Identify the signpost words that indicate evidence, support, details, examples, or opposing arguments.
- Expand your vocabulary by creating lists of words with their synonyms. Use a thesaurus to find new words with the same or similar meanings. When you learn a new word, find an example of how it's used in context, for example in a learner's dictionary.

Multiple-choice, choose single answer

TIP STRIP

1 Read the question before the options and decide what you need to read for. If you are looking for the 'writer's main purpose', you are reading for the overall idea or argument.

2 If you do not understand a word in the question, check to see whether it has been explained in the passage. In this passage, *innovation* refers back to *any new technology or device*.

In the test, there are 2–3 tasks. For each task, you read the text on the left of the screen and look at the options on the right of the screen. You click the button next to the answer you think is correct. The wording in the instructions below is the same as you will see in the actual test. See page 30 for help.

Read the text and answer the multiple-choice question by selecting the correct response. ***Only one response is correct.***

1 Huge reserves of energy have been found in rocks far below the surface of the ground in Britain. It is estimated that the north and southwest regions could hold enough energy in the form of heat to provide power for millions of homes. In fact, up to a fifth of Britain's energy could be provided by this geothermal source. Extracting the heat and converting it into electricity is difficult and expensive. Thousands of bore holes would be needed; but once they were in place, the heat would keep regenerating indefinitely.

What is the writer's main purpose in this paragraph?

- ○ A to show how common the use of geothermal power is in Britain
- ○ B to describe the problems related to using geothermal power in Britain
- ○ C to highlight the potential benefits of geothermal power for Britain
- ○ D to give a detailed description of how geothermal energy is produced in Britain

2 People tend to think that any new technology or device is an act of genius; something that has required vision and insight to create and then develop into a marketable product. The fact is that innovations were often already 'out there' in the public domain in some form or another. They tend to evolve from notions that have been around for years but that had not, until that point, been suitably adapted. One expert calls this the 'long nose' approach to innovation, whereby new concepts come into the world slowly, gradually revealing all they have to offer.

What is the writer's main point about innovation?

- ○ A Many new products fail to interest consumers.
- ○ B New products are not always based on new ideas.
- ○ C Creators of new products require a unique set of skills.
- ○ D New products are easy to distinguish from old ones.

Multiple-choice, choose multiple answers

About the task type

This is a multiple-choice reading task type that tests reading skills. More than one response is correct in answer to a question about a text. You will do 2–3 *Multiple-choice, choose multiple answers* tasks.

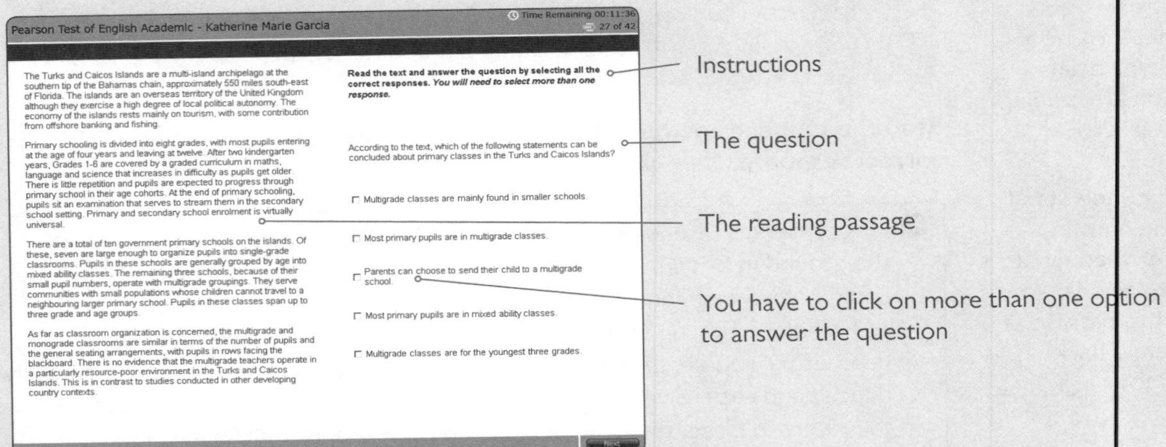

STRATEGIES

Strategies

Read the question first

- Read the question before you read the passage. This will tell you what information you are looking for in the text. It could be the main ideas, the writer's purpose or attitude, some detailed information, or inferences.
- Next, skim the text to get an idea of the general content and the development of the ideas. Don't worry if you don't understand every word.

Read for a purpose

- From the prompt, identify whether the answers you need are located in the whole text or in parts of it, then read carefully the whole text or the relevant parts.
- Remember, the options may use synonyms for words in the passage, not the exact words.
- If you don't know an important word in the text, try to guess its meaning from the context.
- Answer the question by clicking on more than one option or on their checkboxes.

Confirm your choices

- After you have chosen the options, compare each of the other options to the text to eliminate each one. If you change your mind, click on the option again to de-select it then click on the correct option.
- Be aware of the time and don't spend too much time on one task.

Testing focus Scoring ➤ page 152

Subskills tested

Reading: any of the following depending on the task: identifying the topic, theme or main ideas; identifying the relationships between sentences and paragraphs; evaluating the quality and usefulness of texts; identifying a writer's purpose, style, tone or attitude; identifying supporting points or examples; reading for overall organization and connections between pieces of information; reading for information to infer meanings or find relationships; identifying specific details, facts, opinions, definitions or sequences of events; inferring the meaning of unfamiliar words.

Preparation

- Practise skimming longer texts of several paragraphs to answer this question: *What are the writer's main points?* Summarize the main points.
- Practise skimming longer texts to answer this question: *What were the writer's goals in writing this passage?* (to criticize, to argue, to persuade the reader, to describe, to explain, etc.).
- Practise identifying the topic sentences in paragraphs; this helps to identify the main themes.
- Take notes of the information in a text and use arrows to show how the writer's ideas develop.
- Highlight the cohesive devices used in a text, such as pronoun use, article use, substitution, etc.
- Highlight any words you don't know in a text and practise guessing what they mean from the context. Check your guess in a dictionary.
- Work with a friend to see if you agree on what are the main points and the supporting points in a text. Identify the signpost words that indicate evidence, support, details, examples, or opposing arguments.
- Expand your vocabulary by creating lists of words with their synonyms. Use a thesaurus to find new words with the same or similar meanings. When you learn a new word, find an example of how it is used in context, for example in a learner's dictionary.

Multiple-choice, choose multiple answers

TIP STRIP

Read the question before the options and decide what you need to read for; the words *Which of the following are true* indicate that you are reading for detailed information.

In the test, there are 2–3 tasks. For each task, you read the text on the left of the screen and look at the options on the right of the screen. You click the buttons next to all of the answers you think are correct. The wording in the instructions below is the same as you will see in the actual test. See page 32 for help.

1 Read the text and answer the question by selecting all the correct responses. ***You will need to select more than one response.***

Small, localised enterprises are becoming ever-more imaginative in identifying opportunities to boost tourism for their areas. A more unusual attraction is the Old Man of the Lake, which is the name given to a 9-metre-tall tree stump that has been bobbing vertically in Oregon's Crater Lake since at least 1896. For over one hundred years, it has been largely ignored but recently it has become a must-see item on the list of lake attractions. Since January 2012, tour boats regularly include the Old Man on their sightseeing trips around the lake.

At the waterline, the stump is about 60 centimetres in diameter, and the exposed part stands approximately 120 centimetres above the surface of the water. Over the years, the stump has been bleached white by the elements. The exposed end of the floating tree is splintered and worn but wide and buoyant enough to support a person's weight.

Observations indicated that the Old Man of Crater Lake travels quite extensively, and sometimes with surprising rapidity. Since it can be seen virtually anywhere on the lake, boat pilots commonly communicate its position to each other as a general matter of safety.

Which of the following are true of the Old Man of the Lake according to the passage?

- ○ A It has been a tourist attraction for decades.
- ○ B It is a drifting piece of wood.
- ○ C It is close to the edge of Crater Lake.
- ○ D It is owned by a local businessman.
- ○ E It can quickly move about the lake.
- ○ F It can be a danger to boat users.
- ○ G It is too small for someone to stand on.

2 Read the text and answer the question by selecting all the correct responses. ***You will need to select more than one response.***

> To find it, you have to go digging in rainforests, and to the untrained eye, it does not seem special at all – just a thick layer of dark earth that would not look out of place in many gardens. But these fertile, dark soils are in fact very special, because despite the lushness of tropical rainforests, the soils beneath them are usually very poor and thin. Even more surprising is where this dark soil comes from.
>
> 'You might expect this precious fertile resource to be found in the deep jungle, far from human settlements or farmers,' says James Fraser, who has been hunting for it in Africa's rainforests. 'But I go looking for dark earth round the edge of villages and ancient towns, and in traditionally farmed areas. It's usually there. And the older and larger the settlement, the more dark earth there is.'
>
> Such findings are overturning some long-held ideas. Jungle farmers are usually blamed not just for cutting down trees but also for exhausting the soils. And yet the discovery of these rich soils – first in South America and now in Africa, too – suggest that, whether by chance or design, many people living in rainforests farmed in a way that enhanced rather than destroyed soils. In fact, it is becoming clear that part of what we think of as lush pure rainforest is actually long-abandoned farmland, enriched by the waste created by ancient humans.

What is significant about the 'dark soil' that the writer is referring to?

- ○ A It indicates the presence of good soil below it.
- ○ B It is not present in rainforests.
- ○ C It has resulted from agricultural activity.
- ○ D It is more common in South America than Africa.
- ○ E It is being found near where humans have lived.
- ○ F It has confirmed what people have believed for a long time.
- ○ G It is less productive than people once thought.

TIP STRIP

Use key words in the options to help you find the answers in the text. Key words like *indicates*, *presence*, *good soil* point to the information to be confirmed or contradicted in the text.

Re-order paragraphs

About the task type

This is a reading task type that tests reading skills. You have to select the single correct order for a set of sentences presented in incorrect order. You have to do 2–3 *Re-order paragraphs* tasks.

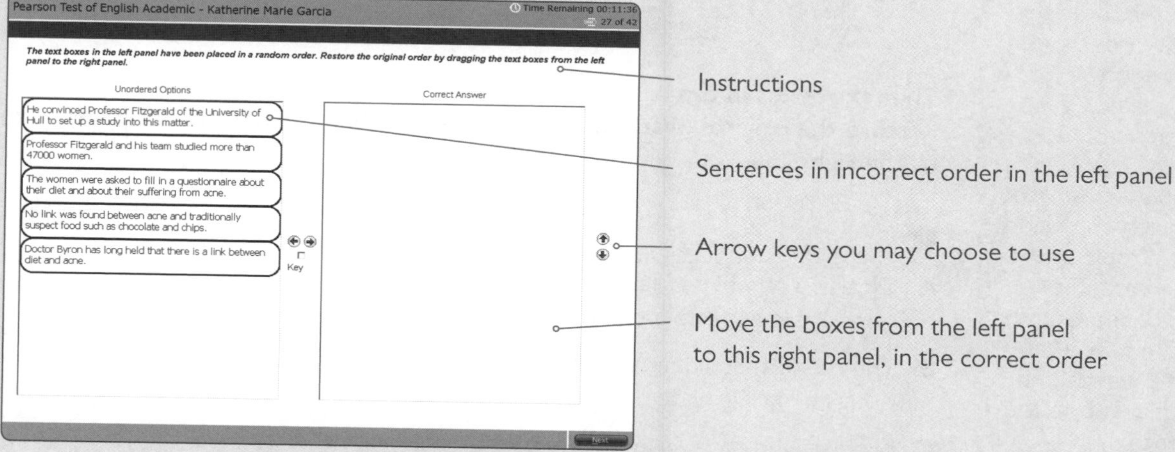

Strategies

Find the topic sentence

- Skim the sentences in the left panel. Look for a sentence that introduces the topic.
- Check that your selected topic sentence 'stands alone', containing no references to any information that must be stated before it.
- Move your topic sentence to the right panel by dragging-and-dropping or using the left/right arrow keys.

Look for the links

- Look for linking words and structures in the other sentences. Look for signal words like *However* or *In addition*, or referencing pronouns replacing nouns already mentioned such as *he* or *it*, or demonstratives such as *this* or *these*. Think about article usage (*a* for first mention, *the* afterwards).
- Use these cohesive markers to put the information in the correct order. Move each sentence to its place in the right panel by dragging-and-dropping or using the arrow keys.

Confirm the order

- Check each sentence. If you change your mind, use the up/down arrow keys or dragging-and-dropping to put the sentence in a different position.
- Read through the sentences in order for one last check, then click 'Next' and move on.

Testing focus Scoring ➤ page 152

Subskills tested

Reading: identifying the topic, theme or main ideas; identifying supporting points or examples; identifying the relationships between sentences and paragraphs; understanding academic vocabulary; understanding the difference between connotation and denotation; inferring the meaning of unfamiliar words; comprehending explicit and implicit information; comprehending concrete and abstract information; classifying and categorizing information; following a logical or chronological sequence of events.

Preparation

- Write a short sentence about a topic. Replace all the nouns with pronouns such as *he*, *she*, *it*, *they*, *them*, etc. Look at the sentence again. Can you see why it is no longer a 'standalone' sentence?
- Look at groups of sentences in magazines or online passages. Highlight the articles *a/an*, *the*. Identify the pattern in article use of first mention/subsequent mention.
- Find short passages of 4–5 sentences in magazines or online. Then:
- Look at the first sentence and ask: *Why is this sentence before the others?*
- Highlight all the words that indicate the cohesion (linking words, pronouns, articles, demonstratives).
- Work with a friend to cut up or re-write the text, moving the sentences into a different order. Exchange texts. Look at each sentence and highlight all the cohesive devices. Use them to re-create the correct order.
- Delete all the referencing pronouns that indicate cohesion. Put the passage aside for a few days, then look at it again and put in the missing words.
- Make a list of signpost words used to show how a text is organized, such as *Firstly, Secondly, However, In addition, On the other hand*, etc.

Re-order paragraphs

TIP STRIP

1 Read through all the text boxes before you begin. As you do this, note the important words – often nouns that express important ideas, e.g. *collisions, erosions, rock formations, Grand Canyon, geological processes*. Use these to help you decide on the main topic of the text; in this case, the formation of the Grand Canyon. Then, you can look for the standalone sentence that will be the first sentence.

2 Use pronouns and linkers to make connections between sentences and help you work out the correct order, e.g. *It was a time when …, As a result, …, these …* .

In the test, there are 2–3 tasks. For each task, you drag paragraphs from the left and drop them into the correct order on the right. The wording in the instructions below is the same as you will see in the actual test. See page 35 for help.

The text boxes in the left panel have been placed in a random order. Restore the original order by dragging the text boxes from the left panel to the right panel.

1

A Clearly, a number of factors have contributed to its remarkable appearance.

B The result is a unique story of land collisions and erosions, and of rising and falling water levels.

C Experts who have analysed the rock formations say that, historically, it goes back nearly two billion years.

D Anyone who has ever visited the Grand Canyon will agree that it is one of the most incredible sights in the world.

E The geological processes that have taken place since then are exposed for everyone to see, not hidden beneath vegetation or a fast-flowing water course.

2

A It was a time when managers had to take a critical look at every aspect of their production process and make improvements where necessary.

B As a result, some people believe it is now time to re-assess many companies in terms of the standards they agreed to some years ago.

C In the late 1900s, food manufacturers were challenged by the organic community to ensure they were using ingredients that had been produced in natural, healthy ways.

D Whether these systems have been maintained seems questionable, particularly as contracts depend so heavily on efficiency and quick sales.

E Over the last half-century, organic farming has become a driving force in the world's food market.

Reading: Fill in the blanks

About the task type

This is a reading task type that tests reading skills. From the box below a text, you have to select a single correct answer for each gap in the text. You will do 4–5 *Reading: Fill in the blanks* tasks.

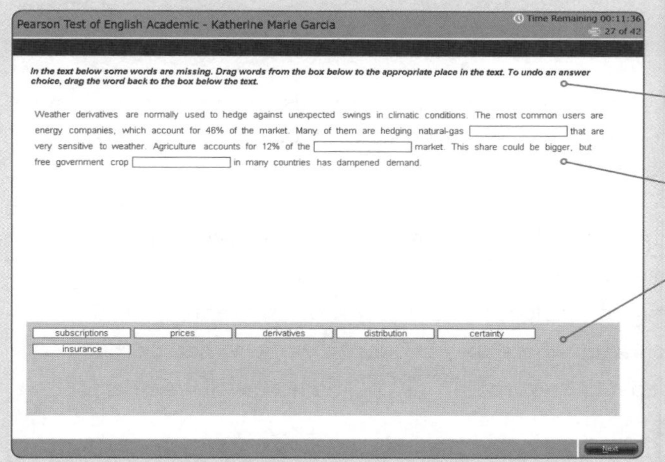

Instructions

Text with missing words

You have to select words from this box and drag them to the gaps in the text above

Strategies

Skim the text first

- Skim the gapped text to get an idea of the topic. Ignore the blanks at this point. Look for the key words that carry the meaning.
- If there are words you don't know, read around them to try to guess the meaning from the context.

Identify the correct words

- Look at the words around the first blank and its place in the sentence. Identify the idea being expressed in the sentence, and think what word will create meaning in the context. Use grammar clues to help you decide between possible options.
- Think about collocation: what word often appears with the word before or after the blank?
- Look for possible words in the box at the bottom of the screen, and try each one by dragging it up to the blank in the text. If it fits the meaning and grammar, leave it there. If not, move it back.
- Once you have filled one blank, move to the next. If you cannot do one, don't worry; just move to the next. The more blanks you fill in, the easier the missing ones will be.

Check one last time

- Check each of the 3 unused words to confirm your choices.
- Read through one last time to check the meaning is consistent.

Testing focus Scoring ➤ page 152

Subskills tested

Reading: identifying the topic, theme or main ideas; identifying words and phrases appropriate to the context; understanding academic vocabulary; understanding the difference between connotation and denotation; inferring the meaning of unfamiliar words; comprehending explicit and implicit information; comprehending concrete and abstract information; following a logical or chronological sequence of events.

Preparation

- Improve your general reading skills by reading short texts and summarizing the main ideas. Stop after 2 or 3 sentences and put the ideas you have read into your own words.
- Try to guess the meaning of words you don't know from the context, then check their meaning in a dictionary. Use a thesaurus to expand your vocabulary with synonyms for the word, and look for examples of how to use the new words, for example in a learner's dictionary.
- Expand your knowledge of collocation (words that frequently occur together, such as *difficult decision*). Keep a diary of collocations you find in your reading and revise them regularly. This will help you to recognize the best word for a blank.
- Make your own collocation lists. Take a common word such as *pollution* and add to it any words you would expect to see it used with, such as *water pollution*, *air pollution*, *urban pollution*. Expand this list by taking the words you have found and adding different collocations, for example, with *water* you can put *water pollution, water sports, water supply, water shortage, clean water, fresh water,* etc.
- Work with a friend to delete some of the words that carry meaning from short texts. Exchange texts and try to guess the missing word, with and without having a list to choose from.

Reading: Fill in the blanks

TIP STRIP

1. Quickly read the paragraph first. Then use grammar clues to help you. For example, *have had* tells you that a plural noun is needed in the first gap.
2. Some gaps will be in common phrases where collocations, such as between adjectives and nouns like *a wide* ______, can help you find the answer.

In the test, there are 4–5 tasks. For each task, you drag the words at the bottom of the text and drop them into the correct space in the text. The wording in the instructions below is the same as you will see in the actual test. See page 37 for help.

In the text below some words are missing. Drag words from the box below to the appropriate place in the text. To undo an answer choice, drag the word back to the box below the text.

1. Technology and flexible work [1] ______ have had a significant impact on today's busy companies. In terms of productivity, it seems the [2] ______ has shifted from managing employees in the workplace to monitoring their total [3] ______, no matter where they choose to work. Whether this trend will continue depends to some [4] ______ on how well it works for everyone concerned.

focus | deals | way | practices | selling | output | extent

2. Elephants have a very [1] ______ communication system, which helps them maintain their close [2] ______ bonds. When they are near each other, they use verbal and visual signals to express a wide [3] ______ of emotions. As they move further [4] ______, they use less common, rumbling [5] ______ that can be heard over two kilometres away.

distant | variety | family | ranging | apart | sounds | complex | round

In the text below some words are missing. Drag words from the box below to the appropriate place in the text. To undo an answer choice, drag the word back to the box below the text.

TIP STRIP

3 Use pronoun references to help you complete the gap. For example, *these huge* refers back to *wind farms*. Select a word from the box that completes the description.

4 You can use your knowledge of grammar and collocation. For example, in Gap 3, choose the verb from the box that collocates with *contribution*.

3 People are naturally concerned about the polluting 1 ______ of energy sources such as oil or coal. But are wind farms the 2 ______? With their enormous rotating blades, these huge 3 ______ are becoming more commonplace in certain 4 ______ of the world. Yet for some people, they are an unwelcome 5 ______ of the landscape.

machines | product | sight | feature | answer | regions | damages | effects

4 Professional astronomers, 1 ______ their amateur counterparts, have no particular interest in the aesthetic quality of their photographs. What 2 ______ to them is the contribution their images can 3 ______ to research, and to the 4 ______ of data scientists in their field 5 ______ for research purposes.

make | equipped | unlike | matters | use | collection | put | concerns

TEST 1

READING

Reading & writing: Fill in the blanks

About the task type

This is a multiple-choice reading task type that tests reading and writing skills. You select one correct word from a list to fill each blank in a text. You will do 5–6 *Reading & writing: Fill in the blanks* tasks.

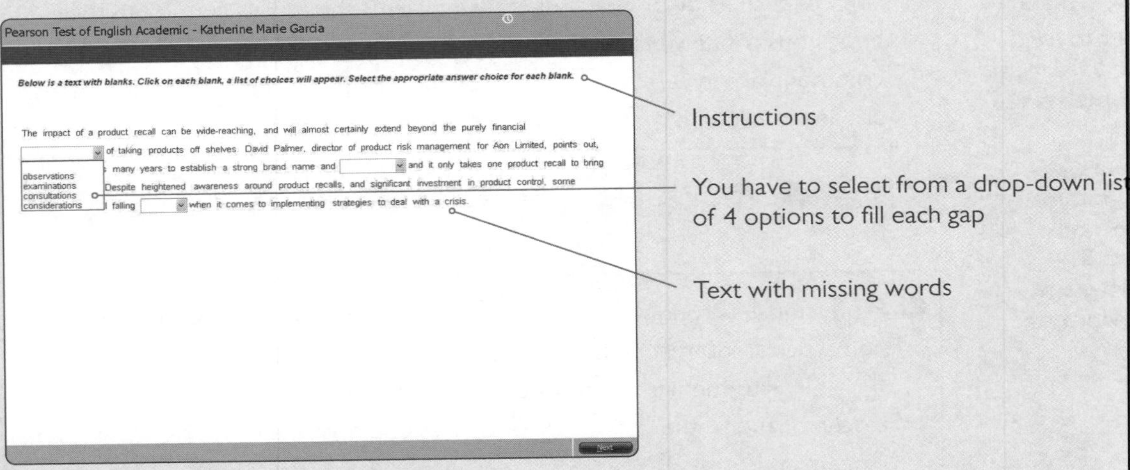

Strategies

Read the text through

- Read the whole text through once for the overall meaning. Then, re-read the sentence with the first blank and think what word would create meaning in the context. Look at the sentence grammar to decide what is needed, e.g. noun, past tense verb, adjective.
- Click on the first blank. From the drop-down list, select the one that will create meaning and is grammatically correct.
- Repeat for the other blanks.

Use your language knowledge

- Think about collocation: what word often appears with the word before or after the blank?
- Consider word form: should the word be the noun form, the verb form, or the adjective form? For example: *allocation, allocate, allocated, allocating*.
- Read the sentence with each word in turn: which one makes the best meaning in context?

Check for grammar and meaning

- Fill each blank in turn. If you cannot do one, leave it and return later. The more blanks you fill, the clearer the text will become.
- When you have finished, check each selection for correct grammar. If it is a verb, is the tense correct? Is it the right form of the word?
- Click 'Next' and move on.

Testing focus Scoring ➤ page 152

Subskills tested

Reading: identifying the topic, theme or main ideas; identifying words and phrases appropriate to the context; understanding academic vocabulary; understanding the difference between connotation and denotation; inferring the meaning of unfamiliar words; comprehending explicit and implicit information; comprehending concrete and abstract information; following a logical or chronological sequence of events.

Writing: using words and phrases appropriate to the context; using correct grammar.

Preparation

- Improve your general reading skills by reading short texts and summarizing the main ideas. Look at the sentence structure and trace the verb tense patterns and the clause structure.
- Revise your knowledge of grammar and word order. Use a grammar book with gap-fill quizzes to practise choosing the grammatically correct word for each gap.
- When reading texts, try to guess the meaning of words you don't know from the context, then check their meaning in a dictionary. Use a thesaurus to expand your vocabulary with synonyms for the word, and look for examples of how to use the new words, for example in a learner's dictionary.
- Expand your knowledge of collocation (words that frequently occur together, such as *difficult decision*). Keep a diary of collocations that you find in your reading and revise them regularly. This will help you to recognize the best word for a blank.
- Notice the discourse structure when you read, how the writers use cohesive devices to indicate the progression of what they are saying. This will help you to choose the correct option based on understanding the construction of a text.
- Work with a friend to delete words such as verbs and nouns from texts. Exchange texts and try to predict what the missing words should be.

STRATEGIES

Reading & writing: Fill in the blanks

TIP STRIP

1. Read the text quickly before you start to get an overall understanding of the content and decide on the main idea or topic. This will help you choose words with the right meaning.
2. Note any small words like prepositions that come after the gap. These will help you rule out some options, for example, in Gap 2, only one of the options has the correct meaning and can be followed by *in*.

In the test, there are 5–6 tasks. For each task, you have a text with several gaps. You select the correct answer for each gap from the drop-down list on the screen. The wording in the instructions below is the same as you will see in the actual test. See page 40 for help.

Below is a text with blanks. Click on each blank, a list of choices will appear. Select the appropriate choice for each blank.

1 It would be very hard to imagine life without electricity. Most of the appliances and machines that are used in homes, offices and factories are powered by electricity and this equipment [1] _____ people's overall quality of life. For that reason, the wider provision of electricity supplies is a critical factor in reducing global poverty [2] _____ . To meet the needs of users around the world, the global consumption of coal has risen more quickly [3] _____ 2000 than any other fuel. For countries that do not have their own supply of natural energy resources, coal has become an essential [4] _____ of producing power. On a global scale, coal is currently used to fire power stations and produces 40% of global electricity. This [5] _____ is very likely to increase, and predictions are that by 2030 coal will fuel 44% of the world's electricity.

1	A helps improving	B helps to improve	C help improve	D help improved
2	A levels	B ranks	C stages	D degrees
3	A for	B in	C since	D at
4	A means	B factor	C aspect	D course
5	A total	B sum	C volume	D figure

2 People are living longer and this longevity is good news for sales teams. It results in a much more [1] _____ customer base for them to work from. Why we are living longer is not the issue for anyone [2] _____ in drawing up plans to market a product. What they focus on is the fact that there are now more age groups to target, which means that a sales pitch can be re-worked a number of times to more exactly fit each one. For example, [3] _____ referring simply to 'adults', there are now 'starting adults', 'young adults' and 'established adults'. [4] _____ markets no longer talk about 'children', but tend to refer to a fuller range of categories that includes 'kids', 'tweens', 'pre-teens' and 'teenagers'. We now have a very diverse population in terms of age, and that can only be a [5] _____ for business.

1	A usual	B precise	C right	D honest
2	A linked	B mixed	C concerned	D involved
3	A rather than	B by	C even when	D while
4	A While	B Similarly	C Even	D Really
5	A desire	B favour	C bonus	D promise

Below is a text with blanks. Click on each blank, a list of choices will appear. Select the appropriate answer choice for each blank.

TIP STRIP

3 Think about whether you need a countable or uncountable noun. For example, there is no article before Gap 1 and, although all the options have similar meanings, only one is used with *reference* to form an uncountable noun phrase.

4 Look at what comes after the gap. For example, in Gap 2, only one option in this set can be followed by an infinitive verb form.

3 Experts have waited a considerable amount of time for this much-needed book. Now we have a new and very thorough survey of wetland plant species. The content is extensive and totally up-to-date and as reference [1] _____, it represents extremely good value. In addition to the editors, there are 35 well-chosen contributors who have put in a tremendous amount of work to [2] _____ the reader with maps and indexes, and colourful photographs. The plant descriptions are straightforward, yet scholarly, and flicking through the pages, [3] _____ the writers' passion for the subject. Each of the eight sections has an overview, [4] _____ current concerns and future conservation plans. Despite a few gaps and the occasional unsatisfactory illustration, this handbook will remind botanists and specialists of the importance of protecting the country's plant life. [5] _____ person interested in the topic, whether student or hardened expert, will find it indispensable.

1	A piece	B report	C book	D material
2	A manage	B assist	C contribute	D hand
3	A it can sense	B one sense	C you can sense	D he senses
4	A highlighting	B focusing	C bringing	D involving
5	A The other	B Any one of	C Every	D All

4 At the moment, there are between six and seven thousand languages in the world. According to linguists, fifty percent of these are in danger [1] _____ extinct. The speed of language loss has accelerated over the past few decades because businesses that need to communicate with a range of people from other cultures [2] _____ to employ more widely used languages, such as English, Chinese, or Spanish. This attitude is understandable, but it means that many local languages are dying out before anyone [3] _____ the opportunity to study them. According to linguists, some of these languages could reveal a great [4] _____ of useful information about language learning and cognitive development. In addition, a local language that has been built on the local culture contains words and phrases that express that culture; lose the language and you arguably may lose the culture, too. And finally, historians will [5] _____ that a language contains evidence of a region's history and should, for that reason alone, be preserved.

1	A have become	B to become	C of becoming	D became
2	A prefer	B fancy	C select	D must
3	A have	B would have	C having had	D has had
4	A size	B deal	C capacity	D load
5	A speak	B tell	C argue	D explore

Below is a text with blanks. Click on each blank, a list of choices will appear. Select the appropriate answer choice for each blank.

TIP STRIP

5 Use reference words such as *this, these, it,* etc. to help you make the correct choice. For example, in Gap 2, *these* refers back to the idea of being *lighter* and *more flexible*. Only one option is the correct group noun.

5 Bamboo is a favoured plant among architects and designers because of its incredible strength and durability. One Colombian architect [1] ______ to it as nature's steel, but in many respects it is even better than steel: it is lighter and more flexible, and these [2] ______ make it the ideal building material in areas that suffer earthquakes and severe weather patterns. Construction workers in places such as Hong Kong rely on bamboo scaffolding whatever the [3] ______ of the tower block they may be working on; over a billion people around the world live in a home that is made of bamboo; and China [4] ______ the plant for thousands of years. The only drawback to this remarkable product is the cost of transporting it. So for those [5] ______ live in cooler regions of the world, the enormous advantages of this natural building material are less accessible.

1	A implies	B mentions	C indicates	D refers
2	A abilities	B qualities	C talents	D values
3	A mass	B top	C summit	D height
4	A has cultivated	B cultivate	C cultivates	D had cultivated
5	A which	B may	C who	D are

Overview: Listening

Part 3 of the PTE Academic test is Listening. This part tests your ability to understand spoken English in an academic environment. It also tests your ability to understand a variety of accents, both native and non-native.

The table shows what you will see in the test, which you will take on a computer. When practising with this book, you will have to write your written answers in the book, your notebook or on your own device, and you could record your spoken answers on your own device, for example a mobile phone.

Part 3: Listening				
Listening (total time 45–57 minutes)				
Task type	**Number of tasks**	**Task description**	**Skills assessed**	**Text/ Recording length**
Summarize spoken text	2–3	After listening to a recording, write a summary of 50–70 words.	listening and writing	60–90 seconds
Multiple-choice, choose multiple answers	2–3	After listening to a recording, answer a multiple-choice question on the content or tone of the recording by selecting more than one response.	listening	40–90 seconds
Fill in the blanks	2–3	The transcription of a recording appears on screen with several blanks. While listening to the recording, type the missing words into the blanks.	listening and writing	30–60 seconds
Highlight correct summary	2–3	After listening to a recording, select the paragraph that best summarizes the recording.	listening and reading	30–90 seconds
Multiple-choice, choose single answer	2–3	After listening to a recording, answer a multiple-choice question on the content or tone of the recording by selecting one response.	listening	30–60 seconds
Select missing word	2–3	After listening to a recording, select the missing word or group of words that completes the recording.	listening	20–70 seconds
Highlight incorrect words	2–3	The transcription of a recording appears on screen. While listening to the recording, identify the words in the transcription that differ from what is said.	listening and reading	15–50 seconds
Write from dictation	3–4	After listening to a recording of a sentence, type the sentence.	listening and writing	3–5 seconds

Each recording is played only once. You may take notes using the Erasable Noteboard Booklet and pen, and use these notes as a guide when answering the tasks.

With the exception of *Summarize spoken text*, listening task types are not timed individually. You can refer to the timer in the upper right-hand corner of the computer screen, *Time Remaining*, which counts down the time remaining for the Listening part.

Summarize spoken text

About the task type

This is a long-answer listening task type that tests listening and writing skills. You have to summarize the key points in a short lecture, in 50–70 words. You will do 2–3 *Summarize spoken text* tasks.

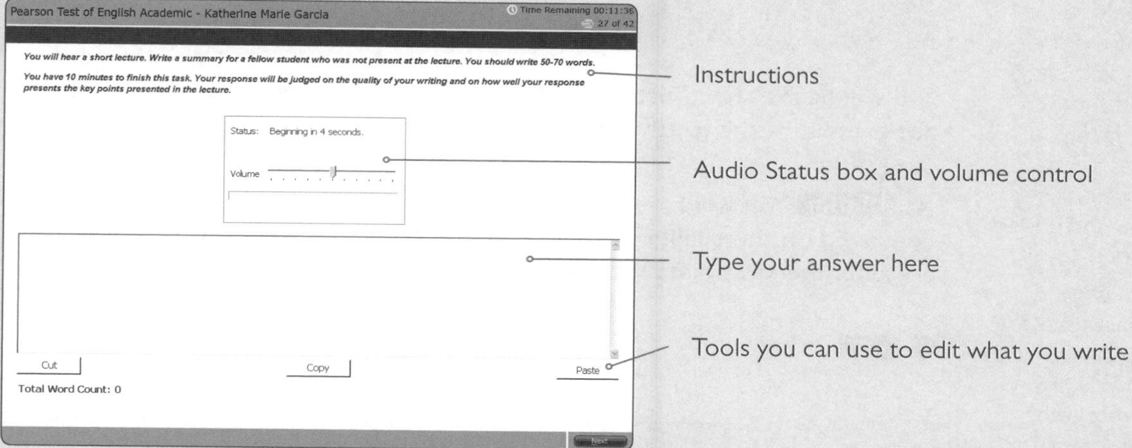

Strategies

Be ready

- The Audio Status box will count down from 12 seconds and the audio will begin.
- Be ready to take notes on the Erasable Noteboard Booklet.

Take notes as you listen

- As you listen, take notes of the main and supporting ideas.
- Don't try to write down everything you hear. Use key words, abbreviations, symbols and arrows to capture the most important ideas and to indicate how the ideas are organized. Effective note-taking will ensure that your summary has all the main points.
- When the recording stops, look at your notes while the audio is fresh in your mind. Plan how you will present the information.

Write your summary

- When the audio stops, you have 10 minutes to write your summary.
- Use your notes to summarize all the main points and add as many supporting details or examples as you can. Top marks will be gained if all relevant aspects of the audio are mentioned.
- Keep to the word limit of 50–70 words, or you will lose marks.
- Save 2 minutes at the end to check your work for grammar and spelling. Mistakes will lose marks.
- After 10 minutes, the screen will stop responding. Click 'Next'.

Testing focus Scoring ➤ page 153

Subskills tested

Listening: identifying the topic, theme or main ideas; summarizing the main idea; identifying supporting points or examples; identifying a speaker's purpose, style, tone or attitude; understanding academic vocabulary; inferring the meaning of unfamiliar words; comprehending explicit and implicit information; comprehending concrete and abstract information; classifying and categorizing information; following an oral sequencing of information; comprehending variations in tone, speed and accent.

Writing: writing a summary; writing under timed conditions; taking notes whilst listening to a recording; communicating the main points of a lecture in writing; organizing sentences and paragraphs in a logical way; using words and phrases appropriate to the context; using correct grammar; using correct spelling; using correct mechanics.

Preparation

- Develop your own techniques for rapid note-taking. Decide on your own abbreviations and symbols and practise using them so they become automatic.
- Find podcasts of lectures with a transcript. Highlight the signal words that indicate the main points and the examples, or evidence, or opposing arguments, then listen for them in the audio to help you understand.
- Find podcasts of lectures online. Listen to 30 seconds of a lecture, noting the key words, then stop the audio and write a sentence that summarizes the main points of what you heard. Repeat this twice until you have listened to 90 seconds. Then, join your sentences into a summary of 50–70 words. Practise until you can listen to 90 seconds without stopping the audio. Summarize 2 or 3 short lectures and time yourself at 10 minutes for each summary.
- Practise writing grammatically correct sentences. Simple sentences that communicate meaning will score better than complex sentences with errors. The best responses use concise, correct sentences that communicate meaning clearly.

Summarize spoken text

TIP STRIP

1 Your grammar, vocabulary and spelling should be accurate. Leave one or two minutes at the end to check your summary. Have you used the right tenses? Have you started each sentence with a capital letter, used commas in lists and ended with a full stop?

2 Your summary should include the main point(s) and important supporting points. When you are summarizing research or an experiment, note down the key stages, paying less attention to examples or minor details.

In the test, there are 2–3 tasks. For each task, you listen to the audio then type your summary into the box on the screen. The wording in the instructions below is the same as you will see in the actual test. See page 45 for help.

You will hear a short lecture. Write a summary for a fellow student who was not present at the lecture. You should write 50–70 words.

10 min. You will have 10 minutes to finish this task. Your response will be judged on the quality of your writing and on how well your response presents the key points presented in the lecture.

1 ▸ 25

....

....

....

....

....

....

2 ▸ 26

....

....

....

....

....

....

Multiple-choice, choose multiple answers

About the task type

This is a multiple-choice listening task type that tests listening skills. More than one response is correct in answer to a question about a lecture. You will do 2–3 *Multiple-choice, choose multiple answers* tasks.

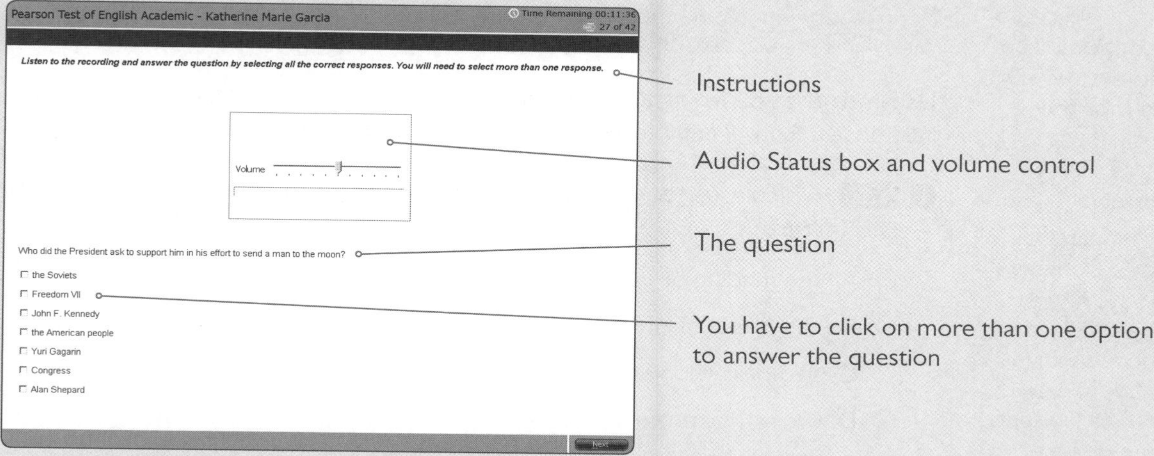

Strategies

Read and think ahead

- Read the question and skim the options before the audio begins. This will tell you what the topic is as well as what information you are listening for. It could be the main ideas, the writer's goals or attitudes, some detailed information, or inferences.

Stay focused

- Keep your attention on the audio. Take notes of key words if you wish, to help you remember the information you hear.
- As you listen, be aware of the development of the speaker's ideas so you can recognize the core information.
- Listen for the general flow of ideas and don't worry if you miss or don't know individual words.
- After the audio finishes, eliminate options that contain incorrect information or have information that was not mentioned.
- Answer the question by clicking on more than one option or on their checkboxes.

Confirm your choice

- After you have chosen the options, check again that each of the other options is incorrect. If you change your mind, click on the option again to de-select it then click on the correct option.
- Be aware of the time and don't spend too much time on one task.

Testing focus Scoring ➤ page 154

Subskills tested

Listening: any of the following depending on the task: identifying the topic, theme or main ideas; identifying supporting points or examples; identifying specific details, facts, opinions, definitions or sequences of events; identifying a speaker's purpose, style, tone or attitude; identifying the overall organization of information and connections between pieces of information; inferring the context, purpose or tone; inferring the meaning of unfamiliar words; predicting how a speaker may continue.

Preparation

- Listen to lectures you find on the web and stop the audio about every minute to answer this question: *What points has the speaker made?* Summarize the main points.
- Listen to lectures you find on the web and stop the audio about every minute to answer this question: *What is the speaker doing here?* (introducing, criticizing, summarizing, persuading, describing, etc.).
- Take notes of the information in a short extract from a lecture and use arrows to show how the speaker's ideas develop.
- Practise activating relevant vocabulary: listen to the opening sentence of a lecture, then stop the lecture and make a list of all the words on that topic that you expect to hear. Circle each one as you listen to the lecture and add other words to your list.
- Find podcasts of lectures with a transcript. Highlight the signal words that indicate the main points and the examples, or evidence, or opposing arguments, then listen for them in the audio. Highlight any words you don't know in the transcript and practise guessing what they mean from the context. Check your guess in a dictionary.
- Expand your vocabulary by creating lists of words with their synonyms. Use a thesaurus to find new words with the same or similar meanings. Look for the words in context, for example in a learner's dictionary.

Multiple-choice, choose multiple answers

In the test, there are 2–3 tasks. For each task, you listen to the audio then click the buttons next to all of the answers you think are correct. The wording in the instructions below is the same as you will see in the actual test. See page 47 for help.

Listen to the recording and answer the question by selecting all the correct responses. *You will need to select more than one response.*

1 ▸ 27 **Which aspects of subway construction will the speaker talk about in this lecture?**

- ○ A the funding of projects
- ○ B the speed of trains
- ○ C geological conditions
- ○ D employing professionals
- ○ E public approval
- ○ F passenger movement

2 ▸ 28 **According to the speaker, which of the following measures helped reduce community problems in Brickendon?**

- ○ A allowing residents to patrol the area
- ○ B interviewing residents about the problems
- ○ C organizing regular community meetings
- ○ D giving families financial support
- ○ E identifying hotspots for crime
- ○ F removing litter from the streets

TIP STRIP

1. Before you listen, decide on the main focus of the question and quickly read through the options. The question is about subway construction (not travel or relocation) so use those words to help you focus your listening.
2. Listen for the ideas, not just words or synonyms for words in the options. If you just match words without understanding the whole option, e.g. *residents*, *families*, *hotspots* you may choose the wrong answers.

Fill in the blanks

About the task type

This is a listening task type that tests listening and writing skills. You have to listen to a recording and write the missing words in a transcription of the recording. You will do 2–3 *Fill in the blanks* tasks.

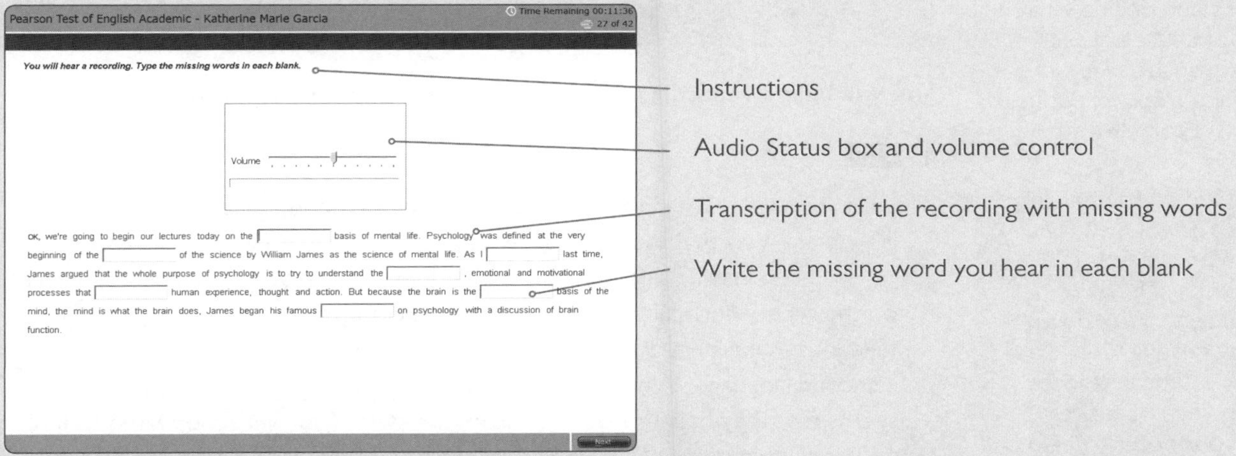

Strategies

Be ready

- Quickly skim the text to gain a general idea of the topic.
- Be ready to write each missing word on your Erasable Noteboard Booklet as you hear each one, or type directly into each blank.
- The Audio Status box will count down from 7 seconds and the audio will then begin.

Write what you hear

- As you hear each missing word during the recording, write or type the word quickly and be ready for the next one. Do not check your spelling at this point.
- Follow the speaker in the transcription so you do not miss a word. Do not get behind.
- Keep writing or typing each missing word until the audio stops.

Check and type

- After the audio stops, read the sentence that has the first missing word and confirm that the word you wrote makes sense.
- Continue for each blank. Type carefully and check your spelling each time. Incorrect spelling will score zero for that blank.
- Use grammar clues to make sure you type the correct form of the word (noun, verb, adjective, etc.).
- Read through one last time for meaning to confirm each word and check your spelling. Click 'Next' to move on.

Testing focus Scoring ➤ page 154

Subskills tested

Listening: identifying words and phrases appropriate to the context; understanding academic vocabulary; comprehending explicit and implicit information; following an oral sequencing of information.

Writing: writing from dictation; using words and phrases appropriate to the context; using correct grammar; using correct spelling.

Preparation

- Practise matching the written form of a word to the sound. Listen to a podcast of a lecture and stop the audio every 10 seconds. Write down the last word you heard, then play that part again to check that the word you wrote makes sense in the sentence.
- Check the pronunciation of any new words you learn by using a dictionary with the words recorded. Make sure you know where the stress falls within the word.
- Confirm the spelling of new words as you learn them. Practise typing new words in lists; this will also help to familiarize you with a QWERTY keyboard (the type of English-language keyboard used in PTE Academic).
- Ask a friend to read short sentences to you from a magazine. Type the sentences you hear on your computer with the spell-checker turned off. Look at what you have written: are there any misspelled words? Run the spell-checker through the sentence to see if you were right.
- Create a word bank for new words with as many forms of the word listed as you can find, such as the noun, verb, adjective and adverb form of words, e.g. *education* (n), *educate* (v), *educated* (adj). You can add synonyms, antonyms and collocations to your word bank to expand your vocabulary. Add to your word bank every day.
- If you hear part of a word, you can work out what form the word must be and how to spell it using grammar and context clues. Use a grammar book with gap-fill quizzes to practise choosing the grammatically correct word for each gap.

Fill in the blanks

TIP STRIP

1. Quickly read the text before the recording begins and decide what it is about. Use important nouns, such as *languages*, *school curriculum*, *business* and *CVs* to help you do this.
2. Note down the missing words as you hear them on the Erasable Noteboard Booklet provided. Write down every missing word you think you hear. When the recording is over, use your notes to help you decide on the correct spelling.

In the test, there are 2–3 tasks. For each task, there is a text with several gaps. You type the correct answer for each gap into the box in the text. The wording in the instructions below is the same as you will see in the actual test. See page 49 for help.

You will hear a recording. Type the missing words in each blank.

1 ▸ 29

Learning a language in the classroom is never easy and, quite [1] ________, it's not the way that most people would choose to learn if they had other [2] ________. Having said that, there are plenty of reasons for keeping languages on the school curriculum. For one thing, a fair number of students go on to take jobs in business and commerce that require a [3] ________ knowledge of a second language. When you talk to young [4] ________ in top companies, it seems that they had a career plan from the start; they were motivated to find additional things to put on their CVs – and of course language is one of those added, but [5] ________ extras.

2 ▸ 30

The assignment that I'm going to set for the holiday period is one that we've given students for a number of years. It's quite [1] ________ and will allow you to get out and about – it's no good being shut up in your rooms all the time! It does have a written [2] ________, too. Um, basically it's a data gathering exercise and there are two choices with regard to how you [3] ________ the data. We'll go through those in a moment. I'm also going to give you a link to an internet site that is – well it's critical that you [4] ________ this before you do anything, as it provides a lot of guidance on data presentation, both in terms of how you plot it – its diagrammatic form and also its [5] ________, which has to be clear.

TEST 1

LISTENING

Highlight correct summary

About the task type

This task type tests listening and reading skills. You will listen to a short lecture then identify the correct summary of the information you have heard. You will do 2–3 *Highlight correct summary* tasks.

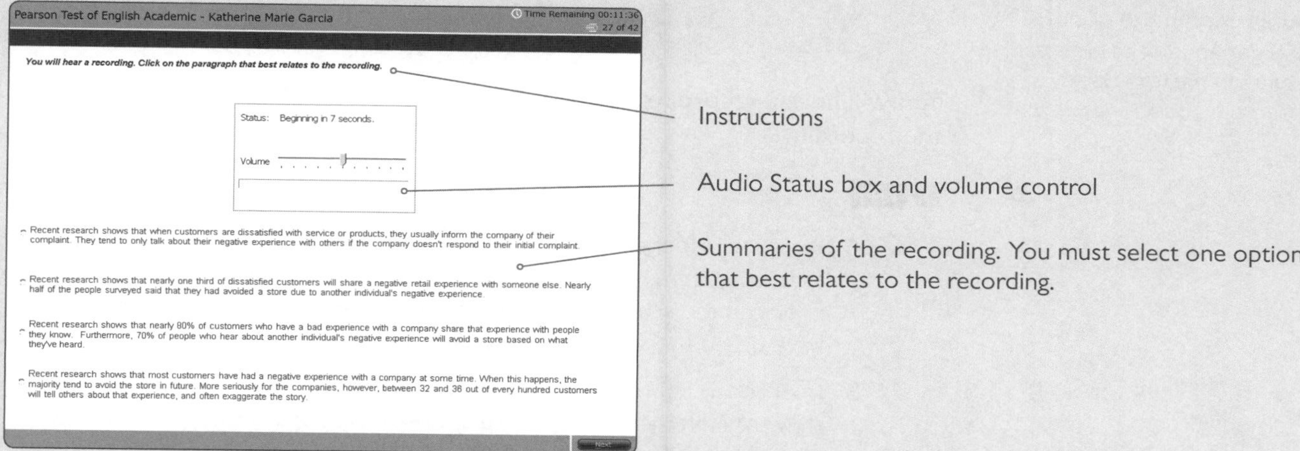

Pearson Test of English Academic - Katherine Marie Garcia
Time Remaining 00:11:36
27 of 42
You will hear a recording. Click on the paragraph that best relates to the recording.
Status: Beginning in 7 seconds.
Volume
Recent research shows that when customers are dissatisfied with service or products, they usually inform the company of their complaint. They tend to only talk about their negative experience with others if the company doesn't respond to their initial complaint.
Recent research shows that nearly one third of dissatisfied customers will share a negative retail experience with someone else. Nearly half of the people surveyed said that they had avoided a store due to another individual's negative experience.
Recent research shows that nearly 80% of customers who have a bad experience with a company share that experience with people they know. Furthermore, 70% of people who hear about another individual's negative experience will avoid a store based on what they've heard.
Recent research shows that most customers have had a negative experience with a company at some time. When this happens, the majority tend to avoid the store in future. More seriously for the companies, however, between 32 and 36 out of every hundred customers will tell others about that experience, and often exaggerate the story.
Instructions
Audio Status box and volume control
Summaries of the recording. You must select one option that best relates to the recording.

Strategies

Be ready

- Use the 10 seconds as the audio counts down to skim the 4 summaries quickly to gain an idea of the topic. You will not have time to read thoroughly.
- Be ready to listen and take notes of key ideas using your Erasable Noteboard Booklet.

Listen and take notes

- As you listen, take notes of the main and supporting ideas.
- Don't try to write down everything you hear. Use key words, abbreviations, symbols and arrows to capture the most important ideas.
- Note any data given in support of an argument, or any implications suggested by the speaker.
- Do not try to read the summaries as you listen. Each one is 40–60 words, so there is too much information. Focus on listening.

Match notes and summary

- When the audio stops, use your notes to select the correct option.
- First, eliminate any options that contain incorrect information.
- Eliminate any options that focus on only one aspect of the information, or that contain information that was not mentioned at all.
- Check the remaining option against your notes to confirm that it covers all aspects of the lecture. Select that option and move on.

Testing focus Scoring ➤ page 154

Subskills tested

Listening: identifying the topic, theme or main ideas; identifying supporting points or examples; understanding academic vocabulary; inferring the meaning of unfamiliar words; comprehending explicit and implicit information; comprehending concrete and abstract information; classifying and categorizing information; following an oral sequencing of information; comprehending variations in tone, speed and accent.

Reading: identifying supporting points or examples; identifying the most accurate summary; understanding academic vocabulary; inferring the meaning of unfamiliar words; comprehending concrete and abstract information; classifying and categorizing information; following a logical or chronological sequence of events; evaluating the quality and usefulness of texts.

Preparation

- Develop your own techniques for rapid note-taking. Decide on your own abbreviations and symbols and practise using them so they become automatic.
- Practise skimming sets of summaries using the practice tests in this book. After 10 seconds, use the words you notice to predict the probable content of the lecture.
- Find podcasts of lectures with a transcript. Highlight the signal words that indicate the main points and the examples, or evidence, or opposing arguments, then listen for them in the audio. Underline words in the transcript that the speaker highlights with stress or intonation; these help to indicate the key points.
- Listen to 30 seconds of a lecture, noting the key points, then stop the audio and write a sentence that summarizes the main information you heard. Repeat this twice until you have listened to 90 seconds. Then, join your sentences into a summary; practice in *writing* summaries will help you to *recognize* a summary. Practise until you can listen to 90 seconds without stopping the audio, then produce a complete summary.

Highlight correct summary

TIP STRIP

Use the ten seconds before the recording begins to skim through the options and get an idea of the main points in each.

In the test, there are 2–3 tasks. For each task, you listen to the audio then click the button next to the summary you think is correct. The wording in the instructions below is the same as you will see in the actual test. See page 51 for help.

You will hear a recording. Click on the paragraph that best relates to the recording.

1 ▶ 31

○ **A** Business students are finding it increasingly difficult to get employment, as the standard of law courses has declined since 2007. Employers have criticized the schools for adopting unsatisfactory teaching methods, and have urged them to ensure students get higher grades.

○ **B** In order to improve the chances of their students obtaining jobs after they have finished their courses, some business schools are adjusting their grades. These adjustments are being made to all grades awarded since 2007 but instead of benefiting the students it is, in some instances, having the opposite effect.

○ **C** Some business schools have realized that their grading system has been inaccurate since 2007 and are currently making changes to correct the errors. Students' grades are being revised, and employers have welcomed this move as it means that they will be able to employ better qualified students.

○ **D** Since 2007, the education of business students has been improving but this has not been reflected in the grades that they are achieving. Business schools have been under pressure from employers to ensure that the grades that students are achieving match their abilities far better than in recent years.

TIP STRIP

Listen for the signposts that indicate the main ideas. Speakers use words and phrases like the first thing I wanted to talk about, on the one side, on the other side to help listeners understand the flow of their ideas.

You will hear a recording. Click on the paragraph that best relates to the recording.

2 ▸ 32

- ○ **A** Many existing buildings in city centres, such as Perth are being cleared to make way for modern developments. Although this is improving the visual impact of the city, it is causing difficulties in areas where there is not enough space to accommodate the expanding population.
- ○ **B** Developers in Perth and other parts of Western Australia are suggesting that it would be better to build much-needed homes within the city centre, as this would be more affordable for local people. It would also make transportation to and from jobs and shops cheaper and quicker.
- ○ **C** Cities like Perth in Western Australia are experiencing a rapid growth in urban development, and the current trend is to expand into surrounding regions. Although some people think this is more cost effective than building within cities, others believe it's having a harmful effect on the environment in these areas.
- ○ **D** The housing shortage in Perth is being addressed by encouraging people to move to other cities in Western Australia where there is more space to develop new housing and infrastructure. This will benefit people struggling to find accommodation and also avoid having to develop on bushland.

Multiple-choice, choose single answer

About the task type

This is a multiple-choice listening task type that tests listening skills. You have to select a single answer to a question about a lecture. You will do 2–3 *Multiple-choice, choose single answer* tasks.

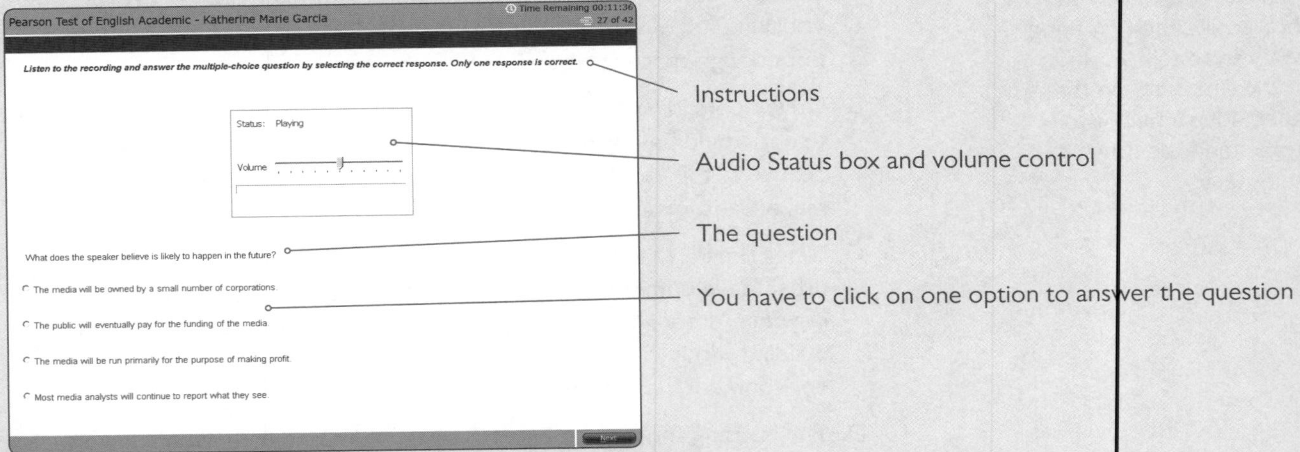

Strategies

Read and think ahead

- Read the question and skim the options before the audio begins. This will tell you what the topic is as well as what information you are listening for. It could be the main idea, the writer's goal or attitude, some detailed information, or an inference that can be drawn.

Stay focused

- Keep your attention on the audio. Take notes of key words if you wish, to help you remember the information you hear.
- As you listen, be aware of the development of the speaker's ideas so you can recognize the core information.
- Listen for the general flow of ideas and don't worry if you miss or don't know individual words.
- After the audio finishes, eliminate options that contain incorrect information or have information that was not mentioned.
- Answer the question by clicking on one option or on its radio button ◯ .

Confirm your choice

- After you have chosen the option, check again that each of the other options is incorrect. If you change your mind, click on the option again to de-select it then click on the correct option.
- Be aware of the time and don't spend too much time on one task. Click 'Next' and move on.

Testing focus Scoring ➤ page 154

Subskills tested

Listening: any of the following depending on the task: identifying the topic, theme or main ideas; identifying supporting points or examples; identifying specific details, facts, opinions, definitions or sequences of events; identifying a speaker's purpose, style, tone or attitude; identifying the overall organization of information and connections between pieces of information; inferring the context, purpose or tone; inferring the meaning of unfamiliar words; predicting how a speaker may continue.

Preparation

- Listen to lectures you find on the web and stop the audio about every minute to answer this question: *What points has the speaker made?* Summarize the main points.
- Listen to lectures you find on the web and stop the audio about every minute to answer this question: *What is the speaker doing here?* (introducing, criticizing, summarizing, persuading, describing, etc.).
- Take notes of the information in a lecture and use arrows to show how the speaker's ideas develop.
- Practise activating relevant vocabulary: listen to the opening sentence of a lecture, then stop the lecture and make a list of all the words on that topic that you expect to hear. Circle each one as you listen to the lecture and add other words to your list.
- Find podcasts of lectures with a transcript. Highlight the signal words that indicate the main points and the examples, or evidence, or opposing arguments, then listen for them in the audio. Highlight any words you don't know in the transcript and practise guessing what they mean from the context. Check your guess in a dictionary.
- Expand your vocabulary by creating lists of words with their synonyms. Use a thesaurus to find new words with the same or similar meanings. When you learn a new word, find an example of how it is used in context, for example in a learner's dictionary.

STRATEGIES

Multiple-choice, choose single answer

In the test, there are 2–3 tasks. For each task, you listen to the audio then click the button next to the answer you think is correct. The wording in the instructions below is the same as you will see in the actual test. See page 54 for help.

TIP STRIP

1. Read the question carefully before you read the options so that you know what you need to listen for. This question is about the main focus so you need to listen to the whole recording and decide which option best describes the overall idea.
2. The words *early views* are important in this question – they tell you that you are listening for opinions on something specific. Listen to what the speakers say about these.

Listen to the recording and answer the multiple-choice question by selecting the correct response. ***Only one response is correct.***

1 ▶ 33 **What is the speaker's main focus?**

- ○ A reasons why Americans have relocated
- ○ B the growth in the American population
- ○ C the expansion of suburban towns
- ○ D trends in where Americans live

2 ▶ 34 **What do the speakers feel about early views on malaria?**

- ○ A They were understandable at the time.
- ○ B They resulted in unnecessary illness.
- ○ C They have contributed to current findings.
- ○ D They will be remembered in the future.

Select missing word

About the task type

This task type tests listening skills. From a set of options, you have to predict what word(s) a speaker will say, based on contextual clues in a recording. You will do 2–3 *Select missing word* tasks.

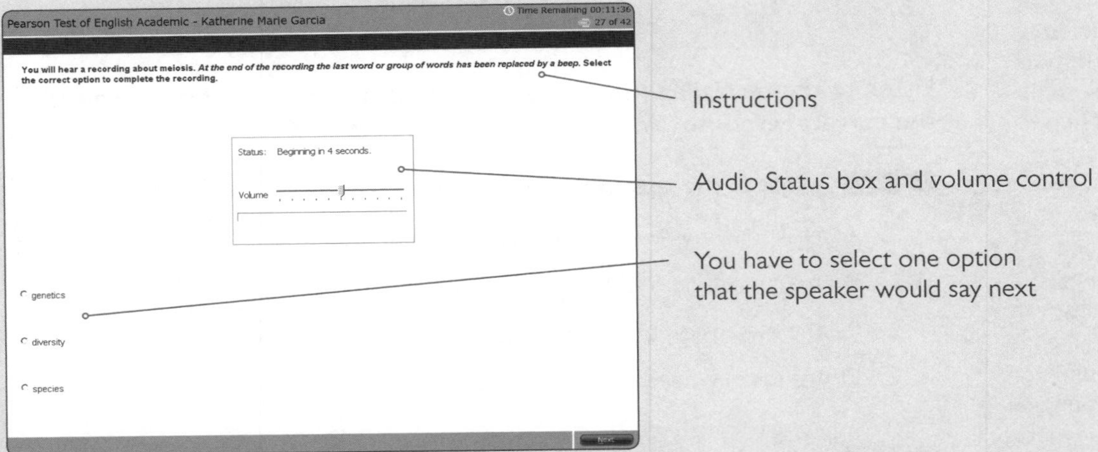

Strategies

Be ready

- The instructions tell you the topic of the recording. As the Audio Status box counts down from 7 seconds, think what vocabulary you might hear.
- Skim the options quickly to gain an idea of the aspect of the topic the speaker might talk about.
- Be ready to focus on what you hear, and nothing else.

Listen attentively

- As you listen, make a mental map of what you are hearing. Do not take notes – it is more important to listen for the development of the speaker's ideas.
- Listen for any signal words the speaker might use to tell you the direction of the talk, e.g. presenting opposite arguments, describing something in detail, supporting a claim, etc.
- Don't worry about any words you don't understand. Focus on the overall ideas.

Predict the ending

- Be aware of the blue bar in the Audio Status box. This shows you when the recording is coming to an end so you will be ready to suggest the word or phrase that has been replaced by a beep.
- As soon as the recording stops, think what would come next and scan the options for the most similar word or phrase. Select it.

Testing focus Scoring ➤ page 155

Subskills tested

Listening: identifying the topic, theme or main idea; identifying words and phrases appropriate to the context; understanding academic vocabulary; inferring the meaning of unfamiliar words; comprehending explicit and implicit information; comprehending concrete and abstract information; following an oral sequencing of information; predicting how a speaker may continue; forming a conclusion from what a speaker says; comprehending variations in tone, speed and accent.

Preparation

- Work with a friend. Find 2 magazine articles and take turns to read out a short paragraph to each other, stopping before the final word or phrase. Try to guess what word or phrase will complete the paragraph.
- Develop your skills of predicting the ideas you will hear. Listen to 20 seconds of a lecture, then stop the audio and say what ideas you think the speaker will talk about next. Play on and check your prediction. Repeat this with longer recordings.
- Find podcasts of lectures with a transcript. Highlight the signal words that indicate the main points and the examples, or evidence, or opposing arguments, then listen for them in the audio. Look at the way these signal words will tell you the direction of the lecture and what the speaker is likely to say next.
- Find podcasts of lectures with a transcript. Play the lecture, stopping the audio about every 30 seconds. Predict what words the speaker will say next, then check the transcript. Compare the written form of the words with how they sound in the lecture.
- Practise predicting what vocabulary you will hear in lectures on different topics. Play the first sentence or two of a short lecture, then make a list of the words and phrases you expect to hear. Play the lecture to check how many words from your list you hear.
- Expand your vocabulary of academic words in context. Keep a record of new words you learn.

Select missing word

TIP STRIP

1 If the options are phrases, read each one quickly while the audio counts down from seven seconds, and decide what you need to listen for. If the answer is A, you should hear a comparison related to writers; B, an overview of how popular something has been; C, reference to how something has changed over time; and D, a description of something that facilitates reading.

2 If the options are single words, consider their meaning and whether they are linked in any way. These options all describe the quality of something. You will need to listen for which quality is discussed by the speaker.

In the test, there are 2–3 tasks. For each task, you listen to the audio then click the button next to the words you think complete the audio. The wording in the instructions below is the same as you will see in the actual test. See page 56 for help.

1 ▶ 35 You will hear a recording about fiction writing. *At the end of the recording the last word or group of words has been replaced by a beep.* Select the correct option to complete the recording.

○ A suits some writers better than others

○ B is becoming more popular

○ C has changed over time

○ D makes reading easier

2 ▶ 36 You will hear a recording about biology. *At the end of the recording the last word or group of words has been replaced by a beep.* Select the correct option to complete the recording.

○ A complex

○ B unreal

○ C confusing

○ D invisible

Highlight incorrect words

About the task type

This task type tests listening and reading skills. As you listen to a recording, you have to identify words in a transcription that differ from what you hear. You will do 2–3 *Highlight incorrect words* tasks.

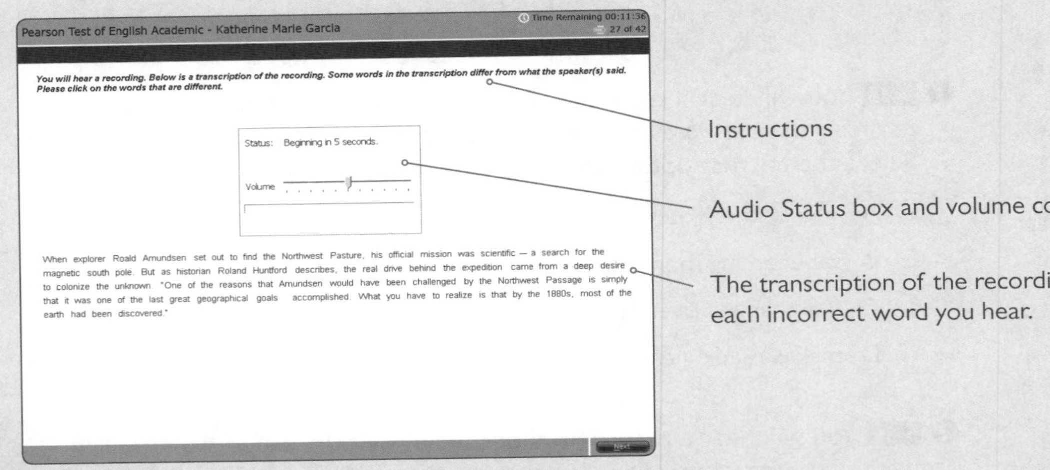

Pearson Test of English Academic - Katherine Marie Garcia
Time Remaining 00:11:36
27 of 42
You will hear a recording. Below is a transcription of the recording. Some words in the transcription differ from what the speaker(s) said. Please click on the words that are different.
Status: Beginning in 5 seconds.
Volume
When explorer Roald Amundsen set out to find the Northwest Pasture, his official mission was scientific – a search for the magnetic south pole. But as historian Roland Huntford describes, the real drive behind the expedition came from a deep desire to colonize the unknown. "One of the reasons that Amundsen would have been challenged by the Northwest Passage is simply that it was one of the last great geographical goals accomplished. What you have to realize is that by the 1880s, most of the earth had been discovered."
Instructions
Audio Status box and volume control
The transcription of the recording. You have to click on each incorrect word you hear.

STRATEGIES

Strategies

Be ready

- Use the 10 seconds before the recording begins to skim the transcription, to familiarize yourself with the topic.
- Move your cursor to the start of the transcription before the audio begins.

Follow the recording

- As soon as the recording begins, move your cursor along each line following the speaker's voice.
- Think how each word you are reading will sound and as soon as you hear a different word, click on the incorrect word.
  The word you have clicked on will be highlighted and will remain highlighted until you click on it again.
- Keep up with the speaker. Do not stop to think about whether your selection was correct or incorrect. If you lose your place it will be difficult for you to catch up and you may miss some words that you should have selected.

Try not to change your mind

- Do not change your mind unless you feel very sure you have made a mistake. Success in this task type depends on real-time decisions.
- Do not guess. You will lose marks for words you click on that were in fact the correct word that was in the recording. There are up to 7 'errors' in each transcription.

Testing focus Scoring ➤ page 155

Subskills tested

Listening: identifying errors in a transcription; understanding academic vocabulary; following an oral sequencing of information; comprehending variations in tone, speed and accent.

Reading: understanding academic vocabulary; following a logical or chronological sequence of events; reading a text under timed conditions; matching written text to speech.

Preparation

- When you learn a new word, use a dictionary that has the words recorded so you can check both the pronunciation of the sounds and where the word stress falls.
- Listen to the way the final sound in one word links to the first sound in the next when people speak. Be prepared for this when you follow the transcription.
- Remember that when people speak, they group the words into meaningful chunks. Be prepared to follow the rhythm of the recording as you read the transcription.
- Find podcasts of lectures with a transcript. In the transcript, highlight the words or phrases you think will be stressed and the words or phrases that will be unstressed or weak. Listen to the podcast in sections and check if you were right.
- In podcasts of lectures with a transcript, highlight in a short section of the transcript all the key words that carry the meaning and think how they are pronounced. Decide where the word stress falls within each word. Check in a dictionary. Then, play the lecture and listen to how the speaker pronounces each of the words you highlighted.
- Listen to podcasts by speakers with different English accents so that you become familiar with the way different speakers pronounce words, especially where they place the word stress, e.g. (UK): *re<u>search</u>*/(US): *<u>re</u>search*. Some consonants will also be different, such as in *schedule*.

Highlight incorrect words

TIP STRIP

1. You will not have time to read the transcription carefully before the recording begins, but you will have time to skim it quickly. As you do this, decide what the general topic of the paragraph is. This will help you follow the ideas as you listen.
2. As you listen, follow the words with the cursor on screen (or your pencil in this book) and click on (or mark) any words that sound different from the transcript.

In the test, there are 2–3 tasks. For each task, you listen to the audio and follow the words in the text on the screen. You click on the words that are different on the screen and the audio. The wording in the instructions below is the same as you will see in the actual test. See page 58 for help.

You will hear a recording. Below is a transcription of the recording. *Some words in the transcription differ from what the speaker said.* Please click on the words that are different.

1 ▸ 37 Transcription:

It seems we now know more about outer space than we do about the Earth's core. This is because temperatures are so great at the centre of the Earth that human beings have not been able to take a close look at it. However, new techniques of analysis may soon change all that. The seismic waves formed by earthquakes and volcanic eruptions penetrate the Earth's layers at different speeds. It is now hoped that by studying these waves, scientists will be able to make new findings and solve some of the mysteries of the inside structure of the Earth.

2 ▸ 38 Transcription:

Many species of birds cover long miles during their seasonal migration to warmer climates. But how successful are they, and do birds that get lost on their route ever survive to find their way back? Much research has been done into how birds navigate and the results show that age is a significant reason. Young birds usually just carry on, if they lose their migratory path, and thus fail to achieve their destination, whereas older, more experienced birds will generally be able to find their first route and continue successfully on their journey.

Write from dictation

About the task type

This task type tests listening and writing skills. You have to write a sentence that you will hear once only, in a recording that lasts 3 to 5 seconds. You will do 3–4 *Write from dictation* tasks.

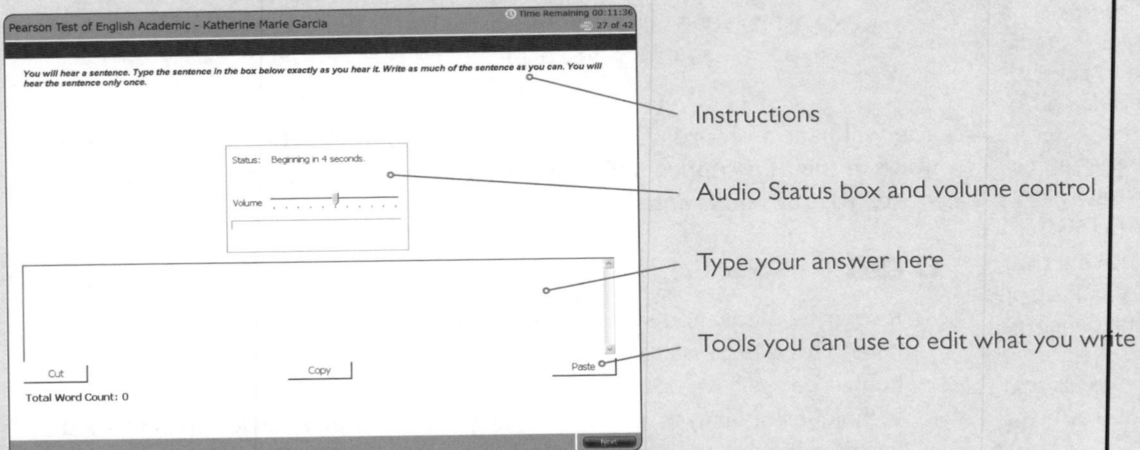

STRATEGIES

Strategies

Be ready

- The Audio Status box will count down from 7 seconds. Focus so that you do not miss any words.
- If you prefer to write the sentence by hand first, be ready to write on your Erasable Noteboard Booklet.
- If you prefer to type directly on the screen, place your cursor in the box on the screen.

Focus on meaning

- When the audio begins, focus on the meaning of the sentence. This will help you to remember it.
- Write or type the content words (nouns, verbs, adjectives and adverbs). Leave the minor words (prepositions, articles) for now.
- Write or type as quickly as you can. Don't worry about spelling at this point. Start writing as soon as the dictation begins and don't stop to check your writing yet.

Construct and check

- Immediately after the recording stops, write or type as much of the sentence as you can.
- Go over the sentence and use your knowledge of grammar, word form and word order to add any words you missed out (e.g. prepositions, articles).
- Check the spelling of every word. Check for verb endings and plurals. Marks are awarded for every correct word spelled correctly. Then click 'Next'.

Testing focus Scoring ➤ page 155

Subskills tested

Listening: understanding academic vocabulary; following an oral sequencing of information; comprehending variations in tone, speed and accent.

Writing: writing from dictation; using correct spelling.

Preparation

- Decide in advance whether you are going to write the sentence by hand or write directly on the screen. Once you have decided which method you prefer, practise dictations using it and don't change your mind on the test day.
- Practise guessing how to spell words you don't know. Write down words you hear in the media, in advertisements, the news, interviews. Try to confirm the spelling of the word you heard using a dictionary.
- Revise your knowledge of the normal spelling conventions. Make a list of words you have trouble spelling, especially words with *ie* or *ei*, or doubled consonants such as *mm*, *ll*, *pp*, *ss*.
- Make a list of words with similar pronunciation but different spelling and different meaning, such as *affect/effect*, *except/accept*, *no/know*, *fair/fare*. Check the meaning of each one.
- Create a word bank for new words with as many forms of the word listed as you can find, such as the noun, verb, adjective and adverb form of words, e.g. *evidence* (n), *evident* (adj), *evidently* (adv). In the test, you may miss part of a word so you may have to work out which form is needed and spell it correctly.
- Practise writing sentences with correct word endings, such as *-ed* endings on past tenses and *-s* endings on plurals and present tenses.
- Listen to podcasts by speakers with different English accents to become familiar with them.
- Remember that this is the final task type in the test. Be aware of the time remaining in Part 3 so that you have enough time to attempt every question. It is better to try every task than to spend too much time on a task you have finished.

Write from dictation

TIP STRIP

1. As you listen, write all the words that you hear on your Erasable Noteboard Booklet. After the recording, write the sentence in the response box.
2. When you write the sentence, write the words you hear and do not paraphrase. You will gain marks for each correct word spelled correctly.
3. Try to spell words correctly and check the grammar before you click on 'Next'. Don't miss endings, such as *-ed* on past verb forms, *-ly* on adverbs or *-s* on plurals.

In the test, there are 3–4 tasks. For each task, you listen and type the sentence you hear into the box on the screen. The wording in the instructions below is the same as you will see in the actual test. See page 60 for help.

You will hear a sentence. Type the sentence in the box below exactly as you hear it. Write as much of the sentence as you can. You will hear the sentence only once.

1 ▸ 39

....

....

....

2 ▸ 40

....

....

....

3 ▸ 41

....

....

....

TEST 2

TEST 2 SPEAKING

Read aloud

TIP STRIP

Read first to get an idea of the overall meaning of the text, e.g. Text 1 is about statistics. Look for the words that contain key information; these are usually stressed, e.g. *statistics*, *economy*, *population*, *environment*, *visible*, *accessible*, *robust*.

Practise saying any difficult words, e.g. *sta<u>tis</u>tics*, *sta<u>tis</u>tically <u>lit</u>erate*. Think about where your voice will rise, fall and pause.

In the test, there are 6–7 tasks. For each task, you read the text aloud into the microphone. The wording in the instructions below is the same as you will see in the actual test. See page 12 for help.

40 sec. Look at the text below. In 40 seconds, you must read this text aloud as naturally and as clearly as possible. You have 40 seconds to read aloud.

1 Statistics reflect vital information about the economy, the well-being of the population, and the environment. Society relies on statistics being visible, accessible and robust, and on statistically literate people making the best use of the information to determine future action. Statistical literacy, then, is the ability to accurately understand, interpret and evaluate the data that inform these issues.

2 Housing fulfils the basic needs that people have for security, privacy and shelter. While the adequacy of housing is an important component of individual well-being, housing also has great impact on the nation's economy, with its influence on investment levels, interest rates, building activity and employment.

3 Being physically active benefits people's health significantly, including reducing the risk of some chronic conditions, helping to control weight, and improving mental health. In recent decades, there has been a decline in physical activity because more people work in offices rather than in manual jobs.

4 Students who wish to take a break from their studies will need to put in an application for Leave of Absence. If your application is successful, you will be notified via email. At the end of your Leave of Absence, you must re-enrol at Student Services and in the subjects you intend to study.

5 There are a number of tests available which can suggest if a person is telling the truth, but knowing which ones are accurate is not easy. A newly created test is claimed to be the most accurate yet in lie detection. However, questions have been raised about its accuracy and ethics.

6 A student exchange program complements formal education, while promoting tolerance, maturity and independence – all highly sought after qualities in today's competitive job market. Living in the host country, not as a tourist or guest but as a member of the community, is what makes the experience both challenging and rewarding.

Repeat sentence

TIP STRIP

Focus on the meaning of the sentence and the key words, e.g. in Sentence 1: *students*, *extension*, *tutors*. Notice the stressed words and where the speaker's voice rises and falls, and imitate this when you speak. Does the speaker's voice go up or down at the end of the sentence?

If you take notes, don't try to write every word. Note the key words using abbreviations, e.g. *sts*, *ext*, *tut*.

In the test, there are 10–12 tasks. For each task, you listen and repeat the sentence you hear into the microphone. The wording in the instructions below is the same as you will see in the actual test. See page 14 for help.

▸ 42–51 15 sec. You will hear a sentence. Please repeat the sentence exactly as you hear it. You will hear the sentence only once.

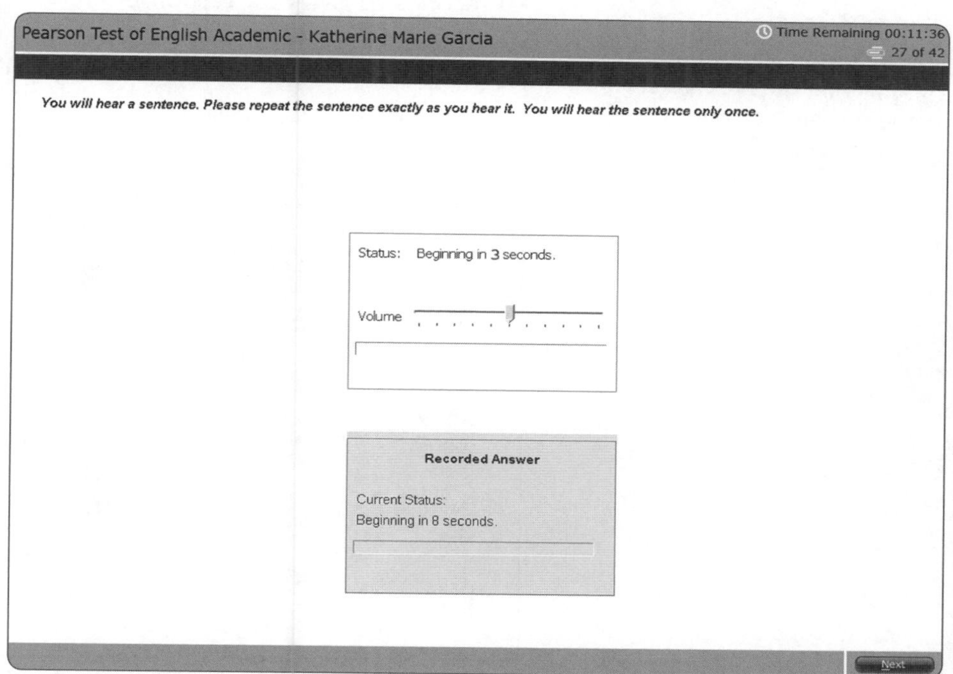

Repeat sentence: Each question is displayed on a new screen.

TEST 2

SPEAKING

Describe image

TIP STRIP

Look at the title of the image. This helps you to begin with a general statement about the information, and then you can describe the major features. In Question 1, the plan shows student accommodation, and the major features are the overall size and number of rooms, their location and their contents.

In the test, there are 6–7 tasks. For each task, you look at the image and describe it into the microphone. The wording in the instructions below is the same as you will see in the actual test. See page 16 for help.

1 40 sec. Look at the plan below. In 25 seconds, please speak into the microphone and describe in detail what the plan is showing. You will have 40 seconds to give your response.

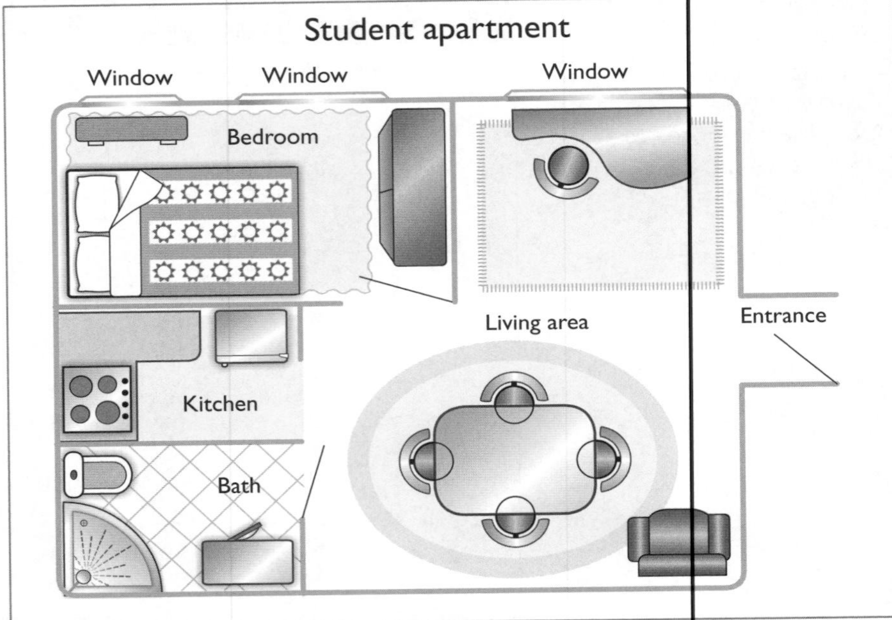

2 40 sec. Look at the graph below. In 25 seconds, please speak into the microphone and describe in detail what the graph is showing. You will have 40 seconds to give your response.

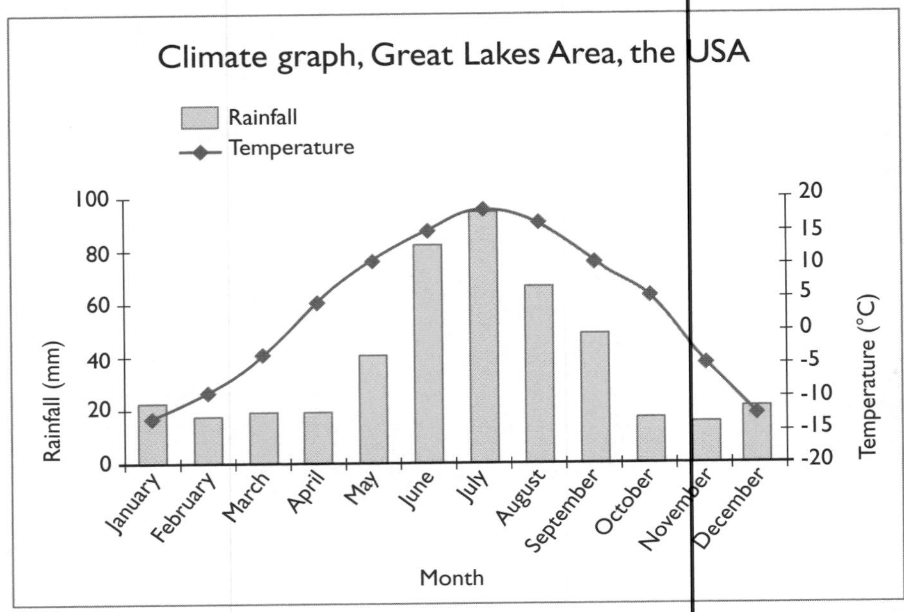

TEST 2
SPEAKING

3 40 sec. Look at the graph below. In 25 seconds, please speak into the microphone and describe in detail what the graph is showing. You will have 40 seconds to give your response.

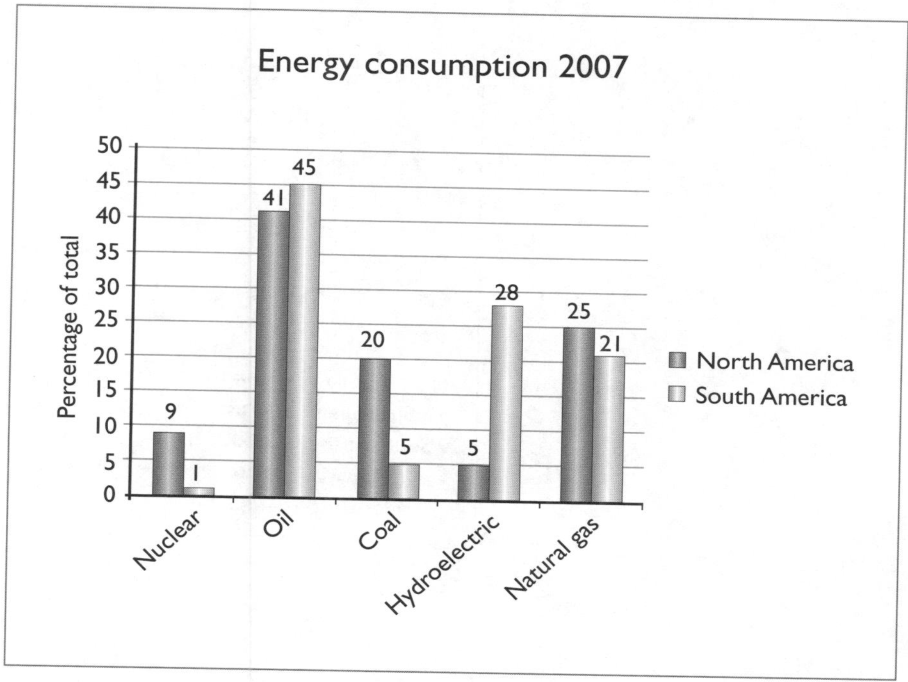

4 40 sec. Look at the table below. In 25 seconds, please speak into the microphone and describe in detail what the table is showing. You will have 40 seconds to give your response.

Language college timetable, week 1

	Day 1	Day 2	Day 3	Day 4	Day 5	Day 6	Day 7
9 a.m. to 12 noon	Tour of college	English language class	English language class	English language class	Full day activities: *Examples: tennis, films, games, surfing*	Weekend with Homestay families	Weekend with Homestay families
	Welcome by Head of college and Morning tea	English language class	English language class	English language class			
1 p.m. to 4 p.m.	English language class	Social activity on site	Excursion to local attraction	Visit to Junior School classroom			
	Social activity on site	Social activity on site		Social activity on site			

5 40 sec. Look at the graph below. In 25 seconds, please speak into the microphone and describe in detail what the graph is showing. You will have 40 seconds to give your response.

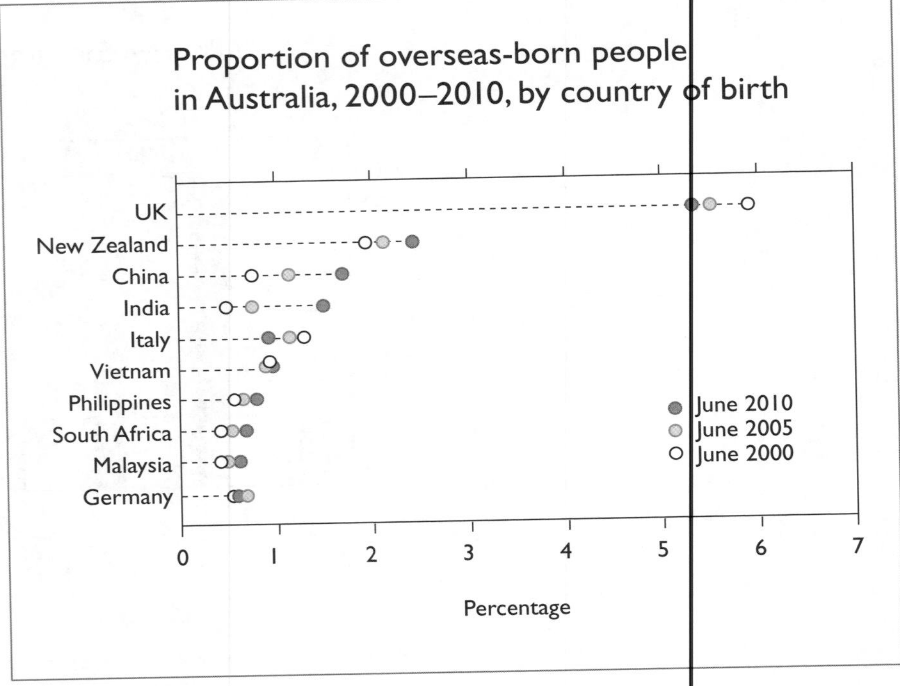

6 40 sec. Look at the diagram below. In 25 seconds, please speak into the microphone and describe in detail what the diagram is showing. You will have 40 seconds to give your response.

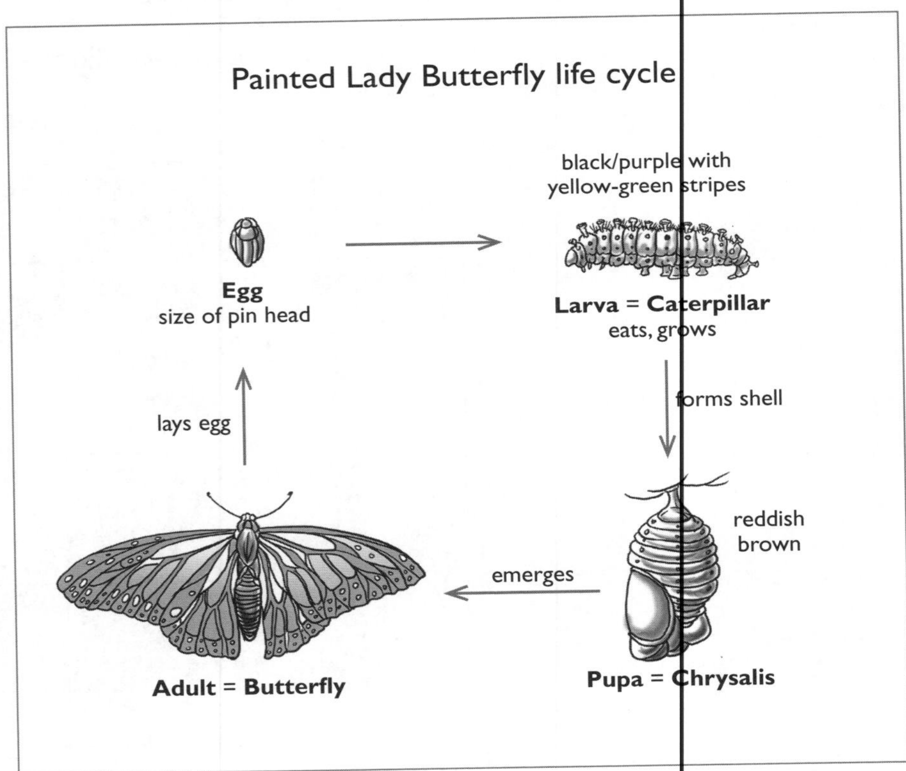

TEST 2 SPEAKING

Re-tell lecture

TIP STRIP

Scan the picture quickly to prepare for the lecture. As you listen, try to get an overall feeling for the meaning and the speaker's attitude.

Take notes but don't try to write every word you hear. Only write key words, e.g. *purpose of museums – relevant in info age? should be educ. – think about visitors, engage – social change, relevant.*

Think about how you will organize what you will say to be ready when the microphone opens.

In the test, there are 3–4 tasks. For each task, you see an image on the screen. Listen to the lecture and then speak into the microphone. The wording in the instructions below is the same as you will see in the actual test. See page 20 for help.

40 sec. You will hear a lecture. After listening to the lecture, in 10 seconds, please speak into the microphone and retell what you have just heard from the lecture in your own words. You will have 40 seconds to give your response.

1 ▸ 52

2 ▸ 53

3 ▸ 54

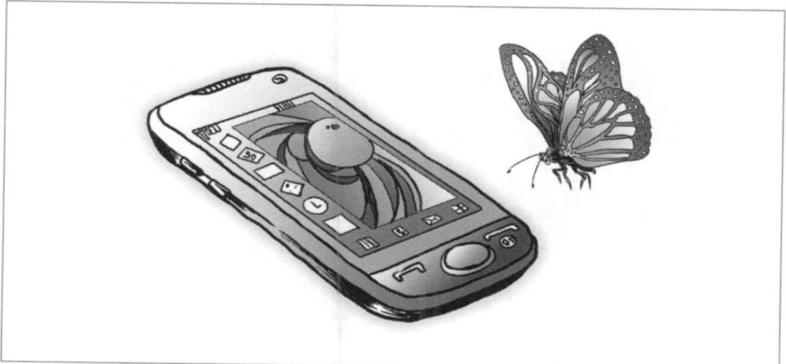

TEST 2

SPEAKING

Answer short question

TIP STRIP

Listen for key words, e.g. in Question 1: *organs, chest, breathe*. If you do not know one of the words, e.g. *organs*, try to answer based on what you know: *What do we use to breathe?* The word *organs* is plural, so we know the answer should be plural.

In the test, there are 10–12 tasks. For each task, you hear a question and speak your answer into the microphone. The wording in the instructions below is the same as you will see in the actual test. See page 22 for help.

▸ 55–64 10 sec. You will hear a question. Please give a simple and short answer. Often just one or a few words is enough.

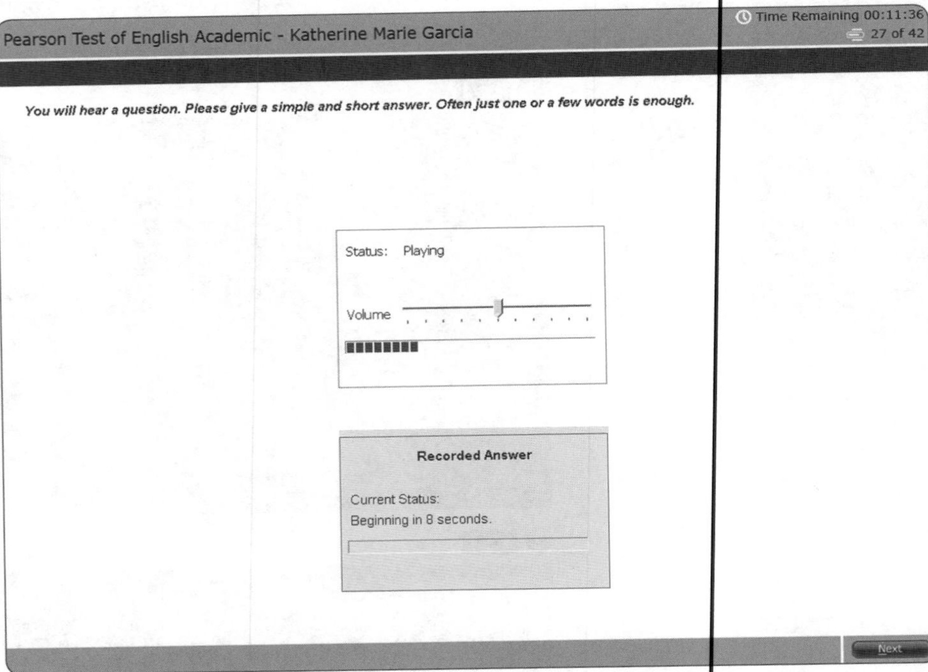

Answer short question: Each question is displayed on a new screen.

TEST 2

SPEAKING

Summarize written text

TIP STRIP

Read the passage for the overall meaning, then find the main idea of each paragraph. For example, in Passage 1 the first paragraph tells us how important sound is to most sea animals, the second paragraph is about the disturbance that noise made by boats causes to creatures underwater and the third paragraph qualifies the second by explaining that the effect of the man-made noises combine, and it is this build-up that causes problems. Shorten these ideas to put them into one sentence.

In the test, there are 2–3 tasks. Each task has a text on the screen. You type your summary of the text into the box at the bottom of the screen. The wording in the instructions below is the same as you will see in the actual test. See page 24 for help.

1 10 min. **Read the passage below and summarize it using one sentence. Type your response in the box at the bottom of the screen. You have 10 minutes to finish this task. Your response will be judged on the quality of your writing and on how well your response presents the key points in the passage.**

Most sea creatures, from whales and dolphins to fish, sharks, shrimps and possibly even anemones respond to sound, and many can produce it. They use it to hunt and to hide, find mates and food, form and guide shoals, navigate 'blind', send messages and transmit warnings, establish territories, warn off competitors, stun prey, deceive predators, and sense changes in water and conditions.

Marine animals click bones and grind teeth; use drum-tight bladders and special sonic organs to chirp, grunt, and boom; belch gases; and vibrate special organs. Far from the 'silent deep', the oceans are a raucous babel.

Into this age-long tumult, in the blink of an evolutionary eye, has entered a new thunder: the throb of mighty engines as 46,220 large vessels plough the world's shipping lanes. Scientists say that background noise in the ocean has increased roughly by 15 decibels in the past 50 years. It may not sound like much in overall terms; but it is enough, according to many marine biologists, to mask the normal sounds of ocean life going about its business. At its most intense, some even say noise causes whales to become disoriented, dolphins to develop 'the bends', fish to go deaf, flee their breeding grounds or fail to form shoals – enough to disrupt the basic biology of two thirds of the planet.

'Undersea noise pollution is like the death of a thousand cuts', says Sylvia Earle, chief scientist of the U.S. National Oceanic and Atmospheric Administration. 'Each sound in itself may not be a matter of critical concern, but taken all together, the noise from shipping, seismic surveys, and military activity is creating a totally different environment than existed even 50 years ago. That high level of noise is bound to have a hard, sweeping impact on life in the sea.'

....

....

....

....

....

2 10 min. Read the passage below and summarize it using one sentence. Type your response in the box at the bottom of the screen. You have 10 minutes to finish this task. Your response will be judged on the quality of your writing and on how well your response presents the key points in the passage.

Humans have been cultivating chillies as food for 6,000 years, but we are still learning new things about the science behind their heat and how it reacts with our body. In the late 1990s, scientists identified the pain nerves that detect capsaicin: the chemical in chillies responsible for most of the burning sensation in our mouth. But it's only during the last few years that scientists have also learnt why chillies evolved to be spicy in the first place, and they have managed to cultivate new varieties that are up to 300 times hotter than the common Jalapeno.

The hottest part of a chilli is not the seeds, as many people think, but the white flesh that houses the seeds, known as the placenta. But why did chillies evolve to be hot in the first place? Most scientists believe capsaicin acts mainly as a deterrent against would-be mammal predators such as rodents. But recent research suggests this may not be the whole story. US scientists working in Bolivia have studied how hot and mild chillies differ in their susceptibility to a certain harmful fungus. It turns out that the hotter the chilli, the better its defences against the fungus, leading the researchers to propose that heat may have evolved to help chillies deal with harmful microbes, as well as hungry mammals.

....

....

....

....

....

Write essay

In the test, there are 1–2 tasks. For each task, the essay question is on the screen. You type your essay into the box on the screen. The wording in the instructions below is the same as you will see in the actual test. See page 27 for help.

TIP STRIP

Identify the key words in the statement and note them on your Erasable Noteboard Booklet. For example, in Question 1: *school – students stay to 18?*

Decide what your opinion is going to be. You do not have to agree or disagree completely but you need to be clear on your position and why you believe it. Make some brief notes for your argument before you start to write.

20 min. **You will have 20 minutes to plan, write and revise an essay about the topic below. Your response will be judged on how well you develop a position, organize your ideas, present supporting details, and control the elements of standard written English. You should write 200–300 words.**

1. 'Students should be required to stay in school until the age of eighteen.'
   To what extent do you agree or disagree with this statement? Support your point of view with reasons and/or examples from your own experience.

2. 'Environmental problems are too great to be managed by individuals so real change can only be achieved at government level.'
   To what extent do you agree or disagree with this statement? Support your point of view with reasons and/or examples from your own experience.

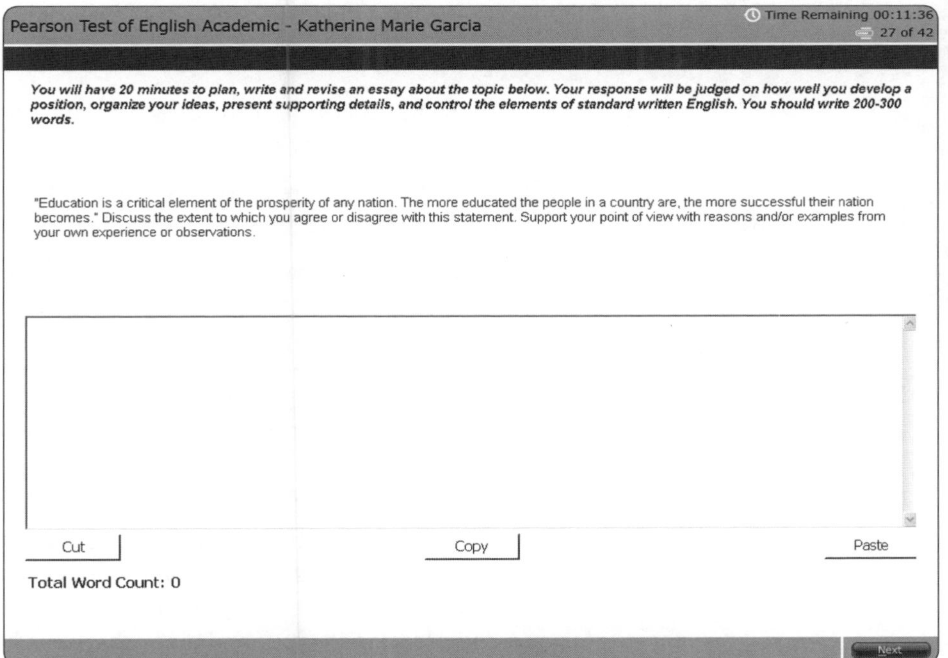

Write essay: Each question is displayed on a new screen.

Multiple-choice, choose single answer

TIP STRIP

The question will tell you what information to look for. In Question 1, you must find a problem in relation to sea snails. Note that the first sentence of the passage refers to *dangers of sea snails*, so you know the problem is one caused by sea snails.

In the test, there are 2–3 tasks. For each task, you read the text on the left of the screen and look at the options on the right of the screen. You click the button next to the answer you think is correct. The wording in the instructions below is the same as you will see in the actual test. See page 30 for help.

TEST 2

READING

Read the text and answer the multiple-choice question by selecting the correct response. ***Only one response is correct.***

1 Submarine operators have been alerted to the dangers of sea snails in a recent study. An international research team says the hardy deep-sea animals latch on to the submarines used by scientists, potentially spreading disease in pristine ecosystems.

The limpet is a sea snail that lives 2,000 metres underwater but can also survive in air when a submarine emerges from the water. If it goes unnoticed, the limpet can find itself in another habitat the next time the submarine is used. As 90 per cent of limpets are infected by parasites, this poses a threat to the ecosystem; but thoroughly cleaning the submarines will solve the problem.

What problem does the article mention in relation to sea snails?

- ○ A Research into sea snails has been harming the animals themselves.
- ○ B Sea snails are being carried by submarines to places where they harm other species.
- ○ C Sea snails are spreading diseases to the research scientists on submarines.
- ○ D Dirty submarines are endangering the well-being of the sea snails that attach themselves.

2 The Graphic Design degree provides students with a nurturing environment for learning, developing aesthetic appreciation and design skills with an emphasis on media and marketing. Students have the chance to develop their personal style, while broadening their technical repertoire as designers.

The academic staff are former working artists, theorists and designers who have been successful in achieving major awards, commissions and research grants. The facilities for the graphic design program include spacious design studios, colour and monochrome darkrooms and photography studios. Students will develop skills at a professional working standard in all computer-based programs that the design industry requires.

What does the Graphic Design degree offer students?

- ○ A experience working on new magazines
- ○ B the opportunity to apply for funds to help with their study
- ○ C teachers who have practical experience in a creative field
- ○ D the use of state-of-the-art cameras

Multiple-choice, choose multiple answers

TIP STRIP

Words in the options may not be exactly the same as the ones in the text. Remember, you do not need to know all these words; you will usually be able to guess the meaning if you know some of them. For example, in Text 1, if you know what a *canoe* is, you can guess that *rigging*, *sails* and *lengthy anchor warps* are equipment for boats.

In the test, there are 2–3 tasks. For each task, you read the text on the left of the screen and look at the options on the right of the screen. You click the buttons next to all of the answers you think are correct. The wording in the instructions below is the same as you will see in the actual test. See page 32 for help.

1 Read the text and answer the question by selecting all the correct responses. ***You will need to select more than one response.***

When the Maori people first came to New Zealand, they brought the mulberry plant from which they made bark cloth. However, the mulberry did not flourish in the new climate so they found a substitute in the native flax. They used this for baskets, mats, and fishing nets and to make intricate fibre ceremonial cloaks. Maori identified almost 60 types of flax, and propagated flax nurseries and plantations to supply the integral material. They chopped the leaves near the base of the flax plant using a sharp mussel shell or shaped rocks. The flesh of the leaf was stripped off right down to the fibre which went through several processes of washing, bleaching, softening, dyeing and drying. Flax ropes and cords had such great strength that they were used to bind together sections of hollowed-out logs to create huge ocean-going canoes, and to provide rigging, sails and lengthy anchor warps for them. It was also used for roofs for housing. The ends of the flax leaves were fanned out to make torches to provide light at night.

For which of the following purposes does the passage say the Maori used flax?

- ○ A special clothing
- ○ B cleaning cloth
- ○ C equipment for boats
- ○ D walls for their huts
- ○ E cooking tools

2 Read the text and answer the question by selecting all the correct responses. *You will need to select more than one response.*

The Neue National Gallery in Berlin was designed by Mies van der Rohe. Built in 1968, it is a jump from the traditional museum concept of a closed building with exhibition rooms. Instead it is an open-plan, flexible space. With only two steel columns on each side, the corners are 'free', giving the building a lightweight look.

The gallery was the first building completed as part of a cluster of buildings dedicated to culture and the fine arts. It is often said that the building is a work of art in itself. The unusual natural illumination in the building, coming from around and below the viewer rather than above, has the effect of shocking the viewer out of their usual way of seeing and encouraging visitors to bring a fresh eye to the art.

The upper level is mainly used for special exhibits, for example, large-scale sculptures or paintings. The vast lower level has space for themed shows, and contains shops, a café, and the museum's permanent collection, which ranges from early modern art to art of the 1960s. The podium roof plaza is an open air gallery for public sculpture.

On request, guests may enter the garden to see figurative and abstract sculptures on display there. Special exhibits are attended by specially trained, very personable staff, who field questions, explain the exhibits, and enthuse about their favourite works.

What does the passage say can be found at the Neue National Gallery?

- ○ A overhead lighting to showcase artwork
- ○ B substantial pillars in the corners of the building
- ○ C artwork on top of the building
- ○ D several separate gallery rooms on each floor
- ○ E helpful guides to give information about the art

Re-order paragraphs

TIP STRIP

Reference words, e.g. *the*, *this* refer to something that has been mentioned before. Use this to help you order the text.

In Question 1, Sentence D introduces the idea of a conference; Sentence B refers to *the conference*, so it must come after the first mention in Sentence D.

Look at the reference to *this assistance* in Sentence C; it follows on from *to assist* in Sentence B and introduces the idea of industry professionals.

Sentence A follows this by mentioning *the industry professionals*.

In the test, there are 2–3 tasks. For each task, you drag paragraphs from the left and drop them into the correct order on the right. The wording in the instructions below is the same as you will see in the actual test. See page 35 for help.

The text boxes in the left panel have been placed in a random order. Restore the original order by dragging the text boxes from the left panel to the right panel.

1

A It is important to register for sessions with the industry professionals as numbers are limited.

B The conference is part of the career counselling centre's campaign, which has been designed to assist final year students transitioning out of university and getting their careers off to a good start.

C Students will be able to speak with industry professionals and graduates who had the benefit of this assistance last year.

D The University will host its second annual Arts and Commerce Career Readiness Conference on campus next month.

2

A Urban planners must consider these threats and work to allay them.

B Historically, in Europe and many other parts of the world, settlements were built on higher ground for the purposes of defence and to be close to fresh water sources.

C If the dangers are only in specific areas then they can make the affected regions into parkland or a green belt, often providing the added advantage of open space.

D Cities have often spread down from these locations onto coastal plains, putting them at risk of floods and storm surges.

Reading: Fill in the blanks

TIP STRIP

Read the text for overall meaning, e.g. Text 1 is about giving graduation gifts. Then look for clues in words like *despite*, which suggests an opposite idea to the positive idea of prosperity in *giving graduation gifts*, and *while*, which suggests another opposite idea: What do families have to be when choosing a gift if they do not have as much money? For the final gap, which word collocates with *lump*?

In the test, there are 4–5 tasks. For each task, you drag the words at the bottom of the text and drop them into the correct space in the text. The wording in the instructions below is the same as you will see in the actual test. See page 37 for help.

In the text below some words are missing. Drag words from the box below to the appropriate place in the text. To undo an answer choice, drag the word back to the box below the text.

1 The practice of giving graduation gifts seems to be alive and well, despite [1] ______ economic times. A recent study in the US has shown that while families may not have as much to spend, they are being more [2] ______ in the gifts they bestow. Lavish celebrations and large lump [3] ______ seem to have gone by the wayside in favour of smaller, more thoughtful gifts.

generous | hard | creative | money | sums | favourable

2 The majority of early pictures in the National Portrait Gallery's [1] ______ are by unknown artists, with fundamental questions, such as when, where and why they were painted still remaining to be answered. Through the application of scientific methods, a new project has the [2] ______ to unlock evidence that will allow researchers to determine answers to these questions. They will use a [3] ______ of cutting-edge scientific techniques, such as X-ray and infra-red reflectography, in order to reveal new [4] ______ about individual paintings.

information | potential | combination | prospect | connection | care | work

TEST 2 READING

In the text below some words are missing. Drag words from the box below to the appropriate place in the text. To undo an answer choice, drag the word back to the box below the text.

3 Gunpowder, also referred to as 'black powder', was the only [1] ______ chemical explosive until the mid-nineteenth century. It [2] ______ potassium nitrate, or 'saltpeter', which is an oxidiser, and a combination of charcoal and sulphur serves as fuel. There is [3] ______ consensus that gunpowder was initially invented in China as early as the ninth century. This [4] ______ to its use in fireworks and in gunpowder weapons.

includes | contains | caused | academic | known | unique | led

4 Marion Dorset (1872–1935) was an influential American biochemist. He began working as a [1] ______ for the U.S. Department of Agriculture in 1894, and worked his way up to become chief of the biochemical [2] ______ in 1904. He made important discoveries in bacterial toxins and animal diseases, and he conducted pioneering work in the [3] ______ of meat products. He co-discovered the virus that causes hog cholera and subsequently developed a [4] ______ to prevent it.

researcher | leader | serum | fluid | inspection | consumption | division

Reading & writing: Fill in the blanks

TIP STRIP

Think about the grammar and vocabulary as well as the meaning for each gap. Look at Text 1, Question 1: Which tense is used for an event that happened in the past and is finished? In Question 2, which verb collocates with *role*? For Question 3, which relative pronoun is used after a non-defining relative clause (after a comma)? For Question 4, which option emphasizes the number of different contributions the Professor made?

TEST 2

READING

In the test, there are 5–6 tasks. For each task, you have a text with several gaps. You select the correct answer for each gap from the drop-down list on the screen. The wording in the instructions below is the same as you will see in the actual test. See page 40 for help.

Below is a text with blanks. Click on each blank, a list of choices will appear. Select the appropriate choice for each blank.

1 Victoria University of Wellington has conferred an honorary degree on a distinguished astrophysicist in a recent graduation ceremony. Professor Warrick Couch [1] ______ the honorary degree of Doctor of Science for his remarkable contribution to our knowledge of galaxies and dark energy. Professor Couch is a distinguished astrophysicist who has [2] ______ a crucial role in the discovery that the Universe is expanding at an accelerating rate, a finding which led to the lead scientists being awarded a Nobel Prize in Physics in 2011, which he attended in recognition of his contribution.

In his research, Professor Couch uses large ground-based and spaced-based telescopes to observe galaxy clusters, [3] ______ are the largest structures in the Universe. He is also involved in a number of national and international committees overseeing the management of these telescopes. [4] ______ his own research activities, Professor Couch has worked to support young researchers and provide public comment on astronomy internationally.

1	A was receiving	B had received	C is received	D received
2	A played	B found	C done	D led
3	A those	B which	C they	D who
4	A In addition to	B As a result of	C Regarding	D Instead of

2 Keith Haring began as an underground artist, literally. His first famous projects were pieces of stylized graffiti [1] ______ in New York subway stations. Haring travelled from station to station, drawing with chalk and chatting with commuters about his work. These doodles helped him develop his classic style and he grew so [2] ______, doing up to 40 drawings a day, that it was not long before fame and a measure of fortune followed.

Soon, galleries and collectors from the art establishment wanted to buy full-sized pieces by Haring. The paintings skyrocketed in price but this did not sit well with Haring's philosophy. He believed that art, or [3] ______ his art, was for everyone. Soon, Haring opened a store which he called the Pop Shop, which he hoped would attract a broad range of people. While somewhat controversial among street artists, some of [4] ______ accused Haring of 'selling out', the Pop Shop changed the way people thought about the relationship between art and business.

1	A drawers	B drawn	C drew	D draws
2	A perceptive	B proactive	C pedantic	D prolific
3	A by contrast	B at least	C actually	D in part
4	A whose	B those	C whom	D them

Below is a text with blanks. Click on each blank, a list of choices will appear. Select the appropriate answer for each blank.

❸ Conservationists have long debated whether the koala should go on the Australian national threatened species list. [1] ______ the koala is clearly in trouble in some parts of the country – in Queensland, for example, high numbers are afflicted by disease – in other parts such as Victoria and South Australia the problem is not that koala populations [2] ______, but that they have grown to the point where they are almost too numerous.

For a species to be classed as vulnerable, its population [3] ______ by more than 30 percent over the last three generations or 10 years. The problem is that when such a stipulation is applied to koalas, the Victorian boom offsets the Queensland bust, and the species stays off the list.

This has repercussions because northern koalas are different to southern ones. They are smaller, for example, and they contain a genetic variation not represented in the South. [4] ______, a split listing has been devised koalas from New South Wales, the ACT and Queensland are now officially 'Vulnerable'; those from Victoria and South Australia are not considered threatened.

1	A Because	B However	C Despite	D While
2	A had been falling	B were falling	C are falling	D had fallen
3	A must have decreased	B will be decreasing	C was decreased	D has decreased
4	A According to this	B For this reason	C For instance	D In contrast

❹ The Department of Fine Arts is a vibrant department comprising active art professionals housed in a modern, well-equipped facility. The faculty enjoys [1] ______ relationships with local museums, numerous galleries and a variety of other art organizations. Fine Arts students benefit from studying with artistically [2] ______ mentors who exhibit and research regionally, nationally and internationally. The department provides students with many opportunities for artistic and personal [3] ______ through daily contact with full-time faculty members who are noted artists and researchers. Classes are small to allow for personalised feedback and guidance.

Well-appointed studios on campus [4] ______ the daily practice of art in combination with the study of liberal arts. During their studies, students gain exposure to world-class visiting artists and exhibitions, and also have local and international travel [5] ______.

1	A corresponding	B collaborative	C combined	D common
2	A activating	B actively	C activity	D active
3	A growing	B growth	C grown	D grow
4	A facilitating	B facilities	C facilitate	D facility
5	A contingencies	B opportunities	C occasions	D needs

Below is a text with blanks. Click on each blank, a list of choices will appear. Select the appropriate answer for each blank.

❺ Lyrebirds, a common bird in rainforest areas of Australia, have an incredible repertoire of sounds that they are able to mimic from their environment, including over 20 other bird calls as well as sophisticated mechanical sounds. They [1] ______ to replicate the sounds of chainsaws and pneumatic drills. The male lyrebird sings a medley of mimicry to impress females – and the more detailed and varied his repertoire is, the more interesting it seems to potential [2] ______. Like females of other bird species, female lyrebirds do not [3] ______ in the imitating, but simply judge the competing males' symphonies. Once learned, it seems a lyrebird rarely forgets a call, and the sounds are passed down through the generations. There are some lyrebirds in Victoria, Australia, that [4] ______ recreate the sounds of axes, saws and old-fashioned cameras which have not been used in the area for years.

1	A have been known	B are being known	C are knowing	D know
2	A companions	B spouses	C mates	D pairs
3	A put forward	B take place	C work out	D take part
4	A indeed	B still	C just	D yet

TEST 2

READING

Summarize spoken text

TIP STRIP

The first part of the lecture usually introduces the topic, e.g. in Question 1: proofreading. Listen for the main ideas and take notes of key words only, using abbreviations, e.g. in Question 1: *proofreading – hard to see own grammar, punct errors – eliminate past errors – look for logical org – paras – read aloud – check refs – have break before proofreading.*

In the test, there are 2–3 tasks. For each task, you listen to the audio then type your summary into the box on the screen. The wording in the instructions below is the same as you will see in the actual test. See page 45 for help.

You will hear a short lecture. Write a summary for a fellow student who was not present at the lecture. You should write 50–70 words.

10 min. You will have 10 minutes to finish this task. Your response will be judged on the quality of your writing and on how well your response presents the key points presented in the lecture.

1 ▶ 65

....

....

....

....

....

....

2 ▶ 66

....

....

....

....

....

....

Multiple-choice, choose multiple answers

TIP STRIP

Read the question before the audio begins to know what to listen for. In Question 1, you are listening for comments about students.

As you listen, eliminate or confirm options, e.g. when you hear: *We've built a reputation for producing both traditional and alternative performances*, which option can be eliminated? When the speaker says: … *for the level of support that's available, and I mean from the tutors as well as from fellow students and alumni*, which option can be confirmed?

In the test, there are 2–3 tasks. For each task, you listen to the audio then click the buttons next to all of the answers you think are correct. The wording in the instructions below is the same as you will see in the actual test. See page 47 for help.

Listen to the recording and answer the question by selecting all the correct responses. ***You will need to select more than one response.***

1 ▶ 67 **What comments are made about students in the Theatre Studies program?**

- ○ A They are encouraged to focus their studies on modern productions.
- ○ B Past students offer them help.
- ○ C Students can work at their own pace.
- ○ D They need to be clear from the start about the area they want to work in.
- ○ E A high percentage complete the degree and get jobs in their field.

2 ▶ 68 **What was significant about the rock art found in the Yunnan province and in Western Europe?**

- ○ A The skill in the rock art is superior to that found in other parts of the world.
- ○ B It suggests that the ancestors of the rock artists may have once lived in the same area.
- ○ C Rock art in both places depicted animals of interest to humans.
- ○ D It showed the people in each place had very different lifestyles.
- ○ E It shows that people in widely separated places thought the same way.

Fill in the blanks

TIP STRIP

Skim the text briefly to get an idea what it is about, e.g. in Question 1, it is about barred owls.

Use the few seconds before the recording starts to look carefully at the gaps and the words preceding each one, so that you do not miss your cue to write the word.

As you write, make sure that the word makes sense in the context, e.g. in Question 1, Gap 1 *small* [ ] suggests that the next word will be a noun.

In the test, there are 2–3 tasks. For each task, there is a text with several gaps. You type the correct answer for each gap into the box in the text. The wording in the instructions below is the same as you will see in the actual test. See page 49 for help.

You will hear a recording. Type the missing words in each blank.

1 ▶ 69

Barred owls can be found in dense forests right across North America. They feed on small 1 [ ], fish, birds and small reptiles – pretty much anything that comes their way. The barred owl grows up to half a metre tall and has emerged as a very 2 [ ] nocturnal predator. Whereas they have been long-thought to live in old-growth forests, they are now building up quite an 3 [ ] population. In Charlotte, North Carolina, barred owls tend to nest in the cavities of the numerous willow oak trees that line the city's streets. Far from being endangered, the owls have expanded their range; and now, in some places, conservationists are worried about the effects they might have on other 4 [ ] species.

2 ▶ 70

Before the beginning of the 1900s, the only way to obtain pearls was by collecting very large numbers of pearl oysters from the ocean floor by hand. The oysters – or sometimes mussels – were brought to the surface, opened, and 1 [ ]. More than a ton of these had to be checked in order to find just three or four quality pearls. Divers often descended to depths of over 100 feet on just one single breath. Now, of course this exposed them to 2 [ ] creatures and dangerous waves, not to mention drowning. In some areas, divers put grease on their bodies to conserve heat and they held a large 3 [ ], like a rock, to descend so they didn't have to exert effort going down. Today, pearl diving has pretty much been supplanted by cultured pearl 4 [ ]. Particles are implanted in the oyster to encourage the formation of pearls, and this allows for more predictable production. The divers who still work, do so mainly for the 5 [ ] industry.

Highlight correct summary

TIP STRIP

Take notes as you listen; just key words and ideas. In Question 1, these could be: *advantages of telecommuting; things companies should consider; employee suitability to work away from office.*

Read through the summaries and eliminate any that contain information that is wrong or that you did not hear in the passage. Then eliminate any summaries that focus on only part of the message or do not cover the main points.

In the test, there are 2–3 tasks. For each task, you listen to the audio then click the button next to the summary you think is correct. The wording in the instructions below is the same as you will see in the actual test. See page 51 for help.

You will hear a recording. Click on the paragraph that best relates to the recording.

1 ▸ 71

○ A Company leaders have to be careful that they do not have one set of practices for those in the office and another for those who telecommute. Besides needing to be fair at all times, managers will find that a telecommuting arrangement will simply not work if workers feel isolated and excluded from the company culture.

○ B Telecommuting has a lot of advantages but to make it work, company leaders need to plan in advance to ensure that they anticipate issues for example training, security and communication. They also need to ensure that they hire workers who are suited to working remotely and ensure equal access to resources and advancement.

○ C When workers ask if they can work from home, companies should consider a telecommuting arrangement, as it has several advantages for businesses as well as workers. There is money to be saved on overheads and training but for telecommuting to function properly, only independent staff should be allowed to work in this way.

○ D Managers should not rush into letting their employees telecommute. It may sound good because businesses can save money on things like office space, but if workers' needs and ambitions are not well catered for in the arrangement, the company culture will ultimately be damaged and they may even be sued.

You will hear a recording. Click on the paragraph that best relates to the recording.

2 ▸ 72

- ○ A While many of us believe that we enjoy making choices, several studies have shown that this is not in fact the case. When faced with choosing from several types of jam, consumers were interested at first but soon became overloaded with choice. They simply abandoned the choice and went back to their favourite brands.
- ○ B The incredible range of choices that consumers now have is making business difficult for companies who have to provide more and more choices to keep up with the market but also for consumers who expect choice but give up without making any choices at all if they feel confused by the wide range on offer.
- ○ C Consumers face more choices than they did in the past and a study showed shoppers are attracted if a number of options are presented to them. However, those options still need to be of a good quality and something that appeals to the consumer or, as in the study, they will walk away without making a purchase.
- ○ D With a wide range of choices, one would expect consumers to buy more products. However, a consumer experiment found that when customers had many choices, they were likely to sample the products but became overwhelmed and did not buy much, whereas they were more likely to buy something when they had far fewer options to choose from.

Multiple-choice, choose single answer

TIP STRIP

Read the questions and options quickly before the recording begins.

In Question 1, you know you will hear statements about something called the 'Beehive' (option 1), which is a building (option 2) in New Zealand (option 3) that people may have disliked once (option 4).

As you listen, try to eliminate or confirm the options.

In the test, there are 2–3 tasks. For each task, you listen to the audio then click the button next to the answer you think is correct. The wording in the instructions below is the same as you will see in the actual test. See page 54 for help.

Listen to the recording and answer the multiple-choice question by selecting the correct response. ***Only one response is correct.***

1 ▶ 73 What does the speaker say about the 'Beehive'?

- ○ A Its name comes from being a centre of activity.
- ○ B Its architect saw the project through to completion.
- ○ C It used to be a symbol of national pride for New Zealand.
- ○ D It has come back into favour in recent years.

2 ▶ 74 What does the speaker say can be done to avoid conflict within study groups?

- ○ A Group members should have compatible personalities.
- ○ B Tasks should be approached in a creative way.
- ○ C The main task should be divided into parts.
- ○ D Long-range goals need to be given priority.

Select missing word

TIP STRIP

Use the instructions to orient yourself to the topic, e.g. in Question 1, the topic is *studying humanities*.

As you listen, notice the direction of the speaker's argument, so that you can anticipate what ideas are coming, e.g. in Question 1, the speaker is arguing a point of view, so the missing words will be part of that argument.

In the test, there are 2–3 tasks. For each task, you listen to the audio then click the button next to the words you think complete the audio. The wording in the instructions below is the same as you will see in the actual test. See page 56 for help.

1 ▶ 75 You will hear a recording about studying humanities. *At the end of the recording the last word or group of words has been replaced by a beep.* Select the correct option to complete the recording.

- ○ A from a number of angles
- ○ B with a specific goal in mind
- ○ C in a less emotional manner
- ○ D in a way that enriches society

2 ▶ 76 You will hear a recording about surfing. *At the end of the recording the last word or group of words has been replaced by a beep.* Select the correct option to complete the recording.

- ○ A could fail
- ○ B took place
- ○ C were at stake
- ○ D were discovered

Highlight incorrect words

TIP STRIP

Skim the transcription briefly to give you a general idea of the passage, and as you listen, read each word carefully. Often, the word you read and the word you hear will be very similar. There is a word like this in the first sentence of Transcription 1.

In the test, there are 2–3 tasks. For each task, you listen to the audio and follow the words in the text on the screen. You click on the words that are different on the screen and the audio. The wording in the instructions below is the same as you will see in the actual test. See page 58 for help.

You will hear a recording. Below is a transcription of the recording. *Some words in the transcription differ from what the speaker said.* Please click on the words that are different.

1 ▸ 77 Transcription:

Well, there are many factors that can cause one species to diverge into two. One of these is when populations get isolated from each other by something like a lagoon forming or forest being cleared. And there's another idea that as individuals adapt to their environment, this might have a knock-on impact on mate choice, a process called sensitive drive speciation. Now this seems to occur in cichlid fish. They have shown that a female preference for either red or blue striped males only exists in clean water, where they are actually able to see.

2 ▸ 78 Transcription:

Social capital is a concept that was introduced by sociologists, many years ago. It's actually the networks and reserves that people use to deliver social outcomes. For instance, it might be holding a sporting event, running a community fair, being part of a club.

It is difficult to measure social capital and one way of looking at it is the amount that people volunteer in their local community. So you can consider the volunteering rate as an index for how healthy a community is. You can also look at something called a well-being index – the way people think about their lives and how accepting they are of others, their general perception of the value of their life.

Write from dictation

TIP STRIP

Write as much as you can, and continue writing so that you do not miss the rest of the sentence. Do not go back and correct words until the sentence has finished.

Before you click 'Next', check the grammar and spelling; and if you are unsure of the spelling, think of the rules of spelling.

In the test, there are 3–4 tasks. For each task, you listen and type the sentence you hear into the box on the screen. The wording in the instructions below is the same as you will see in the actual test. See page 60 for help.

You will hear a sentence. Type the sentence in the box below exactly as you hear it. Write as much of the sentence as you can. You will hear the sentence only once.

1 ▸ 79

....

....

....

2 ▸ 80

....

....

....

3 ▸ 81

....

....

....

TEST 3

Read aloud

In the test, there are 6–7 tasks. For each task, you read the text aloud into the microphone. The wording in the instructions below is the same as you will see in the actual test. See page 12 for help.

40 sec. Look at the text below. In 40 seconds, you must read this text aloud as naturally and as clearly as possible. You have 40 seconds to read aloud.

1. Tidal energy, also known as tidal power, is a renewable source of energy and a form of hydropower used to generate electricity from the energy of the tides. Though not currently widely utilised, due to high costs and limited availability, it can be called the energy resource of the future given the current rate of depletion of energy resources.

2. Certain types of methodology are more suitable for some research projects than others. For example, the use of questionnaires and surveys is more suitable for quantitative research whereas interviews and focus groups are more often used for qualitative research purposes.

3. Most countries are affected by labour migration. In many rural places, the traditional extended family has been undermined by the need for family members to migrate to towns as an economic necessity. Migration, therefore, presents a major challenge everywhere to social and economic policy.

4. One of the major factors influencing future home design will be the probable change in climate, with hotter summers, colder winters, and the possibility of floods. Consequently, houses will be built with better insulation and will also need ways of keeping cool in hot weather, whether that's air conditioning or more shading of windows.

5. Until fairly recent times, the origin of birds was one of evolution's great mysteries. This is no longer the case. Fossil evidence from China now conclusively proves that there is an evolutionary link between birds and several types of extinct prehistoric reptiles which lived millions of years ago, or in other words, dinosaurs.

6. Group work is valuable because of the opportunities it provides for students to develop collaboration and communication skills. As an assessment task, it has the potential to pose difficulties in relation to appropriate acknowledgement of authorship of individual group members. These difficulties can be minimised by ensuring that the task is well designed, with the roles of individuals effectively identified.

Repeat sentence

In the test, there are 10–12 tasks. For each task, you listen and repeat the sentence you hear into the microphone. The wording in the instructions below is the same as you will see in the actual test. See page 14 for help.

▸ 82–91 15 sec. You will hear a sentence. Please repeat the sentence exactly as you hear it. You will hear the sentence only once.

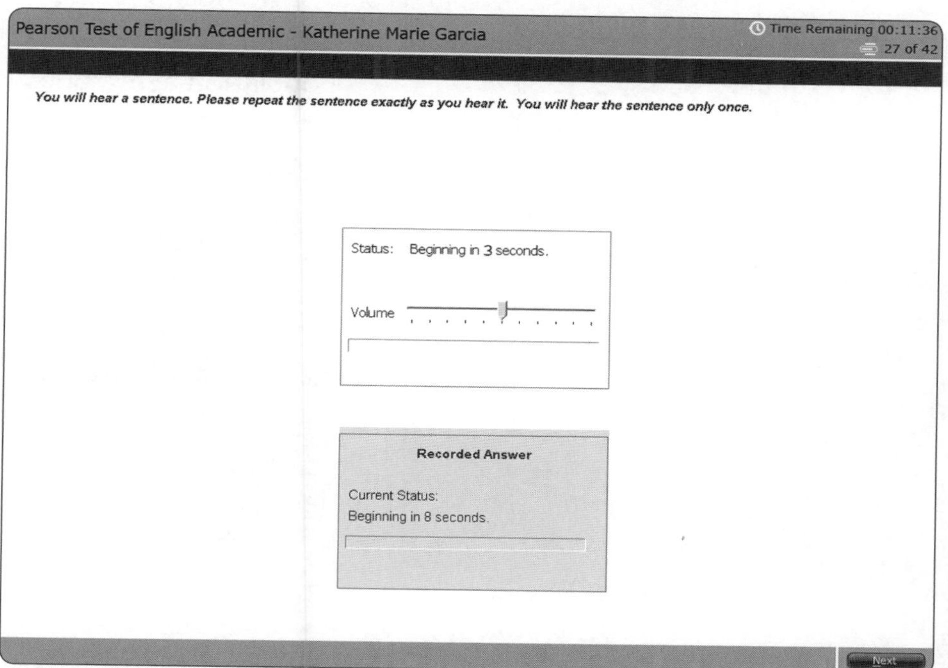

Repeat sentence: Each question is displayed on a new screen.

TEST 3
SPEAKING

Describe image

In the test, there are 6–7 tasks. For each task, you look at the image and describe it into the microphone. The wording in the instructions below is the same as you will see in the actual test. See page 16 for help.

1 40 sec. Look at the chart below. In 25 seconds, please speak into the microphone and describe in detail what the chart is showing. You will have 40 seconds to give your response.

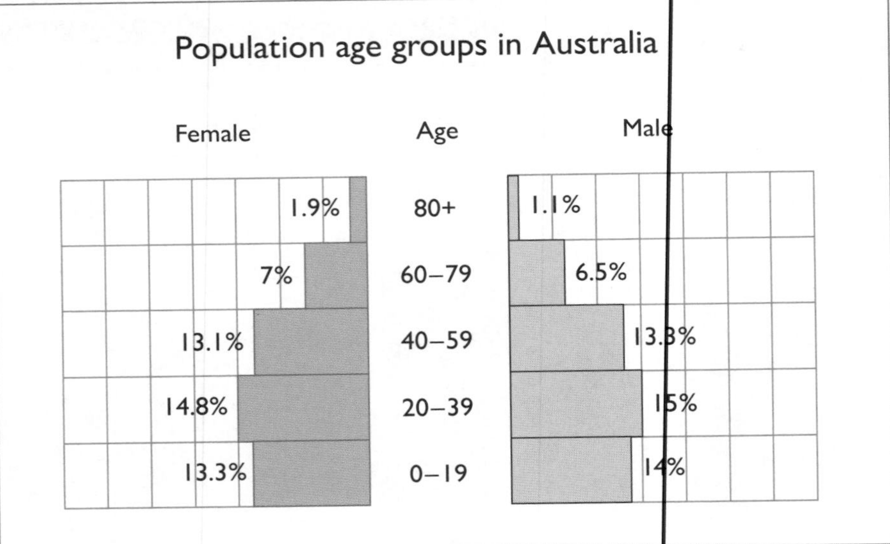

2 40 sec. Look at the diagram below. In 25 seconds, please speak into the microphone and describe in detail what the diagram is showing. You will have 40 seconds to give your response.

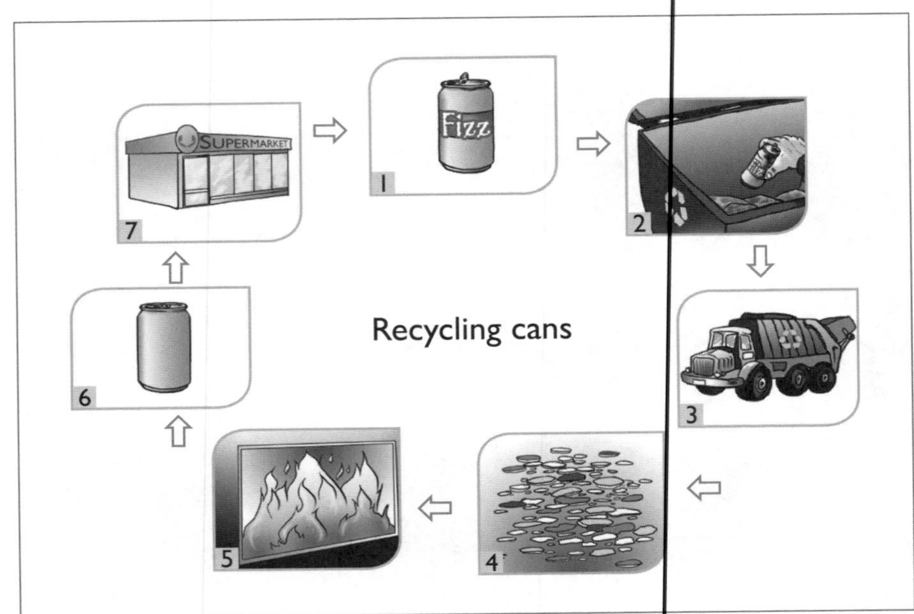

3 40 sec. Look at the chart below. In 25 seconds, please speak into the microphone and describe in detail what the chart is showing. You will have 40 seconds to give your response.

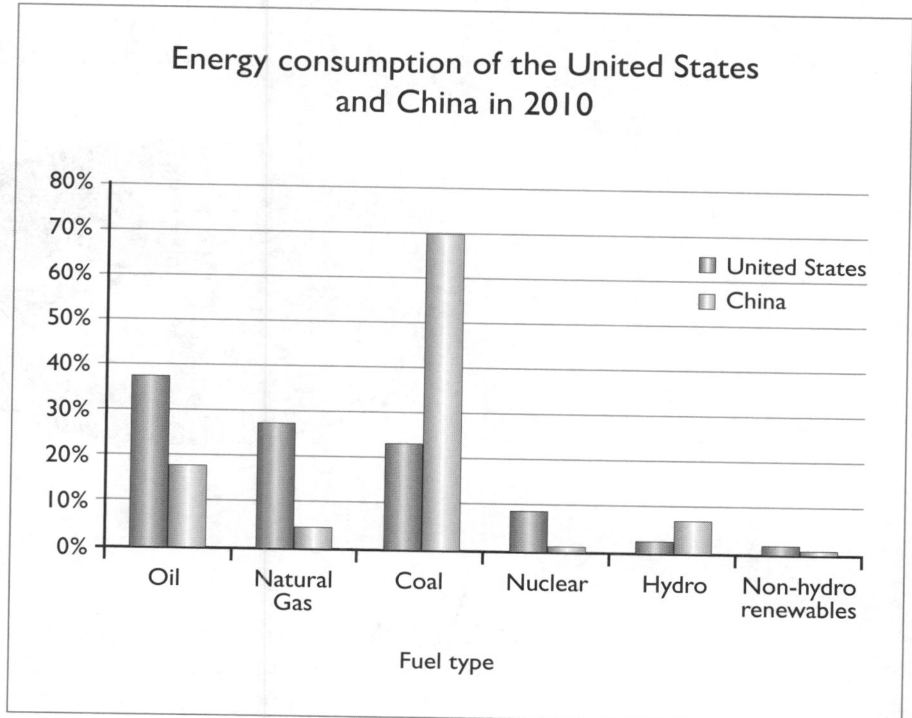

4 40 sec. Look at the diagram below. In 25 seconds, please speak into the microphone and describe in detail what the diagram is showing. You will have 40 seconds to give your response.

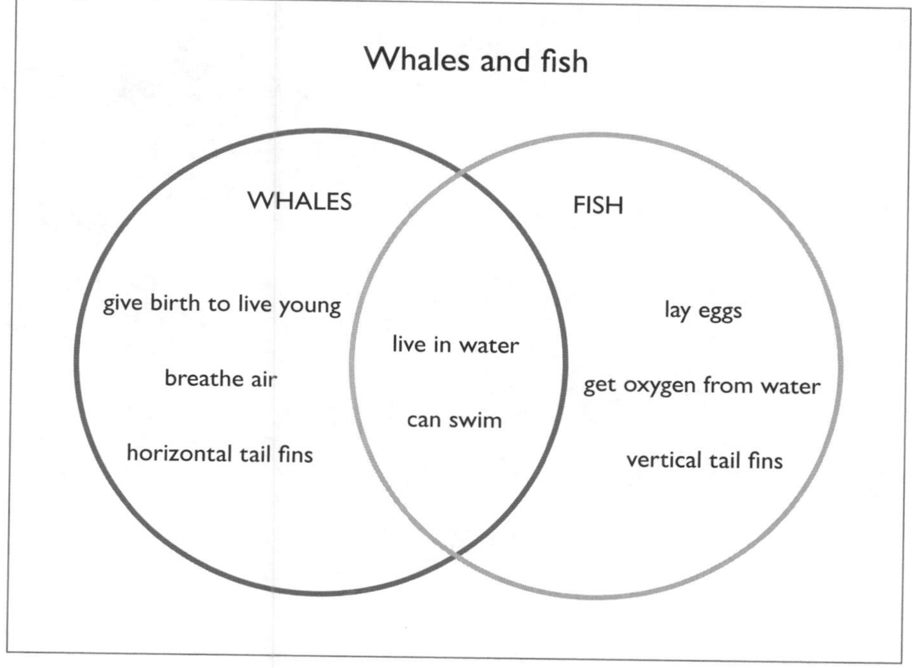

TEST 3

SPEAKING

5 40 sec. Look at the chart below. In 25 seconds, please speak into the microphone and describe in detail what the chart is showing. You will have 40 seconds to give your response.

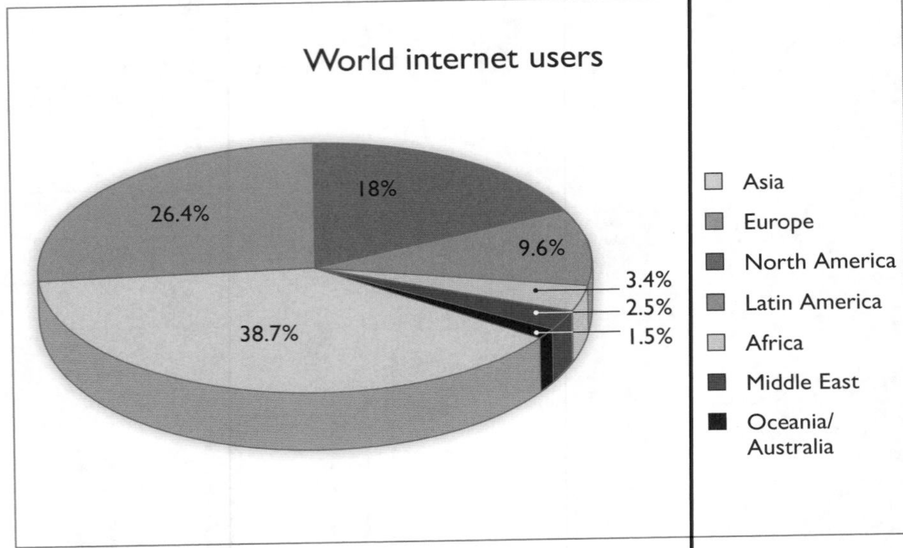

6 40 sec. Look at the diagram below. In 25 seconds, please speak into the microphone and describe in detail what the diagram is showing. You will have 40 seconds to give your response.

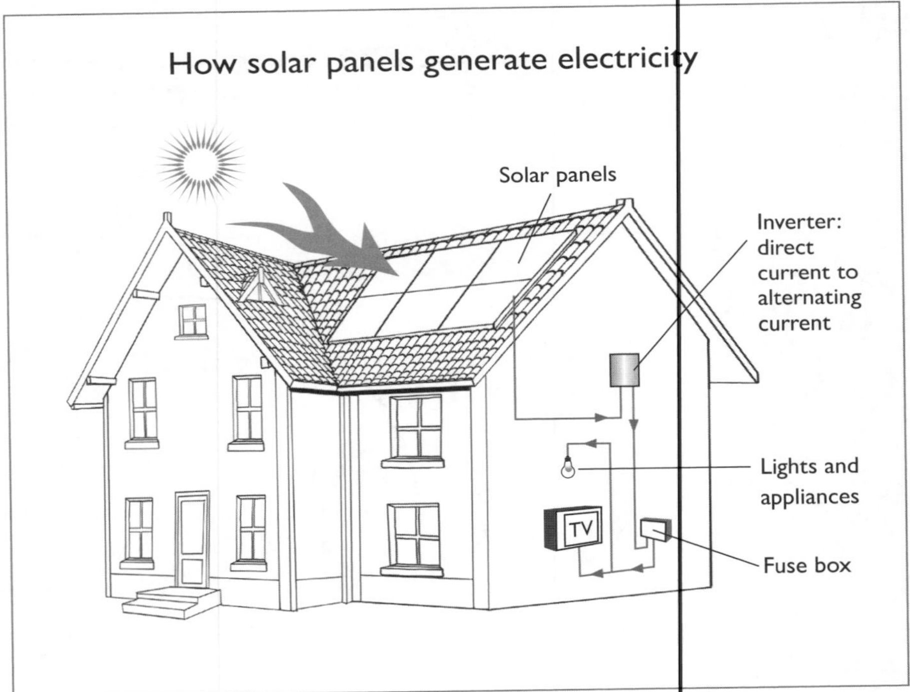

TEST 3
SPEAKING

Re-tell lecture

In the test, there are 3–4 tasks. For each task, you see an image on the screen. Listen to the lecture and then speak into the microphone. The wording in the instructions below is the same as you will see in the actual test. See page 20 for help.

40 sec. You will hear a lecture. After listening to the lecture, in 10 seconds, please speak into the microphone and retell what you have just heard from the lecture in your own words. You will have 40 seconds to give your response.

1 ▸ 92

2 ▸ 93

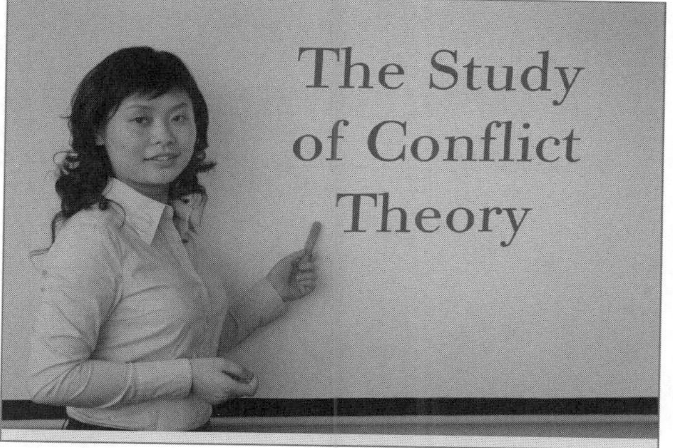

3 ▸ 94

TEST 3

SPEAKING

Answer short question

In the test, there are 10–12 tasks. For each task, you hear a question and speak your answer into the microphone. The wording in the instructions below is the same as you will see in the actual test. See page 22 for help.

▸ 95–104  **10 sec.** You will hear a question. Please give a simple and short answer. Often just one or a few words is enough.

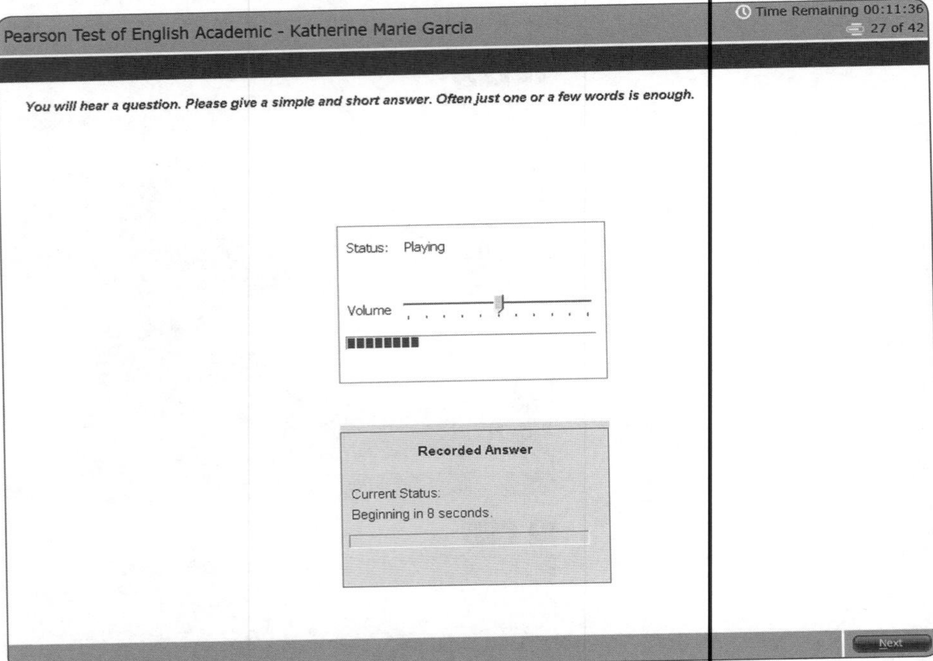

Answer short question: Each question is displayed on a new screen.

TEST 3

SPEAKING

Summarize written text

In the test, there are 2–3 tasks. Each task has a text on the screen. You type your summary of the text into the box at the bottom of the screen. The wording in the instructions below is the same as you will see in the actual test. See page 24 for help.

1 **10 min.** **Read the passage below and summarize it using one sentence. Type your response in the box at the bottom of the screen. You have 10 minutes to finish this task. Your response will be judged on the quality of your writing and on how well your response presents the key points in the passage.**

Inequality between world citizens used to be determined in equal measures by class and location. New research, however, reveals that people's fortunes are being dictated primarily by where they live. As a result, economic migration has become the key way for individuals from developing countries to improve their economic standing, and governments will not be able to alleviate the pressure of migration on their societies until global inequality is reduced.

In *Global Inequality: from class to location, from proletarians to migrants*, Branko Milanovic, of the University of Maryland, examines the differences in income between countries and concludes that a key priority for policy makers should be aid and support for developing countries.

'Not only is the overall inequality between world citizens greater in the early 21st century than it was more than a century and a half ago, but its composition has entirely changed; from being an inequality determined in equal measures by class and location, it has become preponderantly an inequality determined by location only,' finds the report. 'Analysis of incomes across countries for different members of the population reveals a wide gap between the underprivileged in wealthy societies and in less wealthy countries. This fact is of great political and economic significance. Individuals can now make large gains from migrating to wealthier countries.'

TEST 3 WRITING

2 10 min. Read the passage below and summarize it using one sentence. Type your response in the box at the bottom of the screen. You have 10 minutes to finish this task. Your response will be judged on the quality of your writing and on how well your response presents the key points in the passage.

> English is the world's lingua franca, the language of science, technology, business, diplomacy and popular culture. That probably explains why it is the world's most widely spoken language. It probably also explains why native English speakers are so reluctant to learn a second language. It's not worth the effort.
>
> In 2005, the European Commission carried out a survey of the European Union's 25 member states. The two with the lowest rates of bilingualism – defined as being able to hold a conversation in more than one language – were the UK and Ireland. About two-thirds of people in these countries speak only English. It's a similar story wherever English is spoken as the mother tongue. Only about 25 per cent of US citizens can converse in another language. In Australia, the rates are even lower.
>
> Compare that with continental Europe, where multilingualism is the rule rather than the exception. More than half of EU citizens are bilingual, and not just because they live in countries like Luxembourg with multiple official languages. Even in France, which has only one official language and is immensely proud of its linguistic heritage, most people speak a second language.
>
> Again, that is largely down to the dominance of English. Across Europe, English is by far the most commonly learned language. High levels of bilingualism are not driven by a general desire to learn languages but a specific need to learn English.

....

....

....

....

....

Write essay

In the test, there are 1–2 tasks. For each task, the essay question is on the screen. You type your essay into the box on the screen. The wording in the instructions below is the same as you will see in the actual test. See page 27 for help.

20 min. You will have 20 minutes to plan, write and revise an essay about the topic below. Your response will be judged on how well you develop a position, organize your ideas, present supporting details, and control the elements of standard written English. You should write 200–300 words.

1 'Some types of employment are more suitable for men and other types of employment are more appropriate for women.'

To what extent do you agree with this statement? Support your point of view with reasons and examples from your own experience.

2 'Nowadays many young people leave home at an early age to either study or work in another city.'

Do you think this has more advantages or disadvantages for young people? Support your point of view with reasons and examples from your own experience.

Pearson Test of English Academic - Katherine Marie Garcia

Time Remaining 00:11:36

27 of 42

You will have 20 minutes to plan, write and revise an essay about the topic below. Your response will be judged on how well you develop a position, organize your ideas, present supporting details, and control the elements of standard written English. You should write 200-300 words.

"Education is a critical element of the prosperity of any nation. The more educated the people in a country are, the more successful their nation becomes." Discuss the extent to which you agree or disagree with this statement. Support your point of view with reasons and/or examples from your own experience or observations.

Cut | Copy | Paste

Total Word Count: 0

Next

Write essay: Each question is displayed on a new screen.

Multiple-choice, choose single answer

In the test, there are 2–3 tasks. For each task, you read the text on the left of the screen and look at the options on the right of the screen. You click the button next to the answer you think is correct. The wording in the instructions below is the same as you will see in the actual test. See page 30 for help.

Read the text and answer the multiple-choice question by selecting the correct response. *Only one response is correct.*

❶ Governments, business and many types of institutions collect, organise and record statistics. Statistics capture vital information about such things as the economy, population and the environment and therefore allow meaningful comparisons to be made. This can then inform decisions and plans made about such issues which in turn become public policies. While it may be the issues behind the statistics, rather than the statistics as such that command the public's attention, it must be recognised that it is the figures that inform these issues.

The author considers statistics to be important because

- ○ A they are recorded by official organisations.
- ○ B the general public have an interest in them.
- ○ C they are affected by plans and policies.
- ○ D they assist in driving public issues.

❷ There are innumerable different species on the planet. Nobody really knows how many species there are, although many scientists have tried to estimate it. However, the complexity of trying to do this makes it impossible to establish a definitive number with any confidence. This is probably due to the fact that new species are continually appearing, while at the same time existing species evolve and some become extinct. In the past, the number of new species appearing exceeded the number of those dying out. Nowadays, however, due to human activity, this trend has reversed and as a result we are in danger of seriously disturbing our ecosystem.

Why is it difficult to establish the number of species globally?

- ○ A There are too many species to count them all.
- ○ B The number of species is constantly changing.
- ○ C Currently, more species are appearing than are becoming extinct.
- ○ D Human action has upset the balance of the natural environment.

Multiple-choice, choose multiple answers

In the test, there are 2–3 tasks. For each task, you read the text on the left of the screen and look at the options on the right of the screen. You click the buttons next to all of the answers you think are correct. The wording in the instructions below is the same as you will see in the actual test. See page 32 for help.

1 Read the text and answer the question by selecting all the correct responses. ***You will need to select more than one response.***

Snow is formed when temperatures are low and there is moisture – in the form of tiny ice crystals – in the atmosphere. When these tiny ice crystals collide they stick together in clouds to become snowflakes. If enough ice crystals stick together, they'll become heavy enough to fall to the ground.

Precipitation falls as snow when the air temperature is below 2ºC. It is a myth that it needs to be below zero to snow. In fact the heaviest snow falls tend to occur when the air temperature is between zero and 2ºC. The falling snow does begin to melt as soon as the temperature rises above freezing, but as the melting process begins, the air around the snowflake is cooled.

If the temperature is warmer than 2ºC then the snowflake will melt and fall as sleet rather than snow, and if it's warmer still, it will be rain.

The size and make up of a snowflake depends on how many ice crystals group together, and this will be determined by air temperatures. Snowflakes that fall through dry, cool air will be small, powdery snowflakes that don't stick together. This 'dry' snow is ideal for snow sports but is more likely to drift in windy weather.

When the temperature is slightly warmer than 0ºC, the snowflakes will melt around the edges and stick together to become big, heavy flakes. This creates 'wet' snow, which sticks together easily and is good for making snowmen.

Which of the following statements about snow match the information in the passage?

- ○ A Snow is formed from ice.
- ○ B Falling snow melts because of warm air around it.
- ○ C Subzero temperatures are required for snow to fall.
- ○ D Sleet develops at less than two degrees centigrade.
- ○ E Dry snow falls in colder temperatures than wet snow.

TEST 3

READING

❷ **Read the text and answer the question by selecting all the correct responses.** ***You will need to select more than one response.***

Water for public supply can be obtained from underground sources by wells sunk into aquifers, or from surface sources, such as purpose-built reservoirs or lakes (collecting rainwater run-off or water from streams) and rivers. The safety of the water is of utmost concern – several million people die each year after consuming contaminated water. The primary aim in water treatment is the elimination of any pathogenic micro-organisms present. All the above-mentioned sources can be subject to pollution. In the case of underground water, polluted surface water can enter the saturation zone of an aquifer and so lead to its contamination. Pollution can come from waste containing heavy metals and organic compounds, farm run-off containing pesticides, and industrial wastes which may have been deliberately dumped down old coal mine shafts. River water can be affected by farm drainage, sewage works and industrial effluents, and also the run-off water from roads. Thus there is a need to maintain the quality of the aquatic environment to ensure that the water is suitable for treatment for public supply, and that the cost of treatment is kept as low as possible.

Raw water is usually abstracted from a river and pumped to a reservoir for storage and settlement. In the reservoir, the number of bacteria is reduced through natural processes, such as ultraviolet radiation from sunlight. Also, a large portion of the suspended solids settles out. The water is then conveyed from the reservoir to a treatment works.

Which of the following statements are true according to the information in the passage?

○ A There are insufficient sources of fresh water for human consumption.

○ B Industrial pollution can affect both underground and river water.

○ C There are numerous means by which water can become impure.

○ D Rain is a safer source of water for human consumption than aquifers.

○ E Water in reservoirs is chemically treated to remove harmful bacteria.

Re-order paragraphs

In the test, there are 2–3 tasks. For each task, you drag paragraphs from the left and drop them into the correct order on the right. The wording in the instructions below is the same as you will see in the actual test. See page 35 for help.

The text boxes in the left panel have been placed in a random order. Restore the original order by dragging the text boxes from the left panel to the right panel.

1

A One such example is a solar panel which could charge an LED lamp to create hours of light each day. ☐

B In addition to being fairly costly, these create smoke pollution and carbon emissions. ☐

C Therefore, alternatives are being investigated. ☐

D A result of not being connected to the electricity grid in rural areas of some countries means people light their homes using kerosene lamps. ☐

2

A The fear of criticism from colleagues, friends and family is the main factor that obstructs a change in their employment situation. ☐

B However, most of these workers would not consider career alternatives. ☐

C It seems that the lack of psychological reward is the reason for their dissatisfaction. ☐

D Despite the financial stability a high salary brings, research has shown that the majority of top earners are not happy in their jobs. ☐

E Interestingly, it is not the risk of a decrease in salary which prevents this move. ☐

Reading: Fill in the blanks

In the test, there are 4–5 tasks. For each task, you drag the words at the bottom of the text and drop them into the correct space in the text. The wording in the instructions below is the same as you will see in the actual test. See page 37 for help.

In the text below some words are missing. Drag words from the box below to the appropriate place in the text. To undo an answer choice, drag the word back to the box below the text.

1 Using questionnaires to gather information from people is a well-used quantitative research method. It is considered to be an easy 1 ________, but in reality it is actually very difficult to design a good questionnaire. Question type, clarity of language, length of questionnaire and layout are just some of the many 2 ________, which all need to be carefully considered when designing the questionnaire. Another issue, which 3 ________ some deliberation, is how to ensure a high response 4 ________.

option | opportunity | selection | influences | requires | factors | rate

2 Psychology is a suitable course of study for those 1 ________ in all aspects of human thought and behaviour. It can be 2 ________ as the scientific study of how humans function on a biological, social and mental level. There are a range of influential approaches to the subject, which are 3 ________ to such areas as child development, health, education and sports.

practised | defined | affected | interested | applied | diagnosed

3 Migration could be described as the well-defined journey animals make to a familiar 1 ________ at specific seasons or times of the year. All species that migrate do so for a common 2 ________, in order to survive. Migration allows them to spend their life in more than one area and thus 3 ________ problems that can occur in one habitat, such as lack of food, shelter or exposure to harsh weather.

position | purpose | destination | experience | situation | avoid

4 Multinational companies are often criticised for a number of reasons, but we cannot deny their 1 ________ impact. Employment opportunities are generated for locals in the overseas country. When multinational companies set up manufacturing plants, there is often an increased 2 ________ of products for local consumers, which profits the local economy. Training is also sometimes provided in the use of technology; moreover, the experience and knowledge that the employees 3 ________ strengthens their skills and overall employability.

positive | gain | purchase | negative | availability | benefit

TEST 3

READING

Reading & writing: Fill in the blanks

In the test, there are 5–6 tasks. For each task, you have a text with several gaps. You select the correct answer for each gap from the drop-down list on the screen. The wording in the instructions below is the same as you will see in the actual test. See page 40 for help.

Below is a text with blanks. Click on each blank, a list of choices will appear. Select the appropriate choice for each blank.

1 A well-known feature of the European landscape is the castle. Some types of fortifications [1] ______ built thousands of years ago, but the first real castles only started to appear as recently as one thousand years ago. Construction of most of the larger castles in Europe was between around 1100 and 1500. Initially, the [2] ______ of these castles was to lay claim to land won in battle and also for defence. [3] ______, the owners of the castles also realised that their castles were an effective [4] ______ to intimidate local people. Therefore, castles became a symbol of wealth and authority for those owning them, and a useful tool to keep control of territory and the residents living on that territory.

1	A have been	B were	C have	D was
2	A purpose	B feature	C aspect	D plan
3	A Alternatively	B Fortunately	C However	D Thus
4	A process	B form	C way	D use

2 A recent study reveals that the ability to walk quickly in old age is an indicator of a long life. The report examined results from recent research. The [1] ______ in the research were tested on a regular [2] ______ over an extended period of time. The researchers focused on the relationship between walking speed in the post sixty-five age group and longevity. They concluded that there was a direct correlation between walking speed and life span.

A key researcher gave the explanation that this link exists [3] ______ walking involves the use of many bodily functions working in unison. The heart, lungs, skeletal system, joints, muscles, nerves and brain have to work together in order to ensure a consistent speed. Damage to any of these systems may mean a much slower walking speed [4] ______ could signal medical problems.

1	A experimenters	B investigators	C performers	D participants
2	A circumstance	B situation	C condition	D basis
3	A therefore	B instead of	C because	D so
4	A which	B also	C this	D it

Below is a text with blanks. Click on each blank, a list of choices will appear. Select the appropriate answer for each blank.

3 One of the questions we need to ask ourselves is: How much of the news is biased? Can we recognise bias? The fact is, despite the journalistic ideal of 'objectivity', every news story is [1] ____ by the attitudes and background of its interviewers, writers, journalists, photographers and editors. That is not to say that all bias is [2] ____, but it does exist.

So how can we, as readers or viewers, determine bias? Well, in the case of newspapers, it manifests itself in a number of ways, such as what events [3] ____ for inclusion or omission. The [4] ____ of the article, meaning its proximity to the front or back pages, is significant. The use of headlines, photographs and language are further examples.

1	A influenced	B agreed	C judged	D fixed
2	A considered	B accidental	C deliberate	D balanced
3	A being selected	B have selected	C are selected	D selected
4	A placement	B space	C area	D size

4 It is believed that the only purpose of advertising is to make people buy something. It is undeniable that this is the ultimate, overall goal, but there are [1] ____ equally essential, yet more subtle, aims of an advert as well. For example, people may not buy something as a result of an advert, but that advert [2] ____ awareness of that product and brand. Sufficient advertising will reinforce that awareness [3] ____ when people purchase something, they may choose the heavily advertised brand that can be easily remembered over others; purely on the basis that they may have heard or seen that name and they are not as [4] ____ with the other names or brands available.

1	A necessary	B another	C other	D more
2	A will have improved	B will be improved	C was improved	D is improved
3	A except	B but	C yet	D so
4	A memorable	B familiar	C common	D known

Below is a text with blanks. Click on each blank, a list of choices will appear. Select the appropriate answer for each blank.

5 Sixty years ago an American sociologist made a distinction between 'private troubles' and 'public issues'. His theory was that [1] ______ there being many 'troubles' or 'problems' that individuals may experience in their lives, not all of these always emerge as 'public issues' which attract general interest, or are seen as requiring public responses or even action. Personal troubles are seen as 'private' and are [2] ______ within households, families or maybe even small communities. On the other hand, 'public issues' are dealt with publicly, through forms of social intervention or regulation, for example. One [3] ______ that distinguishes whether issues or problems are perceived as private or public is number. [4] ______ only a few people experience some form of trouble, then it is highly likely to remain a private matter; whereas when a large number of people begin to experience this same trouble it will quite possibly [5] ______ a public issue.

1	A otherwise	B although	C besides	D despite
2	A handled	B effected	C advised	D applied
3	A influence	B reason	C effect	D factor
4	A Consequently	B Whether	C Either	D If
5	A become	B involve	C remain	D stay

Summarize spoken text

In the test, there are 2–3 tasks. For each task, you listen to the audio then type your summary into the box on the screen. The wording in the instructions below is the same as you will see in the actual test. See page 45 for help.

You will hear a short lecture. Write a summary for a fellow student who was not present at the lecture. You should write 50–70 words.

10 min. You will have 10 minutes to finish this task. Your response will be judged on the quality of your writing and on how well your response presents the key points presented in the lecture.

1 ▶ 105

......

......

......

......

......

......

2 ▶ 106

......

......

......

......

......

......

TEST 3 LISTENING

Multiple-choice, choose multiple answers

In the test, there are 2–3 tasks. For each task, you listen to the audio then click the buttons next to all of the answers you think are correct. The wording in the instructions below is the same as you will see in the actual test. See page 47 for help.

Listen to the recording and answer the question by selecting all the correct responses. *You will need to select more than one response.*

1 ▶ 107 The purposes of this talk are to

- ○ A explain how humans grade writing.
- ○ B present different methods for grading writing.
- ○ C criticize the use of technology in grading writing.
- ○ D describe the findings of a research project.
- ○ E suggest directions for future research.

2 ▶ 108 What does the speaker say about sharks?

- ○ A They are hunted heavily because their price is high.
- ○ B They are a more popular food source than other fish species.
- ○ C They reproduce more slowly than other fish do.
- ○ D They live for much longer than other species of fish.
- ○ E They are more likely to become extinct than other fish.

Fill in the blanks

In the test, there are 2–3 tasks. For each task, there is a text with several gaps. You type the correct answer for each gap into the box in the text. The wording in the instructions below is the same as you will see in the actual test. See page 49 for help.

You will hear a recording. Type the missing words in each blank.

1 ▸ 109

To be honest, the biggest problem for most undergraduate students, in terms of academic writing, is not only adapting to a far more [1] ______ and formal style, but also learning how to ascertain the difference between important, [2] ______ information and unnecessary, or even irrelevant [3] ______. In my experience, I would say it takes students their first year, if not longer, to [4] ______ what is required and to start to implement those requirements in their writing. What they really should be doing, if they are struggling with written [5] ______, is to seek help from the [6] ______ support services which are available at the University.

2 ▸ 110

An important question about education is, then, why do some types of students achieve success easily and others struggle to do well? Well, one theory is that there is a [1] ______ reason for academic achievement. What I mean by that is, a certain innate, measurable level of [2] ______. Another frequently discussed theory is environmental factors, such as the effect of home and family upbringing. A final reason is related to the teaching and learning [3] ______ within educational institutions, and the way it is organized, administered and [4] ______.

TEST 3

LISTENING

Highlight correct summary

In the test, there are 2–3 tasks. For each task, you listen to the audio then click the button next to the summary you think is correct. The wording in the instructions below is the same as you will see in the actual test. See page 51 for help.

You will hear a recording. Click on the paragraph that best relates to the recording.

1 ▶ 111

- ○ A Research into family history by ordinary people only started to become far more widespread in the early nineteenth century. Prior to that time, it was chiefly rich, important and powerful families who had an interest and involvement in this type of activity.
- ○ B The study of family history began hundreds of years ago in North Africa in order to establish such things as ownership of property. It rapidly became a common practice in many cultures because inheritance played such an important role in society and government.
- ○ C Originally, tracing family history was only used in order to establish the origins of prosperous and powerful families. However, by the middle of the twentieth century, ordinary people were also starting to show an interest in researching their family background too.
- ○ D All social classes of the general population have always been interested in recording their family history, but genealogy became really popular in the early nineteenth century due to the publication of a book concerned with methodology of determining family history.

You will hear a recording. Click on the paragraph that best relates to the recording.

❷ ▸ 112

◯ A Anthropologists have disagreed for some time regarding when and how fire was first used in prehistoric times. Recent findings have now managed to finally persuade them that it was used before they thought and the principle use of fire was for cooking rather than any other purpose.

◯ B Scientists believe they are now nearer to finding an answer to the question of when humans first started to use fire, and it is much earlier than had been thought. Nevertheless, there is still some disagreement among researchers around what early humans actually used the fire for.

◯ C There has been much discussion by anthropologists about when humans started to use fires. As a result of a recent discovery it is thought that they started to make fires 300,000 years ago, but the reason they made them is still not clear.

◯ D Recent findings have convinced the anthropological community that previous conclusions from research done over many decades was correct in estimating when early humans started to use fire although this research was incorrect in its findings about what fire was used for.

Multiple-choice, choose single answer

In the test, there are 2–3 tasks. For each task, you listen to the audio then click the button next to the answer you think is correct. The wording in the instructions below is the same as you will see in the actual test. See page 54 for help.

Listen to the recording and answer the multiple-choice question by selecting the correct response. *Only one response is correct.*

1 ▶ 113 What does the speaker say about dissertations?

- A They are too difficult for students to do.
- B The subject area selected may not have sufficient focus.
- C There is a lack of understanding of how to conduct research.
- D Students will not be allowed to alter their proposed topic.

2 ▶ 114 What is an important rationale for art therapy?

- A Patients are able to develop an artistic skill.
- B Therapists can diagnose problems more successfully.
- C It is the most effective psychological therapy.
- D It is suitable for less orally communicative patients.

Select missing word

In the test, there are 2–3 tasks. For each task, you listen to the audio then click the button next to the words you think complete the audio. The wording in the instructions below is the same as you will see in the actual test. See page 56 for help.

❶ ▶ 115 You will hear a recording about an archaeological discovery. *At the end of the recording the last word or group of words has been replaced by a beep.* Select the correct option to complete the recording.

- ○ A are much older than expected
- ○ B could very possibly be fake
- ○ C belonged to that culture

❷ ▶ 116 You will hear a recording about measuring time. *At the end of the recording the last word or group of words has been replaced by a beep.* Select the correct option to complete the recording.

- ○ A ancient civilisations
- ○ B desert tribes
- ○ C historical periods
- ○ D current days

Highlight incorrect words

In the test, there are 2–3 tasks. For each task, you listen to the audio and follow the words in the text on the screen. You click on the words that are different on the screen and the audio. The wording in the instructions below is the same as you will see in the actual test. See page 58 for help.

You will hear a recording. Below is a transcription of the recording. *Some words in the transcription differ from what the speaker said.* Please click on the words that are different.

1 ▶ 117 Transcription:

One of the most encouraging phenomena in recent years has been the development of lifelong learning in the education sector. Nowadays, students are embarking on courses at all ages. Higher education is no longer viewed as a place for the young. Mature students are appreciated and respected. Recent research has also indicated that older students are dedicated learners, able to contribute a number of skills and talents gained from work, family and other life experiences.

2 ▶ 118 Transcription:

Conducting a video conference is now a popular method of communication in the business world. This telecommunications technology allows two or more locations to communicate by simultaneous video and audio transmissions. It's designed to serve conferences or meetings in many locations.

The advantages are obvious: no more lengthy phone calls or complicated correspondence with business contacts, partners or offices abroad. This relatively low cost, fast, effective communication method has made significant inroads in not just a business environment, but also education, medicine and media.

Write from dictation

In the test, there are 3–4 tasks. For each task, you listen and type the sentence you hear into the box on the screen. The wording in the instructions below is the same as you will see in the actual test. See page 60 for help.

You will hear a sentence. Type the sentence in the box below exactly as you hear it. Write as much of the sentence as you can. You will hear the sentence only once.

1 ▸ 119

....

....

....

2 ▸ 120

....

....

....

3 ▸ 121

....

....

....

TEST 4

Read aloud

In the test, there are 6–7 tasks. For each task, you read the text aloud into the microphone. The wording in the instructions below is the same as you will see in the actual test. See page 12 for help.

40 sec. **Look at the text below. In 40 seconds, you must read this text aloud as naturally and as clearly as possible. You have 40 seconds to read aloud.**

1. The Italian alphabet has fewer letters in comparison with the English alphabet. Italian does not use the letters J, K, W, X or Y – except in borrowed words. However, young Italians are increasingly using the letter K in words that would be written with C or CH in standard Italian orthography.

2. Summerhill School was regarded with considerable suspicion by the educational establishment. Lessons were optional for pupils at the school, and the government of the school was carried out by a School Council, of which all the pupils and staff were members, with everyone having equal voting rights.

3. This term the University is running a series of workshops for final year students on how to do well in interviews. These sessions will help participants prepare effectively for – and perform at their best during – later job interviews. The workshop tutors have an excellent record of success in helping students acquire the positions they desire.

4. Tasmania is a large and relatively sparsely populated island off the south coast of Australia. The island is of particular interest to natural scientists, who go there to research the unique wildlife. Tasmania has, for example, twelve species of bird that are not found anywhere else in the world.

5. Honey has traditionally been credited with significant medical powers, and it has played a major part in many folk remedies. But it seems now its efficacy is not just an old wives' tale. Recent research has shown there is scientific evidence to prove that honey contains elements that prevent bacteria from growing.

6. The College has a fascinating museum dedicated to archaeology and anthropology. It contains information about many of the studies which have been carried out by members of the College over the five hundred years of its existence. There are many unique exhibits brought back from excavations and explorations in all the continents.

Repeat sentence

In the test, there are 10–12 tasks. For each task, you listen and repeat the sentence you hear into the microphone. The wording in the instructions below is the same as you will see in the actual test. See page 14 for help.

▸ 122–131 15 sec. You will hear a sentence. Please repeat the sentence exactly as you hear it. You will hear the sentence only once.

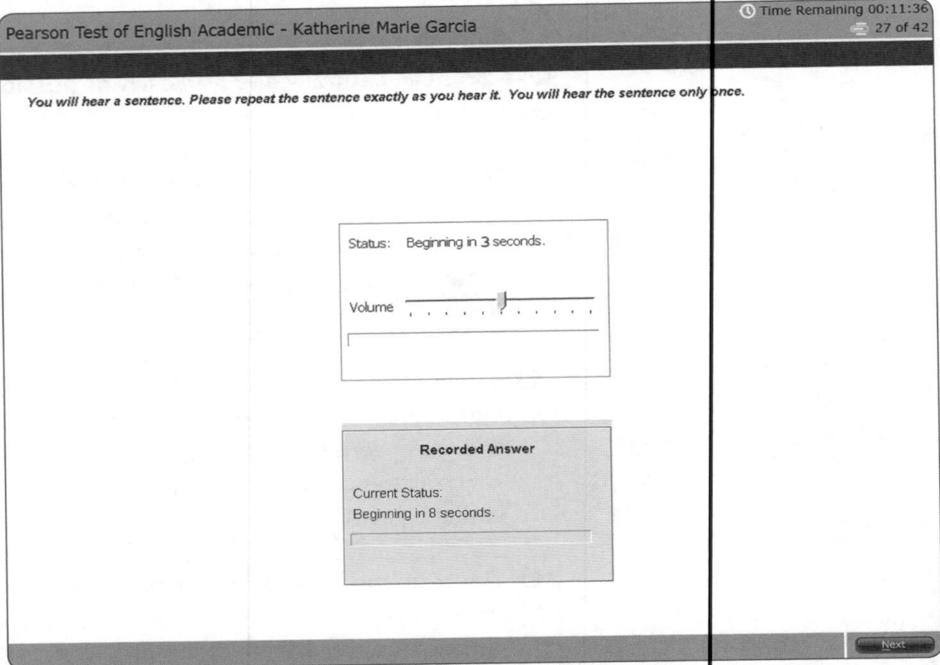

Repeat sentence: Each question is displayed on a new screen.

TEST 4

SPEAKING

Describe image

In the test, there are 6–7 tasks. For each task, you look at the image and describe it into the microphone. The wording in the instructions below is the same as you will see in the actual test. See page 16 for help.

1. 40 sec. Look at the map below. In 25 seconds, please speak into the microphone and describe in detail what the map is showing. You will have 40 seconds to give your response.

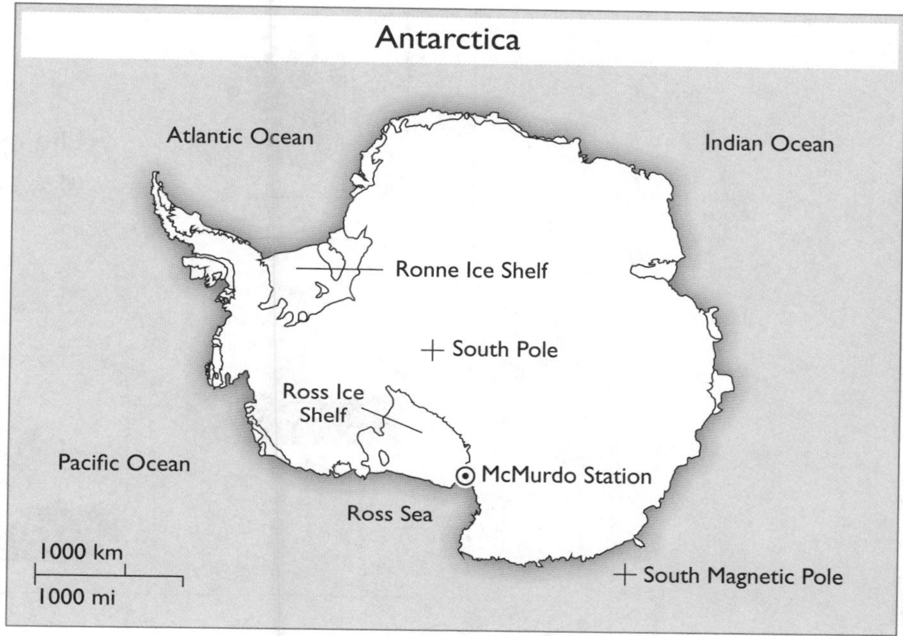

2. 40 sec. Look at the graph below. In 25 seconds, please speak into the microphone and describe in detail what the graph is showing. You will have 40 seconds to give your response.

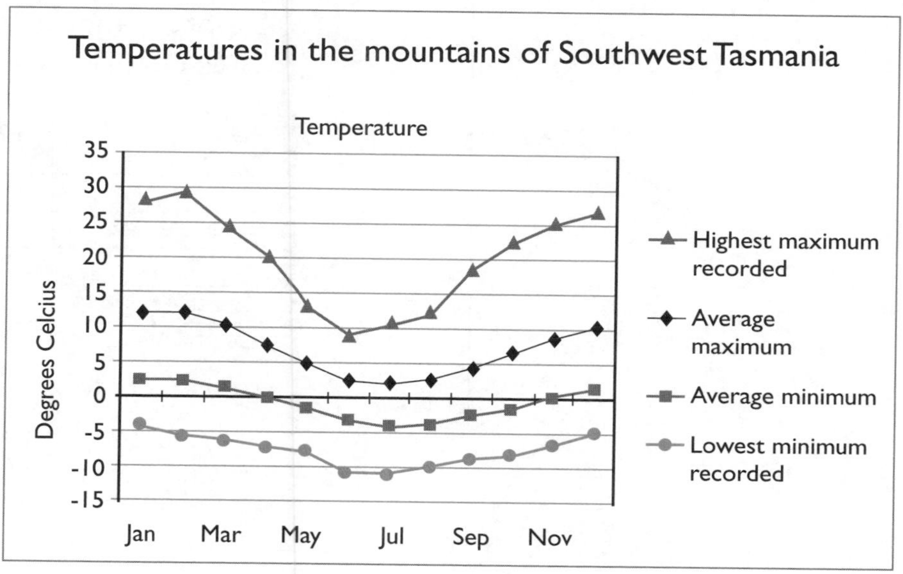

3 40 sec. Look at the diagram below. In 25 seconds, please speak into the microphone and describe in detail what the diagram is showing. You will have 40 seconds to give your response.

4 40 sec. Look at the table below. In 25 seconds, please speak into the microphone and describe in detail what the table is showing. You will have 40 seconds to give your response.

Export of motorcycles from Japan

Last calendar year, by region (%)

	Share (%)	% change on previous year
Asia	7.7	-4.7
Middle East	0.7	-2.9
Europe	34.5	-23.6
North America	35.5	+68.7
Central America	1.2	+11.6
South America	8.0	+19.9
Africa	4.2	-17.8
Oceania	8.2	-16.7
Total	*100.0*	*+2.3*

5 40 sec. Look at the chart below. In 25 seconds, please speak into the microphone and describe in detail what the chart is showing. You will have 40 seconds to give your response.

6 40 sec. Look at the chart below. In 25 seconds, please speak into the microphone and describe in detail what the chart is showing. You will have 40 seconds to give your response.

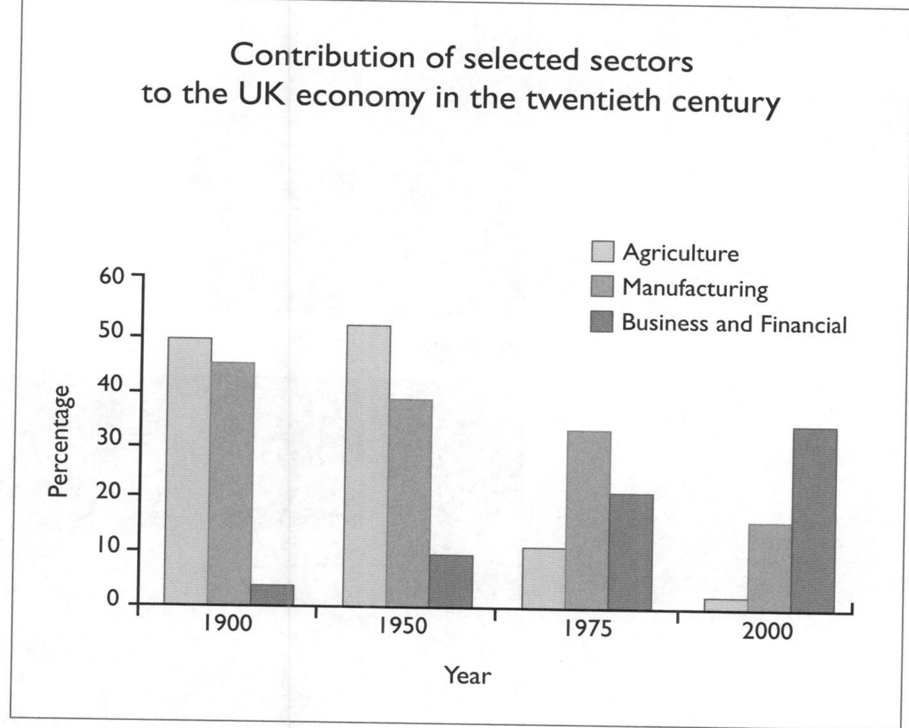

TEST 4
SPEAKING

Re-tell lecture

In the test, there are 3–4 tasks. For each task, you see an image on the screen. Listen to the lecture and then speak into the microphone. The wording in the instructions below is the same as you will see in the actual test. See page 20 for help.

40 sec. You will hear a lecture. After listening to the lecture, in 10 seconds, please speak into the microphone and retell what you have just heard from the lecture in your own words. You will have 40 seconds to give your response.

1 ▸ 132

2 ▸ 133

3 ▸ 134

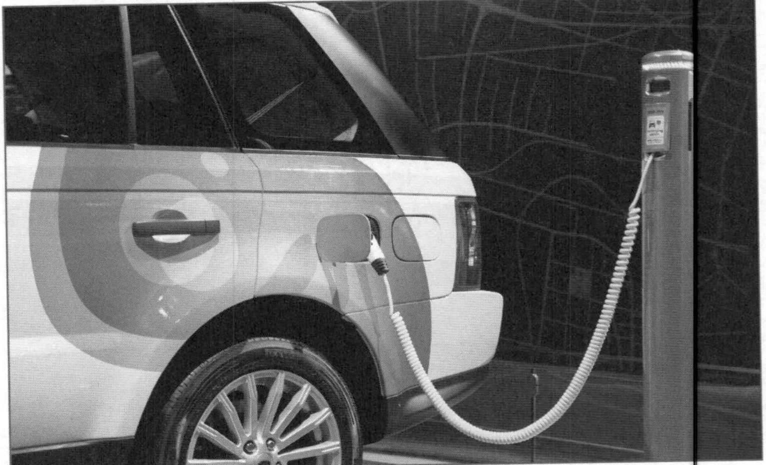

Answer short question

In the test, there are 10–12 tasks. For each task, you hear a question and speak your answer into the microphone. The wording in the instructions below is the same as you will see in the actual test. See page 22 for help.

▸ 135–144 10 sec. You will hear a question. Please give a simple and short answer. Often just one or a few words is enough.

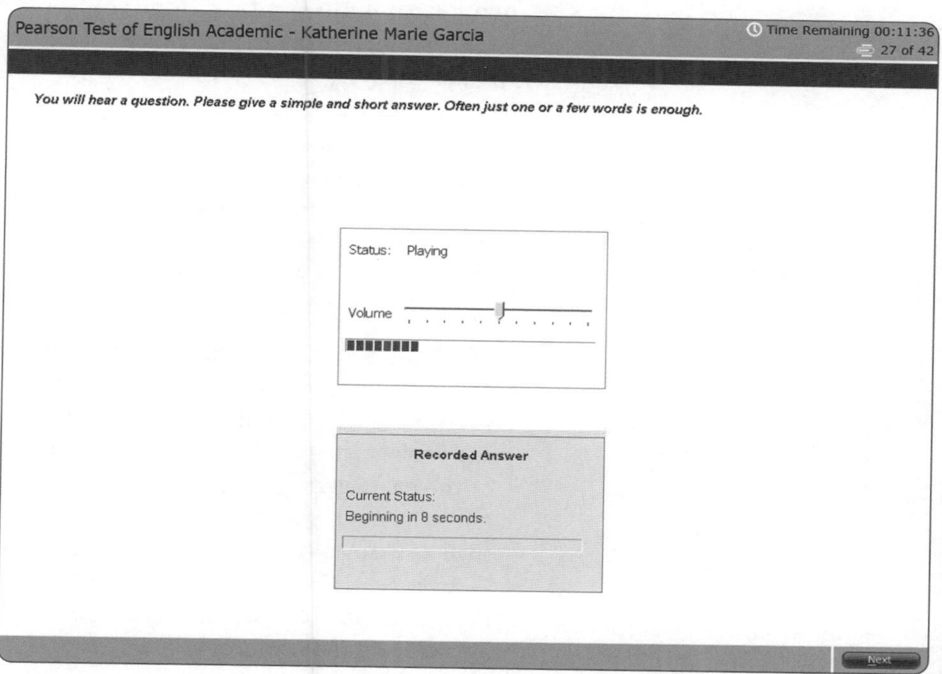

Answer short question: Each question is displayed on a new screen.

Summarize written text

In the test, there are 2–3 tasks. Each task has a text on the screen. You type your summary of the text into the box at the bottom of the screen. The wording in the instructions below is the same as you will see in the actual test. See page 24 for help.

1  **10 min. Read the passage below and summarize it using one sentence. Type your response in the box at the bottom of the screen. You have 10 minutes to finish this task. Your response will be judged on the quality of your writing and on how well your response presents the key points in the passage.**

> Times are fraught, and overstretched executives are constantly on the lookout for a way to clear their minds so they can work in a calmer, more effective, and more responsive way. Cultivating a special state of consciousness called 'mindfulness' – an intense awareness of the here and now – is proving attractive to a growing number of senior managers, both in the US and elsewhere.
>
> Mindfulness is achieved by meditation techniques, often involving sitting on a cushion, eyes closed, concentrating on the inflow and outflow of your breath. Or you might spend 10 minutes studying, sniffing, tasting and finally eating a piece of fruit. That might make it sound like a remnant of the navel-gazing 1960s and 1970s, but the evidence for mindfulness's effectiveness is good enough to have impressed hard-nosed companies such as Google (which has invited mindfulness gurus to speak at the Googleplex), General Mills, PricewaterhouseCoopers, Deutsche Bank, Procter & Gamble, AstraZeneca, Apple, Credit Suisse, KPMG, Innocent, Reuters and many more.
>
> According to Don McCormick, assistant professor of management at California State University and a dedicated meditator, it 'can help individuals to manage workplace stress, perform tasks more effectively, enhance self-awareness and self-regulation, experience work as more meaningful, improve workplace relationships, increase ethical behavior, and make perception more accurate'. It is said to pay dividends for leaders and managers, by improving the quality of their listening and communicating.

....

....

....

....

....

TEST 4

WRITING

❷ 10 min. Read the passage below and summarize it using one sentence. Type your response in the box at the bottom of the screen. You have 10 minutes to finish this task. Your response will be judged on the quality of your writing and on how well your response presents the key points in the passage.

One of the many critiques of academic research that one runs across is that a lot of research done by a faculty at universities across America doesn't 'do' anything: it doesn't lead to some new product that can be marketed; it doesn't create jobs; it doesn't have an obvious social value. After all, people argue, do we really need studies that chart the maturation of catfish? Or that explore the nuances of a minor poet? What is all this for?

As a consequence of attitudes like these, many people – particularly politicians and business persons – argue that the research function should be stripped from academia, or at least those parts of academia that aren't the major research institutions. Then universities wouldn't need so many faculties, and costs could be contained.

Academics like me offer lots of standard objections to this line of thinking: that research keeps one fresh and up-to-date in the discipline; that the faculty often works with students on their research, thus providing students with invaluable training for their future careers and so on.

All of this is true, but I want to add a different point: the power of chance.

In 1990, I took an appointment at the University of Alabama-Huntsville. I had a police officer student who invited me for a ride along. I went – ultimately many times. The book that emerged from the research project I established from that first ride was later included on a list of 'must read' books on public administration by the Government of Canada.

I have no problem with accountability. But if you had asked me what my purpose was when I took my first ride along, and you had demanded to know what use the research could be put to, I would have told you, 'I have no idea'.

....

....

....

....

....

TEST 4

WRITING

3 10 min. Read the passage below and summarize it using one sentence. Type your response in the box at the bottom of the screen. You have 10 minutes to finish this task. Your response will be judged on the quality of your writing and on how well your response presents the key points in the passage.

> Current research into the nature of the relationship between participation in physical activity/sport and educational performance has produced mixed, inconsistent and often non-comparable results. For example, some cross-sectional studies illustrate a positive correlation between participation in sport and physical activity and academic success (e.g. maths, reading, acuity, reaction times). However, critics point to a general failure to solve the issue of direction of cause – whether intelligence leads to success in sport, whether involvement in sport enhances academic performance, or whether a third factor (e.g. personality traits) explains both.
>
> Longitudinal studies also generally support the suggestion that academic performance is enhanced, or at least maintained, by increased habitual physical activity. Yet such studies are criticized for not being definitive because some do not use randomised allocation of pupils to experimental and control groups (to control for pre-existing differences), others tend to use (subjective) teacher-assigned grades to assess academic achievement, rather than standardised and comparable tests; and some programmes include parallel interventions, making it difficult to isolate specific effects.
>
> More generically, one key piece of research illustrates that both acute exercise and chronic training programmes have small, but beneficial, positive impacts on cognitive performance. However, this study concludes that as experimental rigour decreased, effect size increased. Further, generalisation is limited because effect size is influenced by the nature and type of exercise, the type of participants, the nature of the cognitive tests and the methodological quality of the study.

....

....

....

....

....

Write essay

In the test, there are 1–2 tasks. For each task, the essay question is on the screen. You type your essay into the box on the screen. The wording in the instructions below is the same as you will see in the actual test. See page 27 for help.

20 min. You will have 20 minutes to plan, write and revise an essay about the topic below. Your response will be judged on how well you develop a position, organize your ideas, present supporting details, and control the elements of standard written English. You should write 200–300 words.

'Computer technology has had more of a negative than a positive impact on society.'

How far do you agree with this statement? Support your views with reasons and/or examples from your own experience.

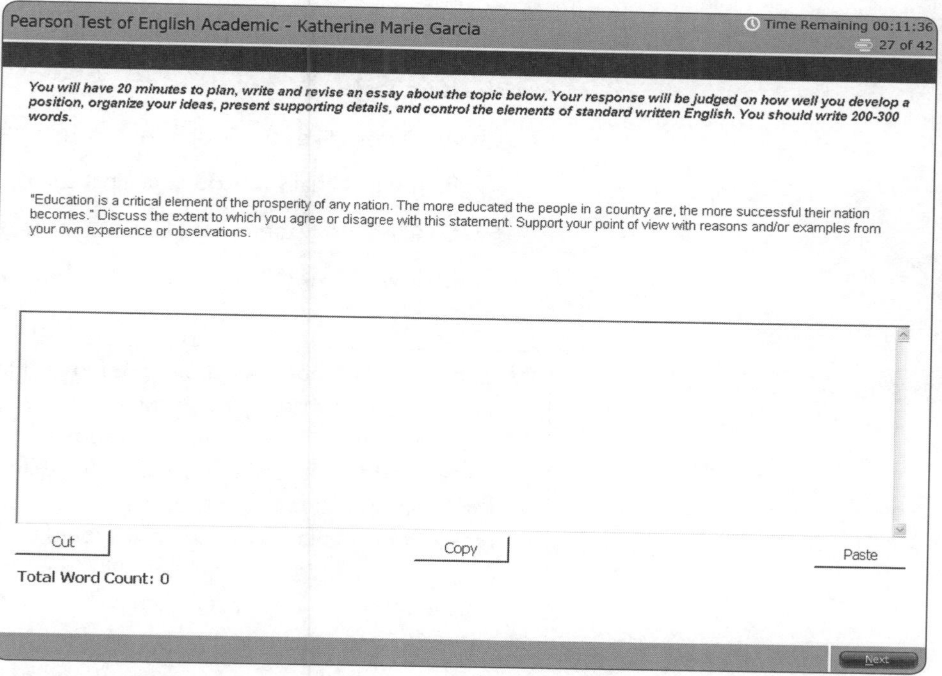

Write essay: Each question is displayed on a new screen.

Multiple-choice, choose single answer

In the test, there are 2–3 tasks. For each task, you read the text on the left of the screen and look at the options on the right of the screen. You click the button next to the answer you think is correct. The wording in the instructions below is the same as you will see in the actual test. See page 30 for help.

Read the text and answer the multiple-choice question by selecting the correct response. ***Only one response is correct.***

❶ It is a curious tradition that the clock on the tower of Christ Church Cathedral in Oxford is always five minutes later than standard British time. The explanation for this lies in the conservative nature of the Cathedral's clergy. It was only when the railways arrived in the middle of the nineteenth century that it became important for clocks throughout the country to be synchronised, however difficult this might be. When the Cathedral was asked to come into line, the clergy discussed the request but decided that this was an idea that needed to prove its worth before being adopted.

Why does Christ Church Cathedral clock give a different time from other British churches?

- ○ A Oxford likes to be different from other places.
- ○ B It was initially a protest against the coming of the railway.
- ○ C Cathedral staff were reluctant to act too quickly.
- ○ D It was very difficult to alter the time on the clock.

❷ Zebras are members of the horse family. However, these 'stripey horses' are not used for riding. Keen riders have occasionally attempted to try. Although zebras have at times let someone sit on their back, the rider soon discovered that a zebra's neck is stiffer than a horse's, lacking the suppleness that enables riders to control the horse. The structure of a zebra's back also makes it less suitable for riding. It would undoubtedly be possible to breed zebras that would ride well, but with the arrival of the internal combustion engine there has not been much incentive to do so.

What is the writer's conclusion about zebras?

- ○ A Zebras are not as similar to horses as they initially appear.
- ○ B People have little motivation to develop a zebra that could be ridden.
- ○ C It is unlikely that people could develop a zebra that would be good to ride.
- ○ D Motorised vehicles are gradually reducing the numbers of zebras that are being bred.

Multiple-choice, choose multiple answers

In the test, there are 2–3 tasks. For each task, you read the text on the left of the screen and look at the options on the right of the screen. You click the buttons next to all of the answers you think are correct. The wording in the instructions below is the same as you will see in the actual test. See page 32 for help.

1 Read the text and answer the question by selecting all the correct responses. ***You will need to select more than one response.***

> Much has been written on the wooden sculptures of West Africa, especially Nigeria, which was pre-eminent in the art, for unlike other crafts, wood-carving has long been acknowledged in the West as an art form. Yet, compared with stone or bronze, wood is not a very durable material in tropical conditions and the oldest carvings in Nigeria are probably no more than two hundred and fifty years old. Many of the earliest, maybe the finest of the wood carvings may also have been destroyed by termites. When one is attacked in this way, no attempt is made to preserve it; a new one is made to replace it, for the creativity of making it is valued above the object *per se*. The finest sculptures were made for religious or ceremonial purposes, and the art of creation was itself a religious act.

What has led to there being no very old wood carvings in West Africa?

- ○ A the nature of the climate there
- ○ B Western collectors' desire for such carvings
- ○ C the fact that other materials were used previously
- ○ D destruction of the carvings because of religion
- ○ E problems caused by insects

2 **Read the text and answer the question by selecting all the correct responses.** ***You will need to select more than one response.***

It is possible to study the curriculum of an educational institution from a number of different perspectives. In the first instance, we can look at curriculum planning, that is at decision-making, in relation to identifying learners' needs and purposes; establishing goals and objectives; selecting and grading content; organising appropriate learning arrangements and learner groupings; selecting, adapting or developing appropriate materials, learning tasks and assessment and evaluation tools.

Alternatively, we can study the curriculum in action, as it were. This second perspective takes us into the classroom itself. Here, we can observe the teaching/learning process and study the ways in which the intentions of the curriculum planners, which were developed during the planning phase, are put into action.

Yet another perspective relates to assessment and evaluation. From this perspective we would try and find out what students had learned and what they had failed to learn, in relation to what had been planned. In addition we might want to find out if they had learned anything which had not been planned.

Which of these ways of looking at an institution's curriculum is outlined in the text?

- ○ A observing what happens during lessons
- ○ B evaluating the materials used
- ○ C analysing the content of tests
- ○ D considering what is taken into account when preparing the curriculum
- ○ E comparing this curriculum with other choices that could have been made
- ○ F reviewing actual learning compared to curriculum goals
- ○ G assessing the effectiveness of teacher preparation for lessons

Re-order paragraphs

In the test, there are 2–3 tasks. For each task, you drag paragraphs from the left and drop them into the correct order on the right. The wording in the instructions below is the same as you will see in the actual test. See page 35 for help.

The text boxes in the left panel have been placed in a random order. Restore the original order by dragging the text boxes from the left panel to the right panel.

1

A There you will see how women are consistently portrayed as weak and in need of male protection.

B This acceptance that men were the superior gender had not developed by chance.

C It had been the view that had been socialized into them from the moment of their birth.

D This will become clear if you look at any girls' magazine or popular film of the period.

E In the 1960s, the greatest obstacle for those who wanted to organize women was said to be women's conviction that they were actually inferior to men.

2

A It is mainly due to the quality of the fabric which effectively resists salt water, direct sunshine and cold winds.

B Traditionally they are navy blue and they are basically square in shape, without a curved armhole or inset sleeve.

C Fishermen's knitted jerseys have always been recognizable in Britain by their colour and their shape.

D This continuing popularity cannot just be put down to a fondness for tradition.

E These navy jerseys are still a familiar sight on any quay or harbour in the land.

Reading: Fill in the blanks

In the test, there are 4–5 tasks. For each task, you drag the words at the bottom of the text and drop them into the correct space in the text. The wording in the instructions below is the same as you will see in the actual test. See page 37 for help.

In the text below some words are missing. Drag words from the box below to the appropriate place in the text. To undo an answer choice, drag the word back to the box below the text.

1 There are two basic branches of the science of astronomy: observational and theoretical. Observational astronomy, as the name suggests, is concerned with observing the 1 _____ and then analyzing the observations, using the 2 _____ of physics. Theoretical astronomy focuses more on developing computer or analytical models to 3 _____ astronomical phenomena. The two 4 _____ complement each other, with observational astronomers attempting to 5 _____ theoretical results, and theoreticians aiming to explain what has been observed.

angles | confirm | describe | effects | fields | principles | reason | skies

2 Behanzin ruled the West African 1 _____ of Dahomey at the end of the nineteenth century, a time when Europeans were doing their utmost to colonise Africa. Behanzin put up extremely 2 _____ resistance. He did this with the 3 _____ of an army, including five thousand female warriors. He is often called King Shark, a name suggesting 4 _____ and wisdom. Famed for being a 5 _____ as well as a warrior, he wrote some of the most beautiful songs ever produced in Dahomey.

aid | battle | kingdom | light | poet | powerful | monarch | strength

3 An investigation into the study habits of undergraduates was carried out by a 1 _____ of researchers at a number of different universities. In all the universities 2 _____ in the study, it was found that there were the 3 _____ significant differences between the habits of arts and science students. Not surprisingly perhaps, arts students read more 4 _____, while science students tended to concentrate on a few 5 _____ texts.

core | heavily | involving | participating | same | staff | team | widely

4 Dolphins are marine mammals found all over the world. There are many 1 _____ species. They are well-known as intelligent creatures and seem to 2 _____ with one another in sophisticated ways. Dolphins are 3 _____ animals in that they live in groups. These can 4 _____ in size from five to several hundred. They often hunt in groups and work together to 5 _____ the fish or squid they like to eat.

capture | communicate | different | grow | learn | range | sociable | strange

Reading & writing: Fill in the blanks

In the test, there are 5–6 tasks. For each task, you have a text with several gaps. You select the correct answer for each gap from the drop-down list on the screen. The wording in the instructions below is the same as you will see in the actual test. See page 40 for help.

Below is a text with blanks. Click on each blank, a list of choices will appear. Select the appropriate choice for each blank.

1 Excavations have recently been carried out on an interesting Mayan house in Central America. The house dates [1] ______ the 9th century, and it has turned out to be of great interest to archaeologists. [2] ______ is particularly remarkable about the house is that its walls are covered with tables [3] ______ detailed astronomical calculations. These tables suggest that Mayan society had considerable understanding of astronomy at a much earlier time [4] ______ was previously thought to be the case. The tables focus on lunar cycles. This was important to the Mayans because they believed that there were six different gods of the moon, [5] ______ of which would take his turn to be in charge of the cycle at any given time.

1	A from	B to	C of	D by
2	A Which	B Where	C What	D Why
3	A showing	B showed	C shown	D show
4	A there	B that	C then	D than
5	A every	B most	C each	D all

2 Meteorologists are making increasing use of information provided on photo websites by ordinary people. There was a presentation dealing with [1] ______ they do this at a recent conference in New York. Scientists based at a university in Indiana looked at thousands of photos of snow scenes [2] ______ online. These provided them with information about snow falls in areas where, because of heavy cloud cover, [3] ______ information from satellite photography was available. It is not necessary to make use of this source of information as far as urban weather is [4] ______ , as there is usually easy access to plenty of other data about towns. But photos taken by the public can be an excellent way of filling in the gaps in knowledge [5] ______ weather events in more distant rural locations.

1	A whether	B what	C that	D how
2	A posting	B posted	C posts	D post
3	A some	B much	C any	D no
4	A concerning	B regarding	C concerned	D regarded
5	A about	B with	C for	D on

TEST 4

READING

Below is a text with blanks. Click on each blank, a list of choices will appear. Select the appropriate choice for each blank.

3 A manakin is an unusual type of bird found in the tropical forests of Colombia and Ecuador. Approximately twenty of the forty different types of manakin [1] ______ a kind of music by moving their body parts. This is particularly done by the male bird when it is hoping to attract a female. Although ornithologists had [2] ______ been aware that the bird somehow managed to make its characteristic noise with its wings, they were unable to work out exactly how the sound was produced. [3] ______, a post-graduate student has recently solved the puzzle. She did so by recording the bird's movements with a camera operating [4] ______ a speed of a thousand frames per second. A standard camcorder records about 30 frames per second. On examining the footage she was able to see that the bird used one special feather to click against other feathers – in much the same way [5] ______ guitarists use a plectrum to pluck the strings of their instrument.

1	A make	B have	C get	D do
2	A once	B ever	C still	D long
3	A However	B Accordingly	C Moreover	D Whereas
4	A for	B by	C at	D in
5	A than	B like	C as	D so

4 A team of young engineering students in Japan are working on the production of a robotic suit. This [1] ______ been designed to help the elderly to move around and lift heavy objects [2] ______ easily. The suit is like a kind of exoskeleton which goes over the top of your body from your shoulders to your calves. It is made of aluminium and has joints at the shoulder and elbow. It is also equipped with artificial muscles. The wearer [3] ______ be helped to stand up, for example, by pressing controls which inject air into the suit [4] ______ that the legs straighten and the person rises. The suit weighs almost ten kilos but users report that this does not seem heavy at all. They said that the increased strength that they got [5] ______ wearing it gave them very positive feelings of empowerment.

1	A was	B has	C had	D is
2	A much	B more	C too	D far
3	A ought to	B used to	C must	D can
4	A until	B on	C so	D by
5	A after	B from	C with	D for

Below is a text with blanks. Click on each blank, a list of choices will appear. Select the appropriate choice for each blank.

❺ Throughout history poetry has often been created to celebrate a wedding. This article will examine the ways in [1] _____ this has happened at different periods of time and in many [2] _____ differing societies. It will look at some examples of wedding poems from a range of eras and cultures, and will [3] _____ them in their specific context, drawing out the particular features that reflect that context. Other writers on this topic have tended to focus on more personal wedding poems, [4] _____ dedicated to the bride or the groom. Here, however, the intention is to consider poems that were written with more of a social purpose [5] _____ mind.

1	A where	B which	C that	D how
2	A widely	B widest	C wider	D wide
3	A take	B get	C see	D set
4	A those	B these	C them	D they
5	A in	B on	C by	D to

TEST 4

READING

Summarize spoken text

In the test, there are 2–3 tasks. For each task, you listen to the audio then type your summary into the box on the screen. The wording in the instructions below is the same as you will see in the actual test. See page 45 for help.

You will hear a short lecture. Write a summary for a fellow student who was not present at the lecture. You should write 50–70 words.

10 min. You will have 10 minutes to finish this task. Your response will be judged on the quality of your writing and on how well your response presents the key points presented in the lecture.

1 ▸ 145

....

....

....

....

....

....

2 ▸ 146

....

....

....

....

....

....

TEST 4

LISTENING

Multiple-choice, choose multiple answers

In the test, there are 2–3 tasks. For each task, you listen to the audio then click the buttons next to all of the answers you think are correct. The wording in the instructions below is the same as you will see in the actual test. See page 47 for help.

Listen to the recording and answer the question by selecting all the correct responses. ***You will need to select more than one response.***

1 ▶ 147 **Which of these tips about doing a good translation does the speaker mention?**

- ○ A Always translate from a second language into your native language.
- ○ B Ask a native speaker if you are not sure of the meaning of something.
- ○ C Take care to choose the right meaning of a word if you use a dictionary.
- ○ D Don't translate technical texts unless you are familiar with the subject.
- ○ E Ask what your translation will be used for.

2 ▶ 148 **Which of these qualities of a building does the speaker mention as being important?**

- ○ A how attractive the building is to look at
- ○ B how original the design of the building is
- ○ C how well the building fits in with surrounding buildings
- ○ D how long the building is likely to last
- ○ E how well the building suits its purpose

Fill in the blanks

In the test, there are 2–3 tasks. For each task, there is a text with several gaps. You type the correct answer for each gap into the box in the text. The wording in the instructions below is the same as you will see in the actual test. See page 49 for help.

You will hear a recording. Type the missing words in each blank.

1 ▸ 149

I'd recommend that you all try to get hold of ***English in the Southern Hemisphere*** by Nolan and Watts, as this provides an excellent [1] ______ of the topics that we're going to be covering in this module. It's really our [2] ______ text. It has particularly strong sections on the history of English in Australia and New Zealand, examining in some depth how the language has [3] ______ in these countries. The sections on phonology and on vocabulary will be [4] ______ when you're doing the written assignment, which I'm going to be telling you about in a moment once I've given you the [5] ______ of a couple of other essential references.

2 ▸ 150

This week we're going to be continuing our discussion of women in society. Last week we looked at a number of [1] ______ relating to women in education. If you remember, we discussed women both at school and at university. Today we're going to be considering the [2] ______ that women play in the workplace. Again, we'll start by taking a historical perspective, and inevitably you'll find that many of the same [3] ______ that impacted on women in education also had a major influence on their working lives. In the second half of the lecture, I'll concentrate on the situation in [4] ______ today, and I'll invite you to suggest how you think things are likely to develop over the next [5] ______. OK, so let's get started.

TEST 4

LISTENING

Highlight correct summary

In the test, there are 2–3 tasks. For each task, you listen to the audio then click the button next to the summary you think is correct. The wording in the instructions below is the same as you will see in the actual test. See page 51 for help.

You will hear a recording. Click on the paragraph that best relates to the recording.

1 ▶ 151

○ A What makes people unique compared to other creatures is their hands. Their flexibility has allowed us to develop the manual skills that have made society what it is today. People should become more aware of the complicated anatomy of each of their hands.

○ B The thumb is the part of our hand which is most complicated in terms of the number of muscles which are required to control it. However, each of our fingers also depends on a set of nerves and muscles which enables it to carry out an extraordinary variety of different actions.

○ C The amazing flexibility of the human hand is truly remarkable. It is the result of a complex anatomy lying under the skin of the hand, and it can be useful to study this anatomy if you want to learn how to use your hands more effectively for sporting or other purposes.

○ D The human hand is extraordinarily flexible. It enables a person to do a remarkable variety of things, some demanding great precision and others requiring considerable strength. This is because of the complex structure of nerves, muscles and ligaments that makes up a hand.

You will hear a recording. Click on the paragraph that best relates to the recording.

❷ ▶ 152

○ A There are fewer Great White sharks in Australian waters than was once believed. This is because tagging has shown that sharks travel considerable distances, and a shark recorded east of Bass Strait one week is often recorded west of Bass Strait the next. However, sharks always return to their place of origin to breed.

○ B A recent research study has shown that Australian Great White shark populations have remained surprisingly distinct as, despite travelling long distances, these sharks do not breed away from their original areas. This means that local shark habitats may have a greater effect on sharks than has been believed up to now.

○ C There is a greater variety in the Great White shark populations in Australian waters than was previously thought to be the case. This means that some types of shark are actually more endangered than was believed. Scientists are therefore developing conservation programs which will help to protect these threatened species.

○ D An investigation of Great White sharks in Australian waters has come up with some unexpected conclusions, as it found that the genetic make-up of sharks in one area was quite distinct from those found elsewhere. This made scientists realize that sharks do not swim as far away from their home areas as used to be thought.

Multiple-choice, choose single answer

In the test, there are 2–3 tasks. For each task, you listen to the audio then click the button next to the answer you think is correct. The wording in the instructions below is the same as you will see in the actual test. See page 54 for help.

Listen to the recording and answer the multiple-choice question by selecting the correct response. ***Only one response is correct.***

1 ▶ 153 **What point does the lecturer make about whales and sound pollution?**

- ○ A Increased sound pollution means whales 'talk' more at night than during the day.
- ○ B Research shows whales communicate to warn each other of sound pollution.
- ○ C Whales may not survive in some situations where there is sound pollution.
- ○ D Sound pollution from submarines has little impact on whales and other creatures.

2 ▶ 154 **What must the students do before next Wednesday?**

- ○ A email the slides for their presentation to the tutor
- ○ B make enough copies of their handouts
- ○ C post an outline of their talk to the course website
- ○ D practise giving their presentation

Select missing word

In the test, there are 2–3 tasks. For each task, you listen to the audio then click the button next to the words you think complete the audio. The wording in the instructions below is the same as you will see in the actual test. See page 56 for help.

1 ▶ 155 You will hear a recording about student assignments. *At the end of the recording the last word or group of words has been replaced by a beep. Select the correct option to complete the recording.*

- ○ A they made an inappropriate choice of topic
- ○ B they used illustrations and evidence well
- ○ C they showed they had grasped the content of the course
- ○ D they did not speak as clearly as they should have done

2 ▶ 156 You will hear a recording about poverty. *At the end of the recording the last word or group of words has been replaced by a beep. Select the correct option to complete the recording.*

- ○ A portraying those living conditions in a literary way
- ○ B bringing the situation to the attention of the public
- ○ C making use of their own experience of poverty
- ○ D helping the poor to gain a good education

Highlight incorrect words

In the test, there are 2–3 tasks. For each task, you listen to the audio and follow the words in the text on the screen. You click on the words that are different on the screen and the audio. The wording in the instructions below is the same as you will see in the actual test. See page 58 for help.

You will hear a recording. Below is a transcription of the recording. *Some words in the transcription differ from what the speaker said.* Please click on the words that are different.

1 ▶ 157 Transcription:

English had barely established itself as a language in England when it began spreading to other countries to be used there as well. First it passed north to Scotland and then west to Wales. It then made its path across the sea to Ireland. That was in the Middle Ages. Over the course of the following centuries it has put down roots all over the earth, from the USA to South Africa, from India to New Zealand. Of course, in all these places it has developed in special ways to suit the new concepts in which it found itself.

2 ▶ 158 Transcription:

Researchers at the University of California claim to have discovered that people who eat chocolate regularly tend to be lighter than those who hardly eat it. The findings may seem suspicious in that chocolate has a great many calories and, in general, the more calories people contain, the more likely they are to put on weight. The recent studies establish that it is more the regularity with which people eat chocolate that is important rather than the amount they consume. Whether they eat a little or a lot seems to make no difference, whereas eating it freely appears to reduce weight more than only having it occasionally.

Write from dictation

In the test, there are 3–4 tasks. For each task, you listen and type the sentence you hear into the box on the screen. The wording in the instructions below is the same as you will see in the actual test. See page 60 for help.

You will hear a sentence. Type the sentence in the box below exactly as you hear it. Write as much of the sentence as you can. You will hear the sentence only once.

1 ▸ 159

....

....

....

2 ▸ 160

....

....

....

3 ▸ 161

....

....

....

SCORE GUIDE

Reported scores: an overview

PTE Academic reports an overall score, communicative skills scores and enabling skills scores.

Overall score

The overall score is based on performance on all test tasks. Each student does between 70 and 91 tasks in any given test and there are 20 different task types. For each task, the score given contributes to the overall score. The score range is 10–90 points.

Communicative skills scores

The communicative skills measured are listening, reading, speaking and writing. Tasks testing these communicative skills also test specific subskills. For integrated skills tasks (i.e. those assessing reading and speaking, listening and speaking, reading and writing, listening and writing, or listening and reading), the task score contributes to the score for the communicative skills that the task assesses. The score range for each skill is 10–90 points.

Enabling skills scores

The enabling skills are used to rate performance in the productive skills of speaking and writing. The enabling skills measured are: **grammar**, **oral fluency**, **pronunciation**, **spelling**, **vocabulary** and **written discourse**. The scores for enabling skills are based on performance on only those tasks that assess these skills specifically. The score range for each skill is 10–90 points.

The enabling skills reported are described as follows:

GRAMMAR	Correct use of language with respect to word form and word order at the sentence level.
ORAL FLUENCY	Smooth, effortless and natural-paced delivery of speech.
PRONUNCIATION	Production of speech sounds in a way that is easily understandable to most regular speakers of the language. Regional or national varieties of English pronunciation are considered correct to the degree that they are easily understandable to most regular speakers of the language.
SPELLING	Writing of words according to the spelling rules of the language. All national variations are considered correct, but one spelling convention should be used consistently in a given response.
VOCABULARY	Appropriate choice of words used to express meaning, as well as lexical range.
WRITTEN DISCOURSE	Correct and communicatively efficient production of written language at the textual level. Written discourse skills are represented in the structure of a written text, its internal coherence, logical development and the range of linguistic resources used to express meaning precisely.

Task scoring: an overview

All tasks in PTE Academic are machine scored. Scores for some task types are based on correctness alone, while others are based on correctness, formal aspects and the quality of the response.

Formal aspects refer to the form of the response, e.g. whether it is over or under the word limit for a particular task type. The quality of the response is represented in the enabling skills, e.g. in the task type *Re-tell lecture* the response is scored on skills such as oral fluency and pronunciation.

Scores for task types assessing speaking and writing skills are generated by automated scoring systems. There are two types of scoring:

Correct or incorrect

Some task types are scored as either correct or incorrect. If responses are correct, one score point will be given, but if they are incorrect, no score points will be awarded.

Partial credit

Other task types are scored as correct, partially correct or incorrect. If responses to these tasks are correct, the maximum score points available will be received. If responses are partly correct, some score points will be given; but less than the maximum available. If responses are incorrect, no score points will be received.

Task scoring

In this section, the scoring criteria used by human raters for PTE Academic are given. This serves to give an understanding of what students need to demonstrate in their responses. The automated scoring engines are trained on scores given by human raters. The scores indicated for each trait, or quality, undergo a number of complex calculations to produce the total task score.

Part 1 SPEAKING AND WRITING

Read aloud

COMMUNICATIVE SKILLS	Enabling skills and other traits scored
READING AND SPEAKING	**Content:** Each replacement, omission or insertion of a word counts as one error. Maximum score: depends on the length of the task prompt. **Pronunciation and oral fluency:** (Detailed criteria on page 151.)

Repeat sentence

COMMUNICATIVE SKILLS	Enabling skills and other traits scored
LISTENING AND SPEAKING	**Content:** Errors = replacements, omissions and insertions only. Hesitations, filled or unfilled pauses, leading or trailing material are ignored in the scoring of content. **3** All words in the response from the prompt in the correct sequence. **2** At least 50 percent of words in the response from the prompt in the correct sequence. **1** Less than 50 percent of words in the response from the prompt in the correct sequence. **0** Almost nothing from the prompt in the response. **Pronunciation and oral fluency:** (Detailed criteria on page 151.)

Describe image

COMMUNICATIVE SKILLS	Enabling skills and other traits scored
SPEAKING	**Content:** 5 Describes all elements of the image and their relationships, possible development and conclusion or implications. 4 Describes all the key elements of the image and their relations, referring to their implications or conclusions. 3 Deals with most key elements of the image and refers to their implications or conclusions. 2 Deals with only one key element in the image and refers to an implication or conclusion. Shows basic understanding of several core elements of the image. 1 Describes some basic elements of the image, but does not make clear their interrelations or implications. 0 Mentions some disjointed elements of the presentation. **Pronunciation and oral fluency:** (Detailed criteria on page 151.)

Re-tell lecture

COMMUNICATIVE SKILLS	Enabling skills and other traits scored
LISTENING AND SPEAKING	**Content:** 5 Re-tells all points of the presentation and describes characters, aspects and actions, their relationships, the underlying development, implications and conclusions. 4 Describes all key points of the presentation and their relations, referring to their implications and conclusions. 3 Deals with most points in the presentation and refers to their implications and conclusions. 2 Deals with only one key point and refers to an implication or conclusion. Shows basic understanding of several core elements of the presentation. 1 Describes some basic elements of the presentation, but does not make clear their interrelations or implications. 0 Mentions some disjointed elements of the presentation. **Pronunciation and oral fluency:** (Detailed criteria on page 151.)

SCORE GUIDE

Answer short question

COMMUNICATIVE SKILLS	
LISTENING AND SPEAKING	Correct/Incorrect: 1 Appropriate word choice in response. 0 Inappropriate word choice in response.

Summarize written text

COMMUNICATIVE SKILLS	Enabling skills and other traits scored
READING AND WRITING	Content: 2 Provides a good summary of the text. All relevant aspects mentioned. 1 Provides a fair summary of the text, but misses one or two aspects. 0 Omits or misrepresents the main aspects of the text. Form: 1 Is written in one, single, complete sentence. 0 Not written in one, single, complete sentence or contains fewer than five or more than 75 words. Summary is written in capital letters. Grammar: 2 Has correct grammatical structure. 1 Contains grammatical errors but with no hindrance to communication. 0 Has defective grammatical structure which could hinder communication. Vocabulary: 2 Has appropriate choice of words. 1 Contains lexical errors, but with no hindrance to communication. 0 Has defective word choice which could hinder communication.

Write essay

COMMUNICATIVE SKILLS	Enabling skills and other traits scored
WRITING	**Content:** 3 Adequately deals with the prompt. 2 Deals with the prompt, but does not deal with one minor aspect. 1 Deals with the prompt, but omits a major aspect or more than one minor aspect. 0 Does not deal properly with the prompt.
	Form: 2 Length is between 200 and 300 words. 1 Length is between 120 and 199 or between 301 and 380 words. 0 Length is less than 120 or more than 380 words. Essay is written in capital letters, contains no punctuation or only consists of bullet points or very short sentences.
	Development, structure and coherence: 2 Shows good development and logical structure. 1 Is incidentally less well structured, and some elements or paragraphs are poorly linked. 0 Lacks coherence, and mainly consists of lists or loose elements.
	Grammar: 2 Shows consistent grammatical control of complex language. Errors are rare and difficult to spot. 1 Shows a relatively high degree of grammatical control. No mistakes which would lead to misunderstandings. 0 Contains mainly simple structures and/or several basic mistakes.
	General linguistic range: 2 Exhibits smooth mastery of a wide range of language to formulate thoughts precisely, give emphasis, differentiate and eliminate ambiguity. No sign that the test taker is restricted in what they want to communicate. 1 Sufficient range of language to provide clear descriptions, express viewpoints and develop arguments. 0 Contains mainly basic language and lacks precision.
	Vocabulary range: 2 Good command of a broad lexical repertoire, idiomatic expressions and colloquialisms. 1 Shows a good range of vocabulary for matters connected to general academic topics. Lexical shortcomings lead to circumlocution or some imprecision. 0 Contains mainly basic vocabulary insufficient to deal with the topic at the required level.
	Spelling: 2 Correct spelling, but there may be one typing error. 1 One spelling error and/or more than one typing error. 0 More than one spelling error and/or numerous typing errors.

Scoring criteria: Pronunciation and oral fluency

PRONUNCIATION
5 Native-like All vowels and consonants are produced in a manner that is easily understood by regular speakers of the language. The speaker uses assimilation and deletions appropriate to continuous speech. Stress is placed correctly in all words and sentence-level stress is fully appropriate.
4 Advanced Vowels and consonants are pronounced clearly and unambiguously. A few minor consonant, vowel or stress distortions do not affect intelligibility. All words are easily understandable. A few consonants or consonant sequences may be distorted. Stress is placed correctly on all common words, and sentence level stress is reasonable.
3 Good Most vowels and consonants are pronounced correctly. Some consistent errors might make a few words unclear. A few consonants in certain contexts may be regularly distorted, omitted or mispronounced. Stress-dependent vowel reduction may occur on a few words.
2 Intermediate Some consonants and vowels are consistently mispronounced in a non-native-like manner. At least two-thirds of speech is intelligible, but listeners might need to adjust to the accent. Some consonants are regularly omitted, and consonant sequences may be simplified. Stress may be placed incorrectly on some words or be unclear.
1 Intrusive Many consonants and vowels are mispronounced, resulting in a strong intrusive foreign accent. Listeners may have difficulty understanding about one-third of the words. Many consonants may be distorted or omitted. Consonant sequences may be non-English. Stress is placed in a non-English manner; unstressed words may be reduced or omitted, and a few syllables added or missed.
0 Non-English Pronunciation seems completely characteristic of another language. Many consonants and vowels are mispronounced, misplaced or omitted. Listeners may find more than half of the speech unintelligible. Stressed and unstressed syllables are realized in a non-English manner. Several words may have the wrong number of syllables.

ORAL FLUENCY
5 Native-like Speech shows smooth rhythm and phrasing. There are no hesitations, repetitions, false starts or non-native phonological simplifications.
4 Advanced Speech has an acceptable rhythm with appropriate phrasing and word emphasis. There is no more than one hesitation, one repetition or false start. There are no significant non-native phonological simplifications.
3 Good Speech is at an acceptable speed but may be uneven. There may be more than one hesitation, but most words are spoken in continuous phrases. There are few repetitions or false starts. There are no long pauses and speech does not sound staccato.
2 Intermediate Speech may be uneven or staccato. Speech (if more than 6 words) has at least one smooth three-word run, and no more than two or three hesitations, repetitions or false starts. There may be one long pause, but not two or more.
1 Limited Speech has irregular phrasing or sentence rhythm. Poor phrasing, staccato or syllabic timing, and/or multiple hesitations, repetitions, and/or false starts make spoken performance notably uneven or discontinuous. Long utterances may have one or two long pauses and inappropriate sentence-level word emphasis.
0 Disfluent Speech is slow and laboured with little discernable phrase grouping, multiple hesitations, pauses, false starts and/or major phonological simplifications. Most words are isolated, and there may be more than one long pause.

Part 2 READING

Multiple-choice, choose single answer

COMMUNICATIVE SKILLS	
READING	Correct/Incorrect: 1 Correct response 0 Incorrect response

Multiple-choice, choose multiple answers

COMMUNICATIVE SKILLS	
READING	Partial credit, points deducted for incorrect options chosen: 1 Each correct response -1 Each incorrect response 0 Minimum score

Re-order paragraphs

COMMUNICATIVE SKILLS	
READING	Partial credit: 1 Each pair of correct adjacent textboxes 0 Minimum score

Reading: Fill in the blanks

COMMUNICATIVE SKILLS	
READING	Partial credit: 1 Each correctly completed blank 0 Minimum score

Reading & writing: Fill in the blanks

COMMUNICATIVE SKILLS	
READING AND WRITING	Partial credit: 1 Each correctly completed blank 0 Minimum score

Part 3 LISTENING

Summarize spoken text

COMMUNICATIVE SKILLS	Enabling skills and other traits scored
LISTENING AND WRITING	Content: 2 Provides a good summary of the text. All relevant aspects are mentioned. 1 Provides a fair summary of the text, but one or two aspects are missing. 0 Omits or misrepresents the main aspects.
	Form: 2 Contains 50–70 words. 1 Contains 40–49 words or 71–100 words. 0 Contains less than 40 words or more than 100 words. Summary is written in capital letters, contains no punctuation, or consists only of bullet points or very short sentences.
	Grammar: 2 Correct grammatical structures. 1 Contains grammatical errors with no hindrance to communication. 0 Defective grammatical structures which could hinder communication.
	Vocabulary: 2 Appropriate choice of words. 1 Some lexical errors but with no hindrance to communication. 0 Defective word choice which could hinder communication.
	Spelling: 2 Correct spelling, but there may be one typing error. 1 One spelling error and/or more than one typing error. 0 More than one spelling error and/or numerous typing errors.

Multiple-choice, choose multiple answers

COMMUNICATIVE SKILLS	
LISTENING	Partial credit, points deducted for incorrect options chosen: **1** Each correct response **-1** Each incorrect response **0** Minimum score

Fill in the blanks

COMMUNICATIVE SKILLS	
LISTENING AND WRITING	Partial credit: **1** Each correct word spelled correctly **0** Minimum score

Highlight correct summary

COMMUNICATIVE SKILLS	
LISTENING AND READING	Correct/Incorrect: **1** Correct response **0** Incorrect response

Multiple-choice, choose single answer

COMMUNICATIVE SKILLS	
LISTENING	Correct/Incorrect: **1** Correct response **0** Incorrect response

Select missing word

COMMUNICATIVE SKILLS	
LISTENING	Correct/Incorrect: 1 Correct response 0 Incorrect response

Highlight incorrect words

COMMUNICATIVE SKILLS	
LISTENING AND READING	Partial credit, points deducted for incorrect options chosen: 1 Each correct word -1 Each incorrect word 0 Minimum score

Write from dictation

COMMUNICATIVE SKILLS	
LISTENING AND WRITING	Partial credit: 1 Each correct word spelled correctly 0 Each incorrect or misspelled word

The PTE Academic Score Scale and the CEF

PTE Academic is aligned to the Common European Framework of Reference for Languages (CEF or CEFR), a widely recognized benchmark for language ability. The CEF includes a set of language levels defined by descriptors of language competencies.

The six-level framework was developed by the Council of Europe (2001) to allow language learners, teachers, universities or potential employers to compare and relate language qualifications gained in different educational contexts.

The CEF describes language proficiency in listening, reading, speaking and writing on a six-level scale, grouped in three bands: A1–A2 (Basic User), B1–B2 (Independent User), C1–C2 (Proficient User).

To stand a reasonable chance at successfully performing any of the tasks described at a particular CEF level, you must be able to show that you can do the average tasks at that level.

As you grow in ability, for example within the B1 level, you will become successful at doing even the most difficult tasks at that level and will also find you can manage the easiest tasks at the next level. In other words, you are entering into the B2 level.

The table below shows PTE Academic scores aligned to the CEF levels A2 to C2. The dotted lines on the scale show the PTE Academic score ranges that predict that you are likely to perform successfully on the easiest tasks at the next level. For example, if you score 51 on PTE Academic, you can probably do the more difficult tasks in the CEF B1 level and the easier tasks at B2.

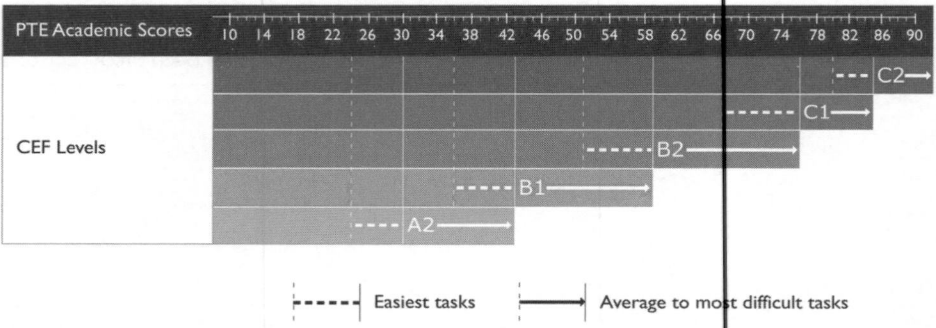

Alignment of PTE Academic scores to CEF levels

SCORE GUIDE

AUDIO SCRIPTS

Test 1, Repeat sentence (page 15)

▶ 2

1 Factors such as cost and function influence the design of a bridge.

▶ 3

2 It's important that humans dispose of their waste in appropriate ways.

▶ 4

3 If you are unable to complete the task in time please notify me by email.

▶ 5

4 The financial report for the last quarter will be available this afternoon.

▶ 6

5 Extra seminars will be scheduled to assist you with revision.

▶ 7

6 Please switch off all electronic devices when you are attending a conference session.

▶ 8

7 It is important that you work as a team on this project.

▶ 9

8 The study showed that people's mood can be affected by news and weather reports.

▶ 10

9 Detailed analysis of population growth has revealed some alarming predictions.

▶ 11

10 Please note that the college laboratories will be closed for cleaning next week.

Test 1, Re-tell lecture (page 21)

▶ 12

1 In today's lecture I'm going to talk about changes in air pollution since the middle of the last century and what has created these changes.

So, um – by the 1950s, air pollution was very visible with frequent thick black fogs known as 'smogs' in many large cities around the world. The main source of this pollution was from factories and it caused severe health problems. For example, a particularly severe smog in London in 1952 caused over four thousand deaths. Obviously something had to be done and in 1956 a Clean Air Act was introduced in Britain. This addressed the pollution from factories and the smogs soon disappeared.

However, as you know, these days air pollution is still a big issue. The main difference between now and the 1950s is that you can't see it – it's invisible. Also, the main source of pollution now is from cars and lorries, and although these don't produce visible signs, this air pollution is still a significant risk to health. And one of the key factors in the rise of this type of pollution is that we have all become much more vehicle-dependent. There are far more cars and lorries, trains and planes than in the 1950s and this is now the main source of air pollution around the world.

▶ 13

2 OK – to help you with your research, I just wanted to give you some tips today on using Focus Groups. These are groups of people that you get together to find out about their opinions and attitudes, for example, to review a piece of work or just basically provide some collective input to help you with whatever you're researching.

First of all, how large should a focus group be? Well, I would say that an ideal number of participants is around six or seven. If it's any bigger, what quite often happens is they break into side-conversations and the focus is lost. If it's any smaller, you may not get the range of views that you need to get a really good discussion.

Secondly, it's important that you have a moderator for the group, who's able to facilitate and guide the discussions. The moderator must ensure that everyone participates and stop anyone dominating. And also, the moderator needs to make sure that the discussions don't go off in the wrong direction.

And thirdly, in order to help the group focus on what's required, some basic materials should be used particularly to kick-start the discussions. This may be in the form of pictures, photos, diagrams, graphs, etc. and will help the group to understand the context of what needs to be discussed.

▶ 14

3 Hello everyone. Today's lecture is about setting up a website. I'm going to be focusing on things that you need to consider to ensure your website really adds value to the people using it.

So – there are three main areas you need to think about. The first and most important thing is who is your target audience? When you're creating a new website you really need to think about who the users are and what information they'll be looking for. What we do when we set up websites is to group users based on their needs. So, for a website in the academic community, for example, we may have groups such as researchers and administrators, and this helps us design the site and add information that is relevant to each group.

The second point is accessibility. The main thing here is to ensure your website can be found. And you can do this by making sure it can be reached from areas on the web where your target audience are also active. So this may mean providing links on other websites or maybe using social media.

And thirdly – retention – making sure your target audience return to your website regularly. You do this by ensuring it gives them a reason to come back. So it's important to keep the site up-to-date and make sure it provides the latest news and interesting information and so on.

Test 1, Answer short question (page 23)

▶ 15

1 Which section of a train timetable will tell you what time your train leaves?

▶ 16

2 What do we call the list of steps that tell you how to put something together?

▶ 17

3 What do we call the meeting where an employer asks a potential employee questions about their work experience?

▶ 18

4 What desk should you go to when you first arrive to stay at a hotel?

▶ 19

5 What is the job title of someone who designs buildings?

▶ 20

6 What term is used for the amount of money you pay a landlord for living in their house or apartment?

▶ 21

7 What do we call the first meal of the day?

▶ 22

8 What word is used for someone who watches a sports event?

▶ 23

9 What object would you use to climb up to the roof of a house?

▶ 24

10 If you don't feel like eating, what do we say you don't have?

Test 1, Summarize spoken text (page 46)

▶ 25

1 'Technological nature' … you may have heard this term … it's a term used to describe a picture of a natural scene that's been produced using computer graphics so that basically it isn't a real view – say of a garden or field – it's a virtual one – it's a picture that looks like a real scene. Now, looking at scenes of nature is known to have an effect on people's health and well-being. So for someone who's ill, for a patient in a hospital, does a virtual view of a garden have the same impact as a real one? Does it have the same beneficial effects when you look at it? Because that would be good. Well, um, if you test this out, if you put a group of people in a room with a real view and another group of people in a room with a virtual view – an unreal view – you can see what happens when they get stressed. If you give both groups a task that is slightly stressful and increases their heart rate and, um, what you'll find is that the people who have the real garden scene outside their window to look at – their heart rate goes back to normal more quickly than those of the people in the other group who only have a virtual view to look at. So, yes, there is a difference – people's recovery from stress is faster in the room with the real view.

▶ 26

2 In criminal trials, memory's a basic … a critical feature of proceedings. Both sides of the legal team – prosecution and defence – are likely to rely to some extent on witnesses and on what they can recall of events that led up to or indeed formed part of the criminal act. Now it's been well established in various circles that memory can be unreliable, particularly if new information is introduced in cross-examination that hasn't been presented up until that point – new facts that witnesses were unaware of. A lot of research has been done to test the effects of this and it can be very problematic. For example, if you show a group of subjects a video of a crime; then you get someone else to read them an account of the same crime, but adding in information, be it ideas or objects, that weren't present on the video. What researchers have found is that when the subjects are asked to re-tell what they saw on the video, they too include a number of things that were never there. In other words, the introduction of new information in a court of law is very likely to skew or distort a witness's memory of the event.

Test 1, Multiple-choice, choose multiple answers (page 48)

▶ 27

1 Last week we looked at urban regeneration and some of the consequences of this, one of which was the relocation of people from urban to suburban areas, to, er, to largely allow them a better standard

AUDIO SCRIPTS

of living – because housing is cheaper in the suburbs, so they have more disposable income. But they have to commute, and commuters need rapid transport to get them from A to B. So subway construction is, well, it's booming in some parts of the world – it's clearly being seen as the 'answer' to the type of migration that I've just mentioned. It often gets huge public support because – well – if a subway's going to help you have a better lifestyle, then what's there to argue about. Well, quite a lot actually. For a start, in order to go ahead with a major project of this kind you need to be absolutely sure that the ground, and more to the point, what lies beneath the ground can support underground transport. And to address questions like that, engineers have to be really experienced, really knowledgeable about the local area, water levels, land formation and so on. And those key issues are what I want to focus on today. Passengers don't think about construction, they trust other, better qualified people to do it for them, and governments have to choose these people very carefully.

▶ 28

❷ In places where there've been serious community tensions – I mean Brickendon's a good example of this. There were 250 reported incidents there in 2009 … often to do with neighbours and arguments, but criminal activity too, um and the police will tell you that if you leave residents to sort things out for themselves the number of incidents rises – it doesn't fall. So the local council realized that they had to do something, so they went round to people's houses and met them and their neighbours and talked to everyone and got a general idea of what the local concerns were. If there were extended families involved, they looked at those particular families more closely and all the relatives and got some of the family intervention services to talk to them. And there were some very positive results. I mean, you can pick out the hotspots – you know, the main areas for crime but the hotspots don't tell you what causes the crime in the first place and so don't address the issues. So this proactive, more direct approach by the council worked well. And this was followed up with other quite practical solutions like cleaning up the area, getting rid of debris in alleyways and just making the place somewhere more agreeable – more liveable.

Test 1, Fill in the blanks (page 50)

▶ 29

❶ Learning a language in the classroom is never easy and, quite frankly, it's not the way that most people would choose to learn if they had other options. Having said that, there are plenty of reasons for keeping languages on the school curriculum. For one thing, a fair number of students go on to take jobs in business and commerce that require a basic knowledge of a second language. When you talk to young employees in top companies, it seems that they had a career plan from the start; they were motivated to find additional things to put on their CVs – and of course language is one of those added, but significant extras.

▶ 30

❷ The assignment that I'm going to set for the holiday period is one that we've given students for a number of years. It's quite practical and will allow you to get out and about – it's no good being shut up in your rooms all the time! It does have a written element, too. Um, basically it's a data gathering exercise and there are two choices with regard to how you collect the data. We'll go through those in a moment. I'm also going to give you a link to an internet site that is – well, it's critical that you review this before you do anything, as it provides a lot of guidance on data presentation, both in terms of how you plot it – its diagrammatic form and also its description, which has to be clear.

Test 1, Highlight correct summary (page 52)

▶ 31

❶ It's been reported recently that some business schools have decided to make changes to students' grades by increasing them by ten percent. This means that a C grade automatically becomes a B, and a B grade automatically becomes an A – under the new grading system. And the change is retrospective, which means that it applies to all grades that have been achieved since the schools' current grading system – er, which was introduced in 2007 – has been in place. Now, there are at least eight business schools who've changed their grading levels, and they decided to award their graduates higher grades so they would be more attractive in the highly competitive job market.

However, changing grades like this has been criticized by the academic and business communities, because many people think the grades have been falsely exaggerated and don't reflect the true ability of the student. In fact, many employers realize when a school has made adjustments to students' grades and so there is no real benefit in doing this. Um, lifting the grades may even be damaging to the students because employers may believe that the graduates were given the high grades when they didn't deserve them.

▶ 32

❷ Urban development is the first thing I wanted to talk about here in Perth. Urban development is going on at a great pace and the standard approach here in Western Australia is for suburban development to happen at the outer edges of the city. You have suburbs slowly spreading out into areas that are cleared, and this is eating into both areas of native bushland and land that used to be used for farming, for agricultural purposes.

The debate here is that on one side there's the idea that we need more housing. We have a housing shortage in Western Australia, and suburban expansion is essential. Suburban expansion on the edges of the city is cheaper and easier to do than building more homes within the city even though it's recognized it creates lots of problems with infrastructure and so on. On the other side of the debate, people say that urban sprawl is destroying bush and consequently the natural wildlife that exists there, and that it's too easy for developers to ignore these facts.

Test 1, Multiple-choice, choose single answer (page 55)

▶ 33

❶ So it seems that – well – despite the fact that more couples are childless and more people are working in the cities, the pull to the suburbs has continued. Over 50 percent of Americans ... that's about 158 million – live in the suburbs now, while in 1990 that figure was around 48 percent. That's actually a difference of 40 million. Rural areas, on the other hand, have not seen the same pattern at all. Populations have declined over the past 20 years and now only 16 percent of our nation lives there.

▶ 34

❷ A Actually, the word 'malaria' means 'bad air' in Italian and centuries ago that's what people thought caused this very infectious disease.

B And who can blame them really? Who can blame them for making that, hmm, false connection? Who'd have thought that a tiny insect, like a mosquito, could cause so much sickness?

A Mmm. Yes. More surprising perhaps is the fact that it's taken scientists so much time since then to come up with a cure.

B Ahah. Well that's what we're going to talk about now. Because it does seem that this is now becoming a real possibility.

Test 1, Select missing word (page 57)

▶ 35

❶ As I mentioned last week, we're going to look today at fiction writing, writing stories, and in particular at authors who have a reputation for creating characters in their books who are known as 'unreliable narrators'. Now what does that mean exactly? Well originally, in the nineteenth century, it tended to simply mean that – as a reader – you just couldn't trust what the narrator of a story was telling you. This might have been because they were not giving you important information, or because they themselves as a character in their own story lacked some kind of personal insight. In later works of literature, this 'unreliability' was used by authors more deliberately, um, with the direct intention of making a story more complicated for a reader to understand – perhaps a crime novel, or a thriller. Nowadays, there's a lot more humour in unreliable narration and it's often used to make first-person characters enjoyable to read about. So, what all that tells us as a general starting point is that this type of narration ——— .

▶ 36

❷ When you first examine something under a microscope, say a leaf from a plant, you're amazed at how much detail there is and it's detail that you simply cannot see without magnification. And what you can see with the naked eye becomes suddenly huge under the lens. How big everything looks is astonishing but it's also amazingly intricate. Suddenly it's as if another world has opened up in front of your eyes and you think, hey, I hadn't realized that something so small, so tiny, could be so ——— .

Test 1, Highlight incorrect words (page 59)

▶ 37

❶ It seems we now know more about outer space than we do about the Earth's core. This is because temperatures are so high at the centre of the Earth that human beings have not been able to take a close look at it. However, new methods of analysis may soon change all that. The seismic waves created by earthquakes and volcanic eruptions penetrate the Earth's layers at different speeds. It is now hoped that by studying these waves, scientists will be able to make new discoveries and solve some of the mysteries of the internal structure of the Earth.

▶ 38

❷ Many species of birds cover long distances during their seasonal migration to warmer climates. But how successful are they, and do birds that get lost on their route ever manage to find their way back? Much research has been conducted into how birds navigate and the results show that age is a significant factor. Young birds usually just carry on, if they lose their migratory path, and thus fail to reach their destination, whereas older, more experienced birds will generally be able to find their original route and continue successfully on their journey.

Test 1, Write from dictation (page 61)

▶ 39

❶ You should draw your graph on a separate page.

▶ 40

❷ Some young people find city life rather stressful.

▶ 41

❸ Weather patterns have changed significantly over the past two hundred years.

AUDIO SCRIPTS

Test 2, Repeat sentence (page 63)

▸ 42

1. Students who wish to apply for an extension should approach their tutors.

▸ 43

2. The research looked at neighbourhood cooperative schemes such as community gardens.

▸ 44

3. Visual aids can make presentations clearer and more interesting.

▸ 45

4. Economy of scale is the increase in efficiency that occurs when more goods are produced.

▸ 46

5. The University is working towards being more environmentally sustainable.

▸ 47

6. Unlike applied arts, fine arts do not serve a practical function.

▸ 48

7. Modern poetry often tests the conventions of language and rhythm.

▸ 49

8. The Law Library is closed on Sundays and public holidays.

▸ 50

9. There are no places left in the morning tutorial.

▸ 51

10. The conference is predicted to draw greater numbers than last year.

Test 2, Re-tell lecture (page 67)

▸ 52

1. I've been asked to speak today about the purpose of museums and I think that's something we often take for granted, that we have museums and we need museums. But with so much information available now online, people have access to whatever it is they want to know so I think we need to consider carefully just what it is that we expect of our museums today. What makes them relevant in the information age.

Clearly, we've got to move beyond the early twentieth century concept of a warehouse full of old, remarkable, untouchable objects. This warehouse idea does very little to inspire people. What museum professionals need to do – what they should be doing, is make their collections and programs work towards the purpose of education. So whether that means having more hands-on exhibits, becoming involved with other community organisations, they should be doing whatever it takes to think about their visitors, to engage people, to educate them. And in that way, they can be instruments of social change. If they have knowledge and understanding of the people who visit, and the people they want to come and visit, they can take this as a starting point for providing exhibitions and services that are relevant to people's lives.

▸ 53

2. I suppose more and more, people are starting to see graffiti as a form of art. Now there are still many who would beg to differ – and they'd point to the destructive scribblings that we see on our bus shelters and our public buildings. These often take the form of tags which are fancy, scribble-like versions of someone's name or nick-name. Tags generally have no aesthetic appeal and they are the scourge of the high street shopkeeper in many a town. I can certainly see where the shopkeepers and property owners are coming from.

But the fact is, graffiti has been around for a very long time indeed. People left their mark on cave walls back in prehistoric times and it's been found too on ancient monuments in Egypt and Rome. But New York style graffiti – which is really the forerunner of a lot of the graffiti that's getting done now – New York graffiti took off in the late 1960s. That's when the advent of the spraycan allowed the humble tag to evolve into more complex styles. In the mid to late 70s, subway trains became the new forum for graffiti artists to display their skills. For many young people it became a medium to express their disillusionment with a system from which they felt excluded. Now of course, the art establishment embraces graffiti artists and some of these artists have actually taken on cult status.

▸ 54

3. We often think of technology and invention and research as being somehow more sophisticated a proposition than nature – but actually, when we think about it, there are lots of really useful concepts that technology can take from the natural world. People are beginning to remember that other organisms on earth are doing things in a very similar way to what we need to do. And they're looking closely at what we can learn from nature.

Take the bright screens on our mobile phones – now, this brightness, this effect that they've managed to achieve there, came partly as a result of research into the iridescence of the wings of butterflies and the antireflective coatings that moths have on their eyes. And it doesn't end there. They're looking at what makes a spider's web so strong, how glow worms produce light with almost zero energy. The list goes on. And this area of research is called biomimicry – that's 'bio', as in biology or life and 'mimicry', copying or imitating. It's a very interesting field of study.

Test 2, Answer short question (page 68)

▶ 55

1 What do we call the organs in our chest that we use to breathe?

▶ 56

2 If someone lives in an urban area, where do they live?

▶ 57

3 What does a king or queen wear on their head at official ceremonies?

▶ 58

4 What do we call a book that contains lists of words with their meanings?

▶ 59

5 What is the source of solar energy?

▶ 60

6 When the writer of a book is unknown, what word is used for the author?

▶ 61

7 What do we call a company or organization that gives money to a sports or arts event in exchange for advertising?

▶ 62

8 What do we call the study of living things?

▶ 63

9 What are winter, spring, summer and autumn?

▶ 64

10 What is a collective term for cows and bulls, especially on a farm?

Test 2, Summarize spoken text (page 81)

▶ 65

1 The Autumn term is in full swing now and deadlines are fast approaching. So, to help you with the final touches on your assignments, I wanted to say a few words about proofreading.

Most people find it easy to spot problems with grammar or punctuation when reading someone else's writing but it's always much harder to see these things when looking at your own. Since you won't always have the luxury of having someone else proofread for you, let's look at a few ways to effectively do it yourself.

When proofreading your own work it's important that you know what kind of errors you're looking for. Think about the kinds of things you've had trouble with in the past and try to eliminate them for a start. Now, most people know to look for things like grammar, spelling and punctuation but don't forget that the big picture is just as important. Make sure your work is organized in a logical way and that each paragraph represents a clear, distinct idea. You might take yourself to a quiet spot and try reading your work aloud – as you do, make sure it flows. Don't forget to check your referencing and citations. If possible try to give yourself at least a day or two to complete the proofreading process. It's easier to spot mistakes if you've had a bit of a break from looking at the paper.

▶ 66

2 Well, our research team spent a year looking at the way local government is functioning, talking to the stakeholders, surveying the community and basically we identified three main issues – three main areas of concern when it comes to government at the local level of the town or city. One of them, and perhaps this is the most important one, is that we need to enable citizens, ordinary people, to take more responsibility, as co-authors of their civic lives. They need to be able to determine what kinds of services and facilities they need and also, think about how they can contribute in those areas, how they can become involved. A second area we looked at was how to create a public service – and public servants – who are able to actually support citizens in what they want and need. Now this should perhaps happen in a more down-to-earth and less bureaucratic way than we've seen in the past. I'm talking about moving towards a more customer-directed approach across the board. Finally, we need to look at the relationships between national government, local government, and citizens, because that has not been functioning as it should. We've had over-directive centralism, and a kind of mistrust has emerged between national and local bodies – and it's the citizens who bear the brunt of this.

Test 2, Multiple-choice, choose multiple answers (page 82)

▶ 67

1 A Today we have Paul Witner, Head of Theatre Studies here to tell us a bit about the Theatre Studies program. Paul, what makes this course different?

B Well I think it's the environment we can offer students. We're a relatively small conservatoire and we offer superb courses in a number of subjects, with an opportunity for performance. We've built a reputation for producing both traditional and alternative performances. I guess the course would appeal to potential students for the level of support that's available, and I mean from the tutors as well as from the fellow students and alumni. There's a real sense of community.

A So, what are you looking for in prospective students?

B I guess we're looking for people who are able to cope with the high demands that the course will put on them. In that way, I think the program reflects the workplace we're preparing them for, so it's incredibly

AUDIO SCRIPTS

intense and we cover a huge range of projects, and they will be introduced to areas of performance design which they might never have considered before. We need students with imagination and dedication, who are able to keep up when the going gets tough. It can be demanding but we have to remember that the college enjoys an excellent reputation for student retention, student satisfaction and student employment after graduation.

▶ 68

❷ For anthropologists and archaeologists, rock art is a kind of window into our ancestors' evolution, migration and lifestyle. These insights that we get from rock art are highly valued by archaeologists because they complement the often scant information provided by excavated objects.

It turns out that there are common themes in rock art between sites in Europe and caves where they have discovered rock art in China. In fact, some recurring motifs in rock art have been observed all over the world. It is truly remarkable that the hunter-gatherers of the Yunnan province in China left very similar creations to the Magdalenians, who lived nearly 9,000 km away in Western Europe and thousands of years prior. Both feature outline images of human predators and prey, from bears and lions to stags, horses and bulls.

Now, both regions were inhabited by hunter-gatherers, on similar terrain. But there's more to it than that. One thing that we think it might reflect, this similarity of rock art in these distant places, is that human beings are essentially the same in their thinking. So, whether it's the ancient people of Europe, or in Asia, they did things and drew things in very similar ways.

Test 2, Fill in the blanks (page 83)

▶ 69

❶ Barred owls can be found in dense forests right across North America. They feed on small mammals, fish, birds and small reptiles – pretty much anything that comes their way. The barred owl grows up to half a metre tall and has emerged as a very adaptable nocturnal predator. Whereas they have been long-thought to live in old-growth forests, they are now building up quite an urban population. In Charlotte, North Carolina, barred owls tend to nest in the cavities of the numerous willow oak trees that line the city's streets. Far from being endangered, the owls have expanded their range; and now, in some places, conservationists are worried about the effects they might have on other native species.

▶ 70

❷ Before the beginning of the 1900s, the only way to obtain pearls was by collecting very large numbers of pearl oysters from the ocean floor by hand. The oysters – or sometimes mussels – were brought to the surface, opened, and searched. More than a ton of these had to be checked in order to find just three or four quality pearls. Divers often descended to depths of over 100 feet on just one single breath. Now, of course this exposed them to hostile creatures and dangerous waves, not to mention drowning. In some areas, divers put grease on their bodies to conserve heat and they held a large object, like a rock, to descend so they didn't have to exert effort going down. Today, pearl diving has pretty much been supplanted by cultured pearl farms. Particles are implanted in the oyster to encourage the formation of pearls, and this allows for more predictable production. The divers who still work, do so mainly for the tourist industry.

Test 2, Highlight correct summary (page 84)

▶ 71

❶ Now, one of the workplace models I want to look at today is telecommuting. Done properly, telecommuting makes good business sense and companies can make huge savings on their overheads.

It can also be a very effective lure to recruit quality employees, but companies need to plan ahead and create the right culture for it to work. It's not as simple as just giving everybody a laptop and sending them off to work from home. Management needs to look at training, security and communication issues before any kind of telecommuting agreement is entered into.

Now, a key part of making it work is ensuring that every employee – and that's whether they're at home or in the office – has equal access to resources and, of course, promotions. The last thing you want is to create a kind of 'us vs. them' scenario. The arrangement breaks down quickly if people start feeling isolated, or limited in their chances of moving up the ladder if they aren't physically in the office.

There has to be foresight, right from the start, in the hiring process. It's vital to screen employees carefully to determine who will be able to prosper working away from the office. Some companies give personality tests to prospective workers – and they do them online or over the phone to see if they're comfortable with that type of set up.

▶ 72

❷ There's no doubt that we have more consumer choices today than ever before. We all think we're good at making choices – some of us even enjoy making them. And you would think, that with all these consumer choices that people would be spending more money, because they can get exactly what they want. Well, actually, that's not always the case. Let me tell you about one study that has produced results about this that are really quite counterintuitive.

An experiment was done in an upmarket specialty grocery store in the US where a tasting booth was set up, first offering consumers 24 different varieties of jam to try and then at another time, they offered six varieties. Now when there were more varieties, more customers stopped to try than when there were only six. But only about three percent of them actually went ahead and selected a product to buy. This is where it's interesting – when there were just six varieties, fewer people stopped to try but what the researchers noticed, and what they didn't expect, was that thirty percent of them bought a jar of jam.

What does this show? Well, it shows that we have choice overload, that up to a point choice is good but beyond that, it overwhelms consumers.

Test 2, Multiple-choice, choose single answer (page 86)

▶ 73

❶ The Beehive is the common name for the Executive Wing of the New Zealand Parliament Buildings, so-called because its shape is very much like a traditional woven beehive. It's ten storeys high with the levels becoming incrementally smaller, the higher up they are.

Scottish architect Sir Basil Spence did the original conceptual design in 1964 but the detailed design of the building was by the Ministry of Works and they carried it through to fruition – it was opened by the Queen in 1977.

When it was built, it was supposed to embody the spirit of New Zealand as a nation but it's never really had that recognition in the way that buildings like, say, the Sydney Opera House have had. In a way, I suppose the Beehive was – for a long time – seen as an unfortunate hangover from the 1960s, but time has passed to the point where people's feelings about it have gone through a kind of ironic celebration to real appreciation now.

▶ 74

❷ Group work is increasingly an important part of university study and students are likely to be asked to produce assignments with other group members. Some of the benefits of group work are that it prepares students for teamwork, something that they will probably encounter in the workplace. Also, work can be shared and it tends to produce more creative solutions to problems.

However, we should be aware that conflicts may occur as individuals negotiate their place in the group and different personalities try to work together. To help overcome potential conflicts, the group can define the major task they need to complete, and then break the larger group objective into smaller tasks. It's important to develop strategies to help the group achieve their short and longer term goals and to do this, individual roles (including leader) need to be assigned.

Test 2, Select missing word (page 87)

▶ 75

❶ It's been suggested that we get rid of the study of humanities altogether. Some say studying subjects like history, philosophy, politics, literature, anthropology, and so on, has no intrinsic value and why should we waste time and energy on courses of study that won't lead directly to a cut and dried career. They say that what the world needs now is specialists, not generalists. Well, I have to say, I couldn't disagree more. Of course we want to produce well-informed, literate, highly functioning citizens who make solid contributions to society. That's an idea that still holds sway – but that's not the reason that I believe studying the humanities is valuable. People who study a breadth of topics, and who have a diverse range of interests, are actually better problem solvers. This broad education means they can approach an issue ——— .

▶ 76

❷ Surfing has been a central part of Hawaiian culture for hundreds of years. But surfing wasn't just a pastime for the Hawaiians in ancient times. It served as a kind of training exercise meant to keep chiefs in top physical condition. Chiefs demonstrated their mastery by their skill in the surf, and commoners gained popularity by the way they handled themselves in the ocean. As well as this, surfing served as a system for conflict resolution. Young males would test their surfing skills in fierce competitions, during which wealth, pride, and even romance ——— .

Test 2, Highlight incorrect words (page 88)

▶ 77

❶ Well, there are many factors that can cause one species to divide into two. One of these is when populations get isolated from each other by something like a lake forming or forest being cleared. And there's another idea that as individuals adapt to their environment, this might have a knock-on effect on mate choice, a process called sensory drive speciation. Now this seems to occur in cichlid fish. They have shown that a female preference for either red or blue striped males only exists in clear water, where they are actually able to see.

▶ 78

❷ Social capital is a concept that was introduced by sociologists, many years ago. It's actually the networks and resources that people use to deliver social outcomes. For instance, it might be holding a sporting event, running a community fête, being part of a club.

It is difficult to measure social capital and one way of looking at it is the extent that people volunteer in their local community. So you can consider the volunteering rate as an indicator for how healthy a community is. You can also look at something called a well-being index – the way people think about their lives and how trusting they are of others, their general perception of the value of their life.

Test 2, Write from dictation (page 89)

▶ 79

❶ The course has been updated to reflect the current situation.

▶ 80

❷ Agenda items should be submitted by the end of the day.

▶ 81

❸ Popular culture is now a serious subject of academic inquiry.

Test 3, Repeat sentence (page 91)

▶ 82

❶ This module develops our understanding of the theory behind advertising campaigns.

▶ 83

❷ Computer software has changed a lot in the last year.

▶ 84

❸ Exam results will be available next week from the course office.

▶ 85

❹ The most modern agricultural equipment is now extremely expensive.

▶ 86

❺ The number of students registering for postgraduate research has risen.

▶ 87

❻ This semester we plan to specialize in educational psychology.

▶ 88

❼ The new drug will be tested in North America.

▶ 89

❽ Books which are overdue will incur a daily fine.

▶ 90

❾ Distance learning has become far more popular these days.

▶ 91

❿ You need to write a proposal for your research.

Test 3, Re-tell lecture (page 95)

▶ 92

❶ Now as we all know, it has long been the habit in many countries that teachers give homework to school children of all ages. Despite the fact that a minority of educators don't agree with this practice, it has never seriously been questioned or challenged before. However, it may be that the tide is turning. These days, more people are becoming convinced that homework is of virtually no benefit, particularly for children in the younger age group. So, why have teachers always given homework? Well, the answer seems to be because they are obliged to. Most teachers don't really believe it has any real value. And the latest research supports the teachers' feelings about this. Not only does homework have very little impact on children's learning but it also puts unnecessary obligations and responsibilities onto the parents. These days not all families have the time or the necessary knowledge to help their offspring. So it would seem that now, senior educators want to start a new initiative. Rather than giving homework, they plan to encourage reading books of any kind, just reading, and they claim that this is a far more effective method of consolidating learning than wading through piles of written homework.

▶ 93

❷ Some years ago a group of academics from different disciplines recognized the necessity of studying conflict as a phenomenon. They were interested in the distinct properties of conflict as it occurred in international relations, national politics, industrial relations, communities or even in the domestic setting. These academics believed that approaches from different disciplines could be applied to the study of conflict with a view to better understanding its causes, effects and solutions.

As a result, research groups developed, and universities and academic journals began to publish papers on 'conflict theory', as it came to be called. Unfortunately many other academics didn't welcome this new discipline; they couldn't reconcile it with traditional scholarly practices because it had both a practical nature and an analytical approach.

Nevertheless, the new discipline continued to develop and the field grew and spread and conflict theory now has the same prestige as other academic areas of research and study, despite the early criticism it attracted.

▶ 94

❸ Now as urban planners, what we really need to start considering is the amount of space allocated for residential areas within a city or town. And when I say 'space' I'm talking about space within a dwelling or home rather than the actual size of residential areas. There's growing concern that the internal space of new homes is becoming far smaller. Too small, in fact.

Maybe you're thinking: Is it important for residents to have sufficient space? Is it merely a preference to have more space or are there more serious implications? Is there, in fact, any evidence to suggest cramped living conditions affect residents' physical or mental well-being or their day to day life?

Well, research from a number of sources indicates that this is an important issue which needs addressing. Cramped conditions can lead to aggressive behaviour, to family tensions, psychological anguish and, in the more extreme cases, physical illness as well. Not only this but there is a proven link between overcrowding and the social and emotional development of children as well as their educational attainment. So, the main issue here is that residents require enough individual space to be able to live and function together but with sufficient private space for personal time within the home.

Test 3, Answer short question (page 96)

▶ 95

1 If something is not expensive, what do we say it is?

▶ 96

2 What do people wear if they can't see very well?

▶ 97

3 If something such as fabric or medicine is artificially made, not natural, what do we say it is?

▶ 98

4 What type of food is an apple?

▶ 99

5 How many months are in a year?

▶ 100

6 What is the opposite of east?

▶ 101

7 When ice is at room temperature, what does it become?

▶ 102

8 Which sweet food is produced by bees?

▶ 103

9 Where can people go to borrow books?

▶ 104

10 Who serves food in a restaurant?

Test 3, Summarize spoken text (page 108)

▶ 105

1 Well, nowadays there's an increasing trend towards eco-tourism holidays. So, what is eco-tourism? Well, it's a form of tourism which should not only protect but also actively improve our environment and its cultures. However, many forms of tourism which are presented as sustainable, nature-based and environmentally friendly are often not what they seem and this is rapidly becoming a somewhat thorny issue. Governments, as well as the tourism industry, promote eco-tourism but there are very well-founded concerns that in many instances it not only lacks adequate scientific foundations but is also not viable as a solution to the world's social and environmental problems, which of course is what eco-tourism is supposed to be about. Many eco-tourism holidays are really nothing more than a marketing ploy and indeed, in the worse cases, can be said to even threaten local cultures, economies and natural resource bases.

The issue is further confused by the multitude of terms to describe types of travel, which supposedly protect the environment. Other than eco-tourism we have adventure travel, sustainable tourism, responsible tourism, nature-based travel, green travel and cultural tourism to name just a few. So the problem we have here is whether a potential traveller who wants a legitimately environmentally friendly travel experience can make the right choice when confronted with this type of marketing.

▶ 106

2 Well, what I want to focus on now is climate change, more specifically on the fact that climate change is a result of human activities. Now there has been some disagreement regarding the extent to which human activity can be blamed for climate change but I want to argue that there is evidence which clearly demonstrates that our own actions really are causing a genuine threat. The available evidence seems to indicate fairly conclusively that land and sea temperatures started to increase around 200 years ago.

So, what's the significance of this? Well, 200 years ago roughly coincides with the beginning of the industrial revolution in the northern hemisphere. In other words, this was when our production of harmful gases really got going as a result of increased industrialisation. Since that time our production of gases has accelerated due to the fact that not only has industry grown in size but it has also now spread to the southern hemisphere, indeed, most parts of the world. So, in the last 200 years, as industry has grown we can see a gradual rise in the temperatures which, to my mind is sufficient proof of the damaging effect of our actions and needless to say it's an issue which we need to address.

Test 3, Multiple-choice, choose multiple answers (page 109)

▶ 107

1 I'd like to start this lecture on the use of technology in education by talking about a subject that's probably close to all your hearts, which is the way that student work is graded, and specifically I want to talk to you about some of the ways written assignments or essays are marked.

Well, as you all know, traditionally writing done by a student is checked, marked and graded by a teacher, a tutor or in some situations an examiner, in other words, a real person. Software to mark essays has been in development for some time and grading software on computers is already used by some universities to mark exams but it is still viewed with suspicion by some. How can a computer mark an essay they ask? Well, a recent study compared the human ability to give grades to student essays to the ability of a computer to do the same job. In the study, over 16,000 essays were used. These essays had already been previously marked by at least one trained human grader.

The study showed that the essay marks given by the computer software were almost the same as those from human graders – which I think you'll agree is a controversial result and it's likely to make us as teachers re-evaluate how we grade written work.

▶ 108

2 A further example of endangered species is the shark. Around 40 million sharks are killed each year. That's quite a lot. Consequently the number of sharks is decreasing. So let's take a closer look at the causes of this.

Firstly, in recent decades sharks have become important. This is largely due to the growing popularity in some parts of the world for the consumption of shark – it has become a very valuable food source.

OK, so maybe you're thinking 'Well, lots of other fish like cod, salmon or tuna are caught for human consumption and they aren't disappearing at the same rate as sharks.' Well, that's true. But the difference here is sharks are not able to repopulate or reproduce themselves quickly like the other types of fish that are commonly fished as a food source. Why? Because sharks are slow breeders. Sharks mature slowly and it takes them years to reach the age for egg production and then they produce only a few eggs so that means just a few new sharks. Humans have a nine month pregnancy or gestation period whereas some shark species are thought to have extremely long gestation periods, as long as three years. This makes them much more vulnerable and in danger of dying out than many other fish species.

Test 3, Fill in the blanks (page 110)

▶ 109

1 To be honest, the biggest problem for most undergraduate students, in terms of academic writing, is not only adapting to a far more structured and formal style, but also learning how to ascertain the difference between important, valid information and unnecessary, or even irrelevant material. In my experience, I would say it takes students their first year, if not longer, to appreciate what is required and to start to implement those requirements in their writing. What they really should be doing, if they are struggling with written assignments, is to seek help from the excellent support services which are available at the University.

▶ 110

2 An important question about education is, then, why do some types of student achieve success easily and others struggle to do well? Well, one theory is that there is a genetic reason for academic achievement. What I mean by that is, a certain innate, measurable level of intelligence. Another frequently discussed theory is environmental factors, such as the effect of home and family upbringing. A final reason is related to the teaching and learning process within educational institutions, and the way it is organized, administered and assessed.

Test 3, Highlight correct summary (page 111)

▶ 111

1

Genealogy can be defined as the compilation of information necessary to construct what is usually known as a family tree, our pedigree or our ancestry. It is a chart which shows the relationships between individual people in an extended family over a period of time.

The first records of genealogy can be traced back to the earliest civilisations in Northern Africa who recorded successions of dynasties and wealthy families reaching back hundreds of years. This was usually done to establish rights to title, land and property. There is evidence that this happened in many places in the world. However, it was the domain of the wealthy and few people outside those circles were even aware that family ancestry could be recorded and traced. This situation changed in the early nineteenth century when genealogy became more generally well-known after the first practical guide to research was published. But it was not until the mid twentieth century that family history was no longer solely devoted to tracing the genealogies of the great, the wealthy, or the famous and it became a more common activity among the general population.

▶ 112

❷ As you know there has been an unresolved debate as to when and why early humans first started to use fire. However, recent new findings from a study in South Africa have been the talk of the anthropological community. So what are these findings? Well, prehistoric ash and the remains of burnt bones are evidence that early humans used fire much longer ago than previously envisaged, 300,000 years earlier than believed, in fact. Scientists have found evidence of multiple fires, ash and bones deep inside a cave which means it is highly improbable the fires were started naturally. One question that still remains unanswered is why they were using fire. Some researchers are citing the burnt bones as proof that our ancestors cooked the meat, but it has also been suggested they ate the meat raw and then tossed the bones into the fire.

Test 3, Multiple-choice, choose single answer (page 113)

▶ 113

❶ So, I want to discuss dissertations now. Our experience is that final year undergraduates and Masters students can struggle to find a suitable topic for their dissertation. Often they're not able to come up with a viable or suitable area to research. Another problem may be that the topic they choose is too broad and needs to be refined.

So, anyway, eventually their proposal is submitted and approved but then, after some background reading or a deeper consideration of research methods they may well want to modify their original proposal, to some extent. Well, that's fine. We expect modifications as the work progresses. This is normal. What we don't want to happen is that the student repeatedly wants to completely change the whole approved topic or original proposal to something completely new, and that does happen at times.

▶ 114

❷ Art therapy can be defined as a form of psychotherapy which uses art as its main means of communication. Patients needn't have any particular talent in art, since the art therapist is not concerned with making an assessment of what the patient produces. The principle aim of this kind of therapy is to facilitate the patient's well-being in order to bring change and growth on a personal level through the use of art materials. Obviously, as always, the relationship between the therapist and the patient is important but art therapy differs from other psychological therapies because it's a process between the patient, the therapist and the art. So, what we've found is, the expressive nature of this therapy is particularly successful with those who have difficulty expressing themselves verbally.

Test 3, Select missing word (page 114)

▶ 115

❶ So, just a few weeks ago excavators of a remote archeological site in southeastern Asia reported an exciting find under the ground. They found evidence of a writing system which dates back thousands of years. Three blocks of flat rock with odd symbols which look like ancient forms of writing were discovered. Well, this find could reveal much about an advanced, independent urban culture which historians believe may have lived in that area. However, many scholars are sceptical about the authenticity of the blocks, which they suspect ——— .

▶ 116

❷ OK, so the date of the invention of the first clock is disputed among historians but it's agreed that the first method for telling the time was the movement of the sun across the sky. When the sun was directly ahead, it was midday and when it was on the horizon, it was early morning or early evening, according to whether it was in the east or the west. However, this method was problematic in terms of accuracy; but nevertheless, it's been used for countless years, from early humanity to ——— .

Test 3, Highlight incorrect words (page 115)

▶ 117

❶ One of the most encouraging phenomena in recent years has been the growth of lifelong learning in the education sector. Nowadays, students are embarking on courses at all ages. Higher education is no longer seen as a place for the young. Mature students are appreciated and valued. Recent research has also indicated that older students are enthusiastic learners, able to contribute a number of skills and attributes gained from work, family and other life experiences.

▶ 118

❷ Conducting a video conference is now a popular means of communication in the business world. This telecommunications technology allows two or more locations to communicate by simultaneous video and audio transmissions. It's designed to serve conferences or meetings in multiple locations.

The advantages are obvious: no more lengthy phone calls or complex correspondence with business contacts, partners or offices overseas. This relatively low cost, fast, effective communication method has made significant inroads in not just a business context, but also education, medicine and media.

Test 3, Write from dictation (page 116)

▶ 119

1. You can request library books by using the electronic catalogue.

▶ 120

2. Course work and exams will form part of the annual assessment.

▶ 121

3. There are new innovations in the field of digital architecture.

Test 4, Repeat sentence (page 118)

▶ 122

1. Studies suggest there may be a correlation between educational achievement and family size.

▶ 123

2. Tomorrow's lunchtime seminar on nuclear engineering has been postponed.

▶ 124

3. During that period heavy industry grew rapidly in the north of the country.

▶ 125

4. Students must hand in their assignments by Friday.

▶ 126

5. Most students on last year's course did well in this module.

▶ 127

6. Tuesday's lecture on social psychology will now take place in the Central Hall.

▶ 128

7. Anyone who has a problem with their accommodation should speak to the Welfare Officer.

▶ 129

8. The fertile plains in the east of the region provide excellent land for farming.

▶ 130

9. Opposition to the government's tax policies was widespread across business sectors.

▶ 131

10. Students with queries about this term's timetables must speak to their tutor immediately.

Test 4, Re-tell lecture (page 122)

▶ 132

1. So today we're continuing to talk about the social history of foodstuffs, and we're going on to consider next the importance of salt and the significant role it has played.

Salt was a highly valued commodity in ancient times. Not because it made food taste nicer, but because of the way it could be used to preserve food. This meant that people were not so dependent on seasonal variations in what was available for them to eat – they could preserve what they produced and consume it as required. It also meant that food could be transported long distances.

Salt was not easy to obtain and so prices for it were high. It was often necessary to transport it long distances and it is believed that one of the reasons for building some of the roads that led to the ancient city of Rome was to make it easier to bring salt to the city from various parts of the Roman empire. Roman rulers took financial advantage of the population's need for salt. When they wanted to raise money for some war or another, they raised the price of salt.

Elsewhere salt was important too. In Africa, for example, caravans consisting of up to forty thousand camels are said to have travelled four hundred miles across the Sahara to transport salt to the inland markets of places like Timbuktu.

▶ 133

2. So today we're going to talk about children's literature and the role it plays in society. Throughout history adults have used the power of stories to entertain and amuse their children. But stories are not used merely to entertain youngsters, they have a significant educational purpose. They serve to teach the moral values of their society. In sociological terms, stories are one of the means by which children are socialized.

How does this work in practice? Well, it often makes use of heroes, the characters in the stories who the children will admire and want to be like. The heroes of children's stories, therefore, exemplify the qualities valued by that society – they will typically demonstrate courage in the face of difficulty, honesty, consideration for others, loyalty to their family and friends, a respect for work and so on. You can see this happening from the fables of ancient societies through fairy tales and folk tales right up to modern day children's stories. For example, the hard-working ant in Aesop's fable is shown to succeed in comparison with the grasshopper who spends the summer singing and has nothing to eat when winter comes. Similarly, it is Cinderella, the honest, hard-working sister, who wins the Prince rather than her cruel, lazy step-sisters. However, there is still usually something to entertain children, even in the most morally instructive of stories.

▶ 134

❸ This week I'd like to start by talking a bit about electric vehicles. Although we tend to think of electric cars as being something completely modern, they were in fact some of the earliest types of motorized vehicle. At the beginning of the twentieth century electric cars were actually more popular than cars with an internal combustion engine as they were more comfortable to ride in. However, as cars fuelled by petrol increased in importance, electric cars declined. The situation became such that electric vehicles were only used for certain specific purposes – as fork-lift trucks, ambulances and urban delivery vehicles, for example.

Although electricity declined in use in road vehicles, it steadily grew in importance as a means of powering trains. Switzerland, for example, was quick to develop an electrified train system, encouraged in this no doubt by the fact that it had no coal or oil resources of its own.

Nowadays there is renewed interest in electricity as a means of powering road vehicles. Why is this the case? Well, undoubtedly economic reasons are of considerable importance. The cost of oil has risen so sharply that there is a strong financial imperative to look for an alternative. However, there are also environmental motivations. Emissions from cars are blamed in large part for – among other things – the destruction of the ozone layer and the resultant rise in temperatures in the polar regions. A desire not to let things get any worse is also encouraging research into designing effective electric transport.

Test 4, Answer short question (page 123)

▶ 135

❶ What is the word in geometry for a shape that has three sides?

▶ 136

❷ What do you call the alphabetical list at the end of a textbook that tells you where to find specific information?

▶ 137

❸ What is the word for the place where a river starts?

▶ 138

❹ Who is the main journalist responsible for producing a newspaper or magazine?

▶ 139

❺ A business doesn't want to make a loss – what does it want to make?

▶ 140

❻ What is the economic sector that deals with farming?

▶ 141

❼ What do you call the very long essay that students have to write for a doctoral degree?

▶ 142

❽ What is the word for a period of one hundred years?

▶ 143

❾ At what ceremony do students receive their degree or diploma at the end of their period of study?

▶ 144

❿ What do we call the date that a piece of work must be finished by?

Test 4, Summarize spoken text (page 136)

▶ 145

❶ People these days increasingly complain of suffering from allergies – to pollen, to cats, to dust, to certain foods like peanuts or shellfish, for example. But what exactly are allergies and why do we develop them? Well, an allergy is the body reacting to something that is trying to harm it. Sometimes the reaction is mild – sneezing or a rash, perhaps – but in extreme cases it can be life-threatening.

In an allergic reaction the body is stimulated to produce histamines, which help to get rid of what is harmful. So, your eyes and nose may stream as a way of losing irritating particles or your skin may itch in order to make you scratch it and so remove any harmful parasites. In some societies these days allergic reactions occur without the person being in a harmful situation. However, in situations where, say, hygiene is less developed, then the body's immune system spends its early years fighting off genuine problems and so does not tend to over-react to harmless irritants at a later stage.

So, how to deal with an allergy? The first step has to be to ascertain what triggers the allergic reaction and then to avoid contact with that allergen as far as is possible. If avoidance is impossible, anti-histamines can be prescribed to minimize the symptoms experienced by the sufferer.

▶ 146

❷ Travelling in the mind's eye, through reading and, more recently, through electronic media, is a European habit of long standing. Ever since the age of discoveries in the Renaissance, Europeans have been interested in reports of life in faraway places. Of all the places in which Europeans were interested, America has received more attention than others for a variety of reasons, the most important of which is that many Europeans themselves emigrated there. The report about America from the person who has been there is a literary genre that Europeans have devoured.

As Europeans watched the United States grow from a British colony to one of the dominant nations of the world, a pattern of conversation developed among them about the meaning of this emerging Colossus of the New World. There emerged a question, aptly stated by Richard Rose: Is America inevitable or inimitable? The question is easier to ask than to answer and both sides of the question are amply represented in American and European writing about America. The one stresses the uniqueness of America, that no nation or people can be compared with the experience of Americans. The other stresses that America is the forerunner of what European, even world, society will be tomorrow.

Test 4, Multiple-choice, choose multiple answers (page 137)

▶ 147

❶ So today I'm going to talk about the key things you need to remember when you go out into the world as translators. The first thing is to be choosy about what commissions you accept. It's not advisable to agree to do every job you're offered even if you're in need of work. You should refuse to do something if you don't know anything about the topic as it would be impossible for you to produce a good piece of writing. And it could be serious – a mistranslation that's going to be used for medical or legal purposes could have disastrous consequences. Having decided you can reasonably take on a commission, if you have the slightest doubt about what something means, then consult a dictionary or someone whose mother tongue is the language you're translating from. It's much better to devote a bit of time and effort to checking something than to risk making a potentially serious error.

▶ 148

❷ Today we are going to talk some more about architecture and what makes for a good design. There are of course a whole range of qualities that most architects would like their buildings to possess. One of these is the durability of the building. Architects must consider how well the building will stand up to the ravages of climate and time. Will it remain robust and in good condition? Clearly, requirements will vary according to the surroundings of the building in question. A design that is suitable for Dubai will have different needs from one for Moscow. Then of course it's essential to consider the appearance of the building. Regardless of what its purpose may be, will people find pleasure in looking at it? An original and still respected writer on architecture, the Roman Vitruvius, wrote in the first century that a building should delight people and should raise their spirits. Again, tastes may vary from one society to the next, but the principle remains the same.

Test 4, Fill in the blanks (page 138)

▶ 149

❶ I'd recommend that you all try to get hold of *English in the Southern Hemisphere* by Nolan and Watts, as this provides an excellent overview of the topics that we're going to be covering in this module. It's really our primary text. It has particularly strong sections on the history of English in Australia and New Zealand, examining in some depth how the language has developed in these countries. The sections on phonology and on vocabulary will be invaluable when you're doing the written assignment, which I'm going to be telling you about in a moment, once I've given you the details of a couple of other essential references.

▶ 150

❷ This week we're going to be continuing our discussion of women in society. Last week we looked at a number of issues relating to women in education. If you remember, we discussed women both at school and at university. Today we're going to be considering the roles that women play in the workplace. Again, we'll start by taking a historical perspective, and inevitably you'll find that many of the same events that impacted on women in education also had a major influence on their working lives. In the second half of the lecture, I'll concentrate on the situation in Europe today, and I'll invite you to suggest how you think things are likely to develop over the next decade. OK, so let's get started.

Test 4, Highlight correct summary (page 139)

▶ 151

❶ I'd like you to think for a moment about your hands and all the things you can do with them. You can use them to write or to drive. You can thread a needle, play the drums, build a wall and so on and so forth. They can be careful and precise – think of someone doing eye surgery, for example. But they can also generate huge forces. And here you might think of the sportsperson throwing a discus or lifting a heavy weight. How is it possible for our hands to be so incredibly flexible? Well, it's all down to the extraordinary complexity of the bones, ligaments, nerves and muscles that lie beneath the skin of our hands. There are, for example, nine muscles alone controlling just one thumb. Some of these are anchored to bones within the hand, while others link to the arm.

▶ 152

❷ A new investigation into shark populations in the waters off Australia has discovered that there are two distinct species of Great White shark, one to the east and one to the west of Bass Strait. This was discovered by tagging large numbers of sharks in the coastal waters all round Australia. Rather to the investigators' surprise, they found that while sharks from the east side certainly travelled to the west side of the continent and vice versa, they always returned to their home areas to breed. The two types of shark were found to have a distinct genetic make-up, indicating that interbreeding has not taken place. The implication of these research findings is that sharks may be more susceptible to changes in local marine environments than had previously been thought.

Test 4, Multiple-choice, choose single answer (page 141)

▶ 153

1 Animals as well as humans are affected by noise. There is evidence to show that some whales, for example, died when they beached themselves after being exposed to excessive sonar – the noise produced by submarines as they navigate underwater. It's been shown that whales produced louder sounds when communicating with each other when sonar equipment was on in their vicinity. This was doubtless because they needed to make themselves heard by their fellows, perhaps to warn each other of danger, or tell one another about a food source. Another example of how noise can affect animal behaviour is given by the European robin. In urban areas this small bird sings at night rather than during the day.

▶ 154

2 So next Wednesday you're all going to be doing your presentations. We'll have to be very strict about timing. Fifteen minutes each – not a minute more. It might make sense to do a practice run-through at home but that's up to you. I'm going to ask you to put an abstract of your presentation on our course website but I'd like you to do that after you've given your talk. Come with your slides on a memory stick – that's the most straightforward way of dealing with things, I think. Oh, and don't forget to bring handouts for everyone. There won't be time to do photocopying that morning. So, any questions?

Test 4, Select missing word (page 142)

▶ 155

1 This year we're planning to use a different type of assessment on this module. In the past students were required to complete two long written assignments and also to do a presentation on a subject of their own choice. We have decided to ask you to write four shorter pieces of written coursework this year. We are also going to be more prescriptive about what you focus on in your presentation. This is because previously many students lost marks unnecessarily simply because ——— .

▶ 156

2 In nineteenth century Britain – and indeed in the first half of the twentieth century – many of the urban poor lived in extremely cramped conditions. Over-crowding, damp, and poor sanitation affected the daily lives of the majority of the population, with serious implications for their own and their children's health. Novelists have a major role to play in reflecting their times to their readers who may otherwise ignore social problems, and the portrayal of the wretched living conditions of the impoverished by such writers as Charles Dickens in the nineteenth century and George Orwell in the twentieth was instrumental in ——— .

Test 4, Highlight incorrect words (page 143)

▶ 157

1 English had barely established itself as a language in England when it began moving to other countries to be used there as well. First it headed north to Scotland and then west to Wales. It then made its way across the sea to Ireland. That was in the Middle Ages. Over the course of the following centuries it has put down roots all over the world, from the USA to South Africa, from India to New Zealand. Of course, in all these countries it has developed in special ways to suit the new contexts in which it found itself.

▶ 158

2 Researchers at the University of California claim to have discovered that people who eat chocolate regularly tend to be lighter than those who rarely eat it. The findings may seem surprising in that chocolate has a great many calories and, in general, the more calories people consume, the more likely they are to put on weight. The recent studies emphasize that it is more the regularity with which people eat chocolate that is significant rather than the amount they consume. Whether they eat a little or a lot seems to make no difference, whereas eating it frequently appears to reduce weight more than only having it occasionally.

Test 4, Write from dictation (page 144)

▶ 159

1 The new theory takes all the latest research results into account.

▶ 160

2 The period was a golden age of English literature.

▶ 161

3 Essential textbooks can be purchased from the campus bookshop.

ANSWER KEY

Test 1, Read aloud (page 13)

See text on page 13.

Test 1, Repeat sentence (page 15)

See audio script on page 157.

Test 1, Describe image (pages 17–19)

1 **(Model answer)**
The graph shows population trends in Europe and Asia as a percentage of world population between 1750 and 2000 (*overview*). Asia had a much bigger percentage of the world population during this period than Europe (*point 1*). Asia's proportion dropped from 65 to 55 percent between 1750 and 1950 but reached 60 percent in 2000 (*point 2*). Europe's population was fairly stable from 1750 to 1850 at just over 20 percent of world population (*point 3*). Then it rose slightly in 1900 before falling by more than half to just over ten percent in 2000.

2 **(Model answer)**
The charts show why males and females stopped going to school (*overview*). In both cases the main reason was that they had completed their studies (*point 1*). This applied to 65 percent of females and 60 percent of males (*point 1a*). The second reason was that they had got a job, but 25 percent of males had work compared with 12 percent of females (*point 2*). Almost the same percentage of females also left school for personal or family reasons, while only four percent of males did (*point 3*). A very small percentage of students left due to illness – three percent of males and five percent of females (*point 4*), and a slightly bigger percentage left for other, non-specified reasons (*point 5*).

3 **(Model answer)**
The chart shows the future trends in the percentage of American citizens over 65 years old (*overview*). In 2010, about 13 percent of US citizens were over 65 (*point 1*). This figure is predicted to rise steadily so that by 2035, it will be 20 percent (*point 2*). Between 2010 and 2030, the rise will be quite steady, whereas between 2030 and 2035, the rise is less significant (*point 3*) – suggesting that the increase in the ageing population may peak shortly after 2035 (*point 4*). However, the rise will have serious implications in areas such as the provision of government services (*implication*).

4 **(Model answer)**
The graph shows revenue growth in millions of dollars for two companies between 2006 and 2024 (*overview*). The revenue of Company X is forecast to rise steadily from $300 m to $1,800 m in 2024 (*point 1*). Company Y's revenue started at zero in 2006 and is likely to increase slowly to about $400 m in 2019 (*point 2*). After that, however, predictions are that the company's growth will surge between 2019 and 2024 to just overtake Company X at $1,900 m (*point 3*).

5 **(Model answer)**
The graph shows reading achievement over three years for two groups of students: successful and struggling readers, measured in words per minute (*overview*). Successful readers make faster overall progress than struggling readers (*point 1: overall trend*). Over three years, they go quite steadily from 20 words per minute to 120 words per minute (*point 1a: support*). Struggling readers make smaller gains and seem to regress a little in the fall (*point 2*), perhaps because they don't read much during the summer break (*point 2a: possible reason*). Overall, they go from about eight words per minute to about 50 in the same period of time (*point 2b: support*)

6 **(Model answer)**
The diagram shows a Shadouf which is a method of collecting water (*overview*). It consists of a raised walkway, that is attached to a post by a pivot, to form a lever (*object description part 1*). On the end of the lever is a rope and a bucket (*object description part 2*). The operator climbs up to the walkway and uses his weight to balance the lever (*process description part 1*). He moves forward so that the lever falls and the bucket tips into the water and then he moves backward again so that his weight raises the lever and the bucket of water rises for collection (*process description part 2*).

Test 1, Re-tell lecture (page 21)

1 **(Model answer)**
The lecture was about air pollution and the changes since the middle of the last century (*main topic*). Air pollution in the 1950s was very visible with thick black smogs causing severe health issues (*point 1*). This air pollution came from factories (*point 2*). A smog in London in 1952 caused a large number of deaths and resulted in a Clean Air Act being introduced (*point 3*). These days, air pollution is invisible but is still a major health risk (*point 4*). It is now largely caused by cars and lorries and is due to the significant increase in vehicles since the 1950s (*point 5*).

❷ (Model answer)
The lecture provided some tips on using Focus Groups to provide help with research (*main topic*). Focus Groups are groups of people who can provide input for your work (*definition of main topic*). She said that ideally there should be six or seven people in a focus group (*point 1*). If it was bigger than that, then it could lose focus and if it was smaller than that, there wouldn't be a big enough range of views (*explanation of point 1*). She recommended having a moderator to guide the discussion and to make sure everyone takes part and keeps focused (*point 2*). And she also recommended having some basic materials to get the discussion going such as pictures and graphs to help understand what the context was (*point 3*).

❸ (Model answer)
The lecturer gave some practical tips on setting up a website. You need to ensure that the website adds value to the users and there are three things to consider (*main topic*). Firstly, who is the target audience and what information are they looking for? (*point 1*) And what you can do is to group users according to their needs and then design the site based on this (*explanation of point 1*). Secondly, it's important that the website can be reached by your target audience (*point 2*) – so you may need to use social media or provide links on other sites (*examples for point 2*). And thirdly, you need to make sure your users have a reason to return to the site (*point 3*) so you need to ensure the information is interesting and up-to-date (*explanation of point 3*).

Test 1, Answer short question (page 23)

❶ departures

❷ instructions

❸ interview

❹ reception/check-in

❺ architect

❻ rent

❼ breakfast

❽ spectator

❾ ladder

❿ appetite

Test 1, Summarize written text (pages 25–26)

❶ (Model answer)
Tea, the second most popular drink in the world (*point 1*), is grown in over 50 countries now (*point 2*), but these countries have to have the right climate and geographical features if they are going to produce sufficient high-quality plants (*point 3*) to manufacture into the wide range of teas that are exported around the world for general consumption (*point 4*).

❷ (Model answer)
The increasing demand for fish, particularly in developed countries (*point 1*), and the rapidly declining fish stocks in the world's oceans because of overfishing to meet demand (*point 2*), should be of concern to governments (*point 3*), who need to do more to protect the earth and its ecosystems, and avoid unnecessary species extinction (*point 4*).

Test 1, Write essay (page 28)

❶ (Model answer)
As medical care improves and the life expectancy of men and women increases, there are a number of consequences that will arise for future generations. Some of these will be beneficial, but some could cause issues (*introduction to topic*).

Most people would like to live longer, provided they can maintain a good quality of life (*positive development – main idea*). This requires good health, money and the desire to participate in an active lifestyle (*explanation of main idea*). Some elderly people have had the opportunity through their working life to save for their retirement, while others may be fit, healthy and enthusiastic about working well into their sixties or seventies (*support for main idea*). For all these people, living longer is likely to be a positive experience (*summing up of positive development*).

However, there are other elderly people who have not been able to provide for their old age or who, despite improved medical care, struggle to lead a healthy life (*disadvantage for individual – main idea*). My grandfather, for example, was a builder all his life. He never managed to save for his retirement and, despite medication to stabilize his health problems, he is unable to continue working (*example – main idea*). For him, old age is a constant worry.

As far as society is concerned, another negative consequence of people living longer is the effect this could have on the workplace (*disadvantage for society – main idea*). Currently, most people retire in their sixties and this allows the younger generation to move into the jobs they have left. As people stay on at work, the turnover of jobs declines making it more difficult for younger people to get work (*explanation of disadvantage for society*).

On balance, I believe that improving medical care in order to extend life expectancy is a good thing (*point of view*). However, governments must ensure that young people are not deprived of jobs and that old people who cannot support themselves are well looked after (*summary of main ideas*).

1 (Model essay outline)

Will people see this as positive?

- Most people want to live longer, as long as they are healthy. If healthy and no money worries: more time to be active, or work.

Disadvantages:

- Individuals: People are living longer but they are not always healthy or wealthy/need medical care and this costs money.
- Society: People retire later and fewer jobs are available for young people.

Conclusion:

- Longer life expectancy good but governments must support aged and also ensure employment for all.

2 (Model answer)

Over the last few decades, there has been a drive to encourage students to continue their studies at university. Efforts have been made to increase the capacity of universities and schools often believe that the more students they prepare for university, the better (*introduction to topic*).

I don't believe this is necessarily a good thing (*point of view*). For some students, university is a stepping stone to the ultimate goal of a career. For others, the choice will be work that requires practical expertise rather than academic abilities and they will not need to go to university to achieve this (*reasons for point of view*). The challenge for schools is to strike the right balance between academic study and preparing young people for employment (*main idea – role of schools*).

The ultimate aim of education is to ensure the population has an adequate level of skill sets and that individuals are capable of being effective in the workplace (*main idea – aim of education*). Schools should be focusing on making sure students are able to communicate well, are numerate, have a foundation of general knowledge and an ability to find things out for themselves (*examples to support main idea*).

In my view, communication is the most important of these skills (*main idea – communication*). Being able to write an essay, report or email, and being able to speak clearly and coherently are essential both for employment and for university study (*examples to support main idea*). At my university, students who cannot express themselves well in writing find it hard to do their assignments and this causes them a lot of anxiety (*personal experience*).

To conclude, I believe schools should keep to their primary function of teaching the core skills I have outlined above (*point of view*). If they do this, they should succeed in preparing their students for life after school – whether it be at university or in the world of work (*summing up of point of view*).

2 (Model essay outline)

Arguments against:

- Only some students want to go to university. Many students prefer practical work – university not needed.

Schools should provide balance:

- Aim of education: prepare people for workplace – directly or after study.
- Should focus on: communication, numeracy, basic general knowledge and how to find things out.

Communication most important: needed for both university and work.

Conclusion:

- Schools should prepare students for both outcomes by teaching core skills.

Test 1, Multiple-choice, choose single answer (page 31)

1 C (to highlight the potential benefits of geothermal power for Britain): focus is on future possibilities (*could, would be, would keep*), and problems are not the main point.

2 B (New products are not always based on new ideas.): *innovations were often already 'out there' in the public domain* (the remainder develops this idea).

Test 1, Multiple-choice, choose multiple answers (pages 33–34)

1 B (It is a drifting piece of wood.): *bobbing vertically, the floating tree, buoyant, travels quite extensively.*

E (It can quickly move about the lake.): *travels … with surprising rapidity.*

F (It can be a danger to boat users.): *boat pilots commonly communicate its position to each other as a general matter of safety.*

2 C (It has resulted from agricultural activity.): *people living in rainforests farmed in a way that enhanced rather than destroyed soils; rainforest is … farmland, enriched by the waste created by ancient humans.*

E (It is being found near where humans have lived.): *I go looking for dark earth round the edge of villages and ancient towns, and in traditionally farmed areas. It's usually there.*

ANSWER KEY

Test 1, Re-order paragraphs (page 36)

❶ D Anyone who has ever visited the Grand Canyon will agree that it is one of the most incredible sights in the world (introduces central idea and stands alone).

A Clearly, a number of factors have contributed to its remarkable appearance (*its* = the Grand Canyon, *remarkable appearance* links to *incredible sights*).

C Experts who have analysed the rock formations say that, historically, it goes back nearly two billion years (*it* = the Grand Canyon; *rock formations* links to *remarkable appearance*).

E The geological processes that have taken place since then are exposed for everyone to see, not hidden beneath vegetation or a fast-flowing water course (*since then* = *two billion years*).

B The result is a unique story of land collisions and erosions, and of rising and falling water levels (*the result* – of the *geological processes*).

❷ E Over the last half-century, organic farming has become a driving force in the world's food market (introduces topic of organic farming; broadest time scale).

C In the late 1900s, food manufacturers were challenged by the organic community to ensure they were using ingredients that had been produced in natural, healthy ways (narrows time reference; develops idea of how organic farming became a *driving force*).

A It was a time when managers had to take a critical look at every aspect of their production process and make improvements where necessary (*It was a time* = *late 1900s; critical look* continues idea of *challenged*).

D Whether these systems have been maintained seems questionable, particularly as contracts depend so heavily on efficiency and quick sales (*these systems* = *improvements*).

B As a result, some people believe it is now time to re-assess many companies in terms of the standards they agreed to some years ago (*as a result* links to the query raised in D).

Test 1, Reading: Fill in the blanks (pages 38–39)

❶ 1 practices: collocation with *work;* agrees with grammar of verb phrase

2 focus: collocation with *shifted*

3 output: the other words don't create meaning in context

4 extent: collocation in phrase *to some extent*; forms phrase meaning *partly*

❷ 1 complex: adjective required; the other words don't create meaning in context

2 family: collocation with *close* and *bonds;* the other words don't create meaning in context

3 variety: singular noun required; collocation with *wide*

4 apart: adverb required; collocation with *move further*

5 sounds: plural noun required; matches meaning of *rumbling* and *heard*

❸ 1 effects: the other nouns don't create meaning in context (the plural *sources* suggests a plural)

2 answer: the other nouns don't create meaning in context

3 machines: plural noun required that substitutes for *wind farms;* the other nouns don't create meaning in context

4 regions: the other nouns don't create meaning in context

5 feature: collocation with *landscape* (*sight* would require *in the landscape*)

❹ 1 unlike: contrastive word needed meaning *different from*

2 matters: the other verbs don't create meaning in context (cannot be *concerns* because of *to*)

3 make: collocation with *contribution*

4 collection: collocation with *data*; the other nouns don't create meaning in context

5 use: verb required; present tense for general statement

Test 1, Reading & writing: Fill in the blanks (pages 41–43)

❶ 1 B (helps to improve): singular with uncountable *equipment* and followed by infinitive

2 A (levels): collocation with *global poverty*

3 C (since): time word used with Present Perfect tense in this context

4 A (means): followed by *of* + *-ing* and collocates with *producing*

5 D (figure): referring to 40 percent, which is a proportion (so not *sum, total, volume*)

❷ 1 B (precise): refers ahead to *there are now more age groups to target … a sales pitch can be re-worked a number of times to more exactly fit each one.*

2 D (involved): in this context none of the others are used with *in*

3 A (rather than): a contrast is being presented

4 B (Similarly): introduces another example of the same thing

5 C (bonus): the others don't create meaning in context

3 1 D (material): the others don't create meaning in context
2 B (assist): the others require *to* or don't create meaning in context
3 C (you can sense): *it* and *he* have no reference; *one sense* is ungrammatical
4 A (highlighting): the others don't create meaning in context or require a preposition
5 C (Every): determiner used with singular noun (*all* used with plural; *the other* contrasts; *any one of* comes before an article or pronoun)

4 1 C (of becoming): the others are grammatically incorrect
2 A (prefer): used with *to* (infinitive form)
3 D (has had): *anyone* is singular; need Present Perfect in clause that refers to past and present time
4 B (deal): collocation *a great deal of* + noun
5 C (argue): the others don't create meaning in context

5 1 D (refers): the only one followed by *to*
2 B (qualities): reference indicates this as the only group noun
3 D (height): the others are not appropriate in the context
4 A (has cultivated): Present Prefect to refer to a period of time that is still continuing
5 C (who): relative pronoun is needed to complete relative clause; for people it must be *who* or *that*

Test 1, Summarize spoken text (page 46)

1 **(Model answer)**
Technological nature refers to a computerized picture of a natural scene (*point 1: topic*). To find out if this has the same beneficial effect as a real scene, put a group of people in a room with a real view and another group in a room with a virtual view (*point 2: research*). The group in the room with the real view will recover more quickly from stress than the other group (*point 3: results*).

2 **(Model answer)**
Lawyers rely on what their witnesses can remember of an event in a criminal trial (*point 1*). If new information is introduced to a witness, it may make their memory unreliable (*point 2*). This has been illustrated in research. If subjects watch a video of a crime and then hear an account that includes new information not shown on the video, their memory of the video can also include new and unreliable information (*point 3*).

Test 1, Multiple-choice, choose multiple answers (page 48)

1 C (geological conditions): *you need to be absolutely sure that the ground, and more to the point, what lies beneath the ground can support underground transport*
D (employing professionals): *engineers have to be really experienced, really knowledgeable … And those key issues are what I want to focus on today.*

2 B (interviewing residents about the problems): *they went round to people's houses and met them … and talked to everyone and got a general idea of what the local concerns were.*
F (removing litter from the streets): *this was followed up with other quite practical solutions like cleaning up the area, getting rid of debris in alleyways*

Test 1, Fill in the blanks (page 50)

1 1 frankly 2 options 3 basic 4 employees 5 significant

2 1 practical 2 element 3 collect 4 review 5 description

Test 1, Highlight correct summary (pages 52–53)

1 B *they decided to award their graduates higher grades so they would be more attractive in the highly competitive job market … lifting the grades may even be damaging to the students because employers may believe that the graduates were given the high grades when they didn't deserve them.*

2 C *Urban development is … going on at a great pace and the standard approach here in Western Australia is for suburban development to happen at the outer edges of the city … Suburban expansion on the edges of the city is cheaper and easier to do than building more homes within the city … urban sprawl is destroying bush and consequently the natural wildlife that exists there*

Test 1, Multiple-choice, choose single answer (pages 55)

1 D (trends in where Americans live): *the pull to the suburbs has continued … Rural areas … have not seen the same pattern at all.*

2 A (They were understandable at the time.): *who can blame them really? … Mmm. Yes.*

Test 1, Select missing word (page 57)

1 C (has changed over time): *originally, in the nineteenth century, it tended to simply mean … In later works of literature, this 'unreliability' was used by authors more deliberately … Nowadays, there's a lot more humour in unreliable narration*

2 A (complex): *you're amazed at how much detail there is … it's also amazingly intricate.*

Test 1, Highlight incorrect words (page 59)

❶ It seems we now know more about outer space than we do about the Earth's core. This is because temperatures are so **great** (high) at the centre of the Earth that human beings have not been able to take a close look at it. However, new **techniques** (methods) of analysis may soon change all that. The seismic waves **formed** (created) by earthquakes and volcanic eruptions penetrate the Earth's layers at different speeds. It is now hoped that by studying these waves, scientists will be able to make new **findings** (discoveries) and solve some of the mysteries of the **inside** (internal) structure of the Earth.

❷ Many species of birds cover long **miles** (distances) during their seasonal migration to warmer climates. But how successful are they, and do birds that get lost on their route ever **survive** (manage) to find their way back? Much research has been **done** (conducted) into how birds navigate and the results show that age is a significant **reason** (factor). Young birds usually just carry on, if they lose their migratory path, and thus fail to **achieve** (reach) their destination, whereas older, more experienced birds will generally be able to find their **first** (original) route and continue successfully on their journey.

Test 1, Write from dictation (page 61)

See audio script on page 160.

Test 2, Read aloud (page 62)

See text on page 62.

Test 2, Repeat sentence (page 63)

See audio script on page 161.

Test 2, Describe image (pages 64–66)

❶ (Model answer)
The plan shows the layout of a student apartment (*overview*). There is one large living area with a table and chairs, and an armchair (*point 1*) with a small kitchen and small bathroom to one side (*point 2*). There is a separate bedroom with a bed and wardrobe and two windows (*point 3*). The study area is on the right of the entrance and is part of the living area. It has a desk near the window and would probably also have bookshelves (*point 4*). The apartment seems quite convenient for a student living on their own (*drawing a conclusion*).

❷ (Model answer)
The graph shows the rainfall and temperature over the period of a year in the Great Lakes area of the USA (*overview*). We can see that the two seem to broadly correspond, in that the rainfall gets heavier as the temperature increases (*point 1*). Both the temperature and the rainfall are at their height in July – the rainfall is heaviest at over 90 mm and the temperature at about eighteen degrees (*point 2*). Both decrease towards the end of the year, although rainfall rises slightly in December and January (*point 3*). The temperature drops below zero around October and the rainfall is at its lowest in October and November with under 20 mm (*point 4*).

❸ (Model answer)
The bar graph compares energy consumption in North and South America in 2007 (*overview*) and shows that in both regions, oil was the main source of energy at 45 percent of the total for South America and 41 percent for North America (*point 1*). Both areas used a lot of natural gas, nearly a quarter of their total consumption (*point 2*). Of the other sources of energy, the main differences were that South America used a lot more hydroelectric energy than North America, 28 percent compared to five percent (*point 3*), but in North America 20 percent of its energy came from coal compared to only five percent in South America (*point 4*). Neither region depended much on nuclear energy, less than ten percent (*point 5*).

❹ (Model answer)
This is a language college timetable for a week, and it shows a balance of classes and social activities (*overview*). After a tour of the college and a welcome morning tea on Day 1, there are English language classes on Days 1 to 4, and the classes are from 9–12, except on Monday, when they have a lesson after lunch (*point 1*). In the afternoons usually they have social activities on site or visits to a local attraction or a Junior School classroom (*point 2*). On Day 5, there are activities for the whole day. Some things they might do include tennis, films, games and surfing lessons (*point 3*). At the weekend, the students spend time with their homestay families (*point 4, 5*).

❺ (Model answer)
The graph shows how the proportions of overseas-born people in Australia have changed from 2000 to 2010 (*overview*). The largest proportion of immigrants is from the UK at between five and six percent followed by New Zealand with between two and three percent (*point 1*), but UK numbers have decreased whereas New Zealand numbers have increased (*point 2*). The proportions of people born in China and India have both noticeably increased over the period to almost two percent (*point 3*). There has been little change in the proportions of people born in Vietnam, the Philippines, South Africa, Malaysia and Germany, which all stayed around or below one percent (*point 4*).

ANSWER KEY

6 (Model answer)
This is a diagram of the life cycle of a Painted Lady Butterfly as it transforms from an egg to an adult butterfly (*overview*). It starts off as an egg, the same size as a pin head (*point 1*). After that it turns into larva and becomes a black to purple caterpillar with yellow-green stripes (*point 2*). This caterpillar eats and grows until it enters the pupa or chrysalis stage. At this point it is reddish brown in colour (*point 3*). In the last stage of the process it emerges from the chrysalis as an adult butterfly, which lays an egg, beginning the cycle again (*point 4*).

Test 2, Re-tell lecture (page 67)

1 (Model answer)
The speaker is asking what the purpose of a museum is and whether we really need museums today when there is so much information available online (*point 1*). He suggests that museums are not just places to store things but they have to develop an educational purpose (*point 2*). This means they have to engage people and do things like get involved with community organisations (*point 3*) and in this way they may become relevant and involved in social change (*point 4*).

2 (Model answer)
The lecture is about graffiti (*topic*) and how some people don't see it as art and some people hate it (*point 1*) but it has been around for a very long time (*point 2*). There are examples of graffiti from ancient Egypt and Rome (*support for point 2*). Modern graffiti really began in New York after the invention of the paint spraycan (*point 3*) and a lot of young people see it as an expression of how they feel (*point 4*). These days, graffiti is accepted as an important art form (*point 5*).

3 (Model answer)
Nature can teach us a lot and technology especially has taken a lot of ideas from nature (*point 1*). This kind of research is called biomimicry, and it means copying or imitating something in nature but using it in a modern piece of technology (*details for point 1*). For example, the bright screens on mobile phones are copied from butterfly wings and moths' eyes (*example of point 1*). There is also research looking at what makes spider webs so strong (*point 2*).

Test 2, Answer short question (page 68)

1 lungs
2 a city/a town
3 a crown
4 a dictionary
5 the sun
6 anonymous
7 a sponsor
8 biology/ecology
9 seasons
10 cattle

Test 2, Summarize written text (pages 69–70)

1 (Model answer)
Many ocean creatures are dependent on underwater sound to live and breed (*point 1*), but in the last 50 years noises made by humans from ship engines, seismic research and military activity have increased background ocean noise levels by about 15 decibels (*point 2*), which may have a very negative and disruptive effect on sealife when its impact is considered altogether (*point 3*).

2 (Model answer)
Scientists are beginning to understand why chillies evolved to be so hot when eaten (*point 1*), and although many scientists still believe the hotness is to deter mammals from eating the plant (*point 2*), recent research suggests it also developed as a defence against harmful microbes (*point 3*).

Test 2, Write essay (page 71)

1 (Model answer)
Raising the school leaving age to 18 would mean that high school graduates would be more well-rounded as individuals and more employable (*opening statement agreeing*). While it may be true that some people are destined to do jobs that do not require a high level of education, the fact is that in today's competitive world, it is becoming more and more difficult to get opportunities without a solid education. As a lot of unskilled work can be done by machines, it is not easy for young, unqualified people to gain employment. As far as skilled work is concerned, employers are less likely than in the past to give young people a chance (*first argument agreeing*).

Although young people are maturing earlier than before and are therefore better equipped to make their own decisions, the world has also become more complicated. People change jobs more often than they did in the past so a good general education is needed. One role of school is to provide a social and moral foundation and this is certainly important in the crucial teenage years as young people face situations that their parents never had to deal with (*second argument agreeing*).

There will always be examples of high school dropouts who have become very successful in their chosen fields but it is important to remember that these individuals are a very small minority. They are generally talented, entrepreneurial and know what they want to do from a very young age. The majority of students would benefit from a longer time at school and society as a whole would benefit if the general level of education were raised (*conclusion agreeing*).

❶ (Model essay outline)

Agree:
- employers won't give chances to unqualified people = competitive world
- social and moral education in crucial teenage years
- raises general level of education in society

Disagree:
- some people not academic = don't need more education
- young people maturing early = can make own decisions
- some successful people = high school dropouts

❷ (Model answer)

Pollution, global warming and the resulting threats to plant and animal species are a modern reality and are occurring on a world scale. While it is true that the environment is a matter of concern for governments all over the world, that does not absolve individual citizens from taking responsibility for finding solutions to the problems (*introduction*).

Local, national and international authorities and governments certainly need to play a part in dealing with problems relating to the environment. This can be done in many ways, whether it is regulating waste management, providing incentives to environmentally friendly companies or funding research into possible solutions. To a great extent, it is up to governments to set the scene for citizens to do the right thing as far as the environment is concerned (*argument for government responsibility*).

However, individuals also have an influence and can do their bit to bring about change, not least by voting for a government that will safeguard the environment. There are many things that people can do, for instance saving electricity in the home, reusing and recycling whatever we can and cutting down on carbon dioxide emissions by limiting the use of private vehicles. Those actions are the very least that individuals should do. To take it a step further, individuals can create innovations that will help manage our resources and minimize our waste. They can lobby politicians to take a strict stand against companies that pollute the environment (*argument for individual responsibility*).

Besides having a moral obligation to fellow human beings and other species to look after our habitat, on a practical level individuals are the ones who will make government policies a reality (*conclusion*).

❷ (Model essay outline)

Responsibility: both government and individual

Government:
- waste management
- encouraging companies to change
- funding solutions

Individual:
- vote for government that cares
- cut energy use
- re-use, re-cycle
- don't drive cars
- be active politically

Conclusion: joint responsibility – individuals make government policies work

Test 2, Multiple-choice, choose single answer (page 72)

❶ B (Sea snails are being carried by submarines to places where they harm other species.): *latch on to the submarines … potentially spreading disease in pristine ecosystems.*

❷ C (teachers who have practical experience in a creative field): *The academic staff are former working artists, theorists and designers*

Test 2, Multiple-choice, choose multiple answers (pages 73–74)

❶ A (special clothing): *ceremonial cloaks*

C (equipment for boats): *canoes … rigging, sails and lengthy anchor warps for them*

❷ C (artwork on top of the building): *the podium roof plaza is an open air gallery for public sculpture.*

E (helpful guides to give information about the art): *specially trained, very personable staff who field questions, explain the exhibits*

Test 2, Re-order paragraphs (page 75)

❶ D The University will host its second annual Arts and Commerce Career Readiness Conference on campus next month (*conference* introduced).

B The conference is part of the career counselling centre's campaign, which has been designed to assist final year students transitioning out of university and getting their careers off to a good start (*the conference*).

C Students will be able to speak with industry professionals and graduates who had the benefit of this assistance last year (*to assist – this assistance*).

A It is important to register for sessions with the industry professionals as numbers are limited (*the industry professionals*).

❷ B Historically, in Europe and many other parts of the world, settlements were built on higher ground for the purposes of defence and to be close to fresh water sources (*building cities on higher ground* introduced).

D Cities have often spread down from these locations onto coastal plains, putting them at risk of floods and storm surges (*these locations = higher ground*).

A Urban planners must consider these threats and work to allay them (*these threats = floods and storm surges*).

C If the dangers are only in specific areas then they can make the affected regions into parkland or a green belt, often providing the added advantage of open space (*they = urban planners*).

Test 2, Reading: Fill in the blanks (pages 76–77)

1 1 hard: *despite* suggests a contrast (so not *favourable*)
2 creative: relates to families having less money (final sentence shows not *generous*)
3 sums: collocation with *lump* (you cannot say *lump money*)

2 1 care: the others don't create meaning in context
2 potential: collocation with *to* + infinitive, future indicated by *will allow*
3 combination: examples given of many techniques
4 information: collocation with *reveal* (research will answer *fundamental questions*)

3 1 known: adjective needed (*academic* does not collocate, *unique* is the same as *only*)
2 contains: sentence describes contents
3 academic: collocation with *consensus* (scholars agree)
4 led: verb showing causal relationship and must be used with *to*

4 1 researcher: *working as a* ... requires a job (*leader* not possible)
2 division: *chief* suggests a section of the Department of Agriculture
3 inspection: suggested by *toxins* and *diseases*
4 serum: *it* = *hog cholera*, which the serum will prevent

Test 2, Reading & writing: Fill in the blanks (pages 78–80)

1 1 D (received): needs Past Simple (finished event in the past)
2 A (played): collocation with *role*
3 B (which): relative pronoun refers to *galaxy clusters* and begins the relative clause
4 A (In addition to): Couch's own research added to work he has done for others

2 1 B (drawn): an example of ellipsis (graffiti *that was drawn*)
2 D (prolific): a lot of work (*up to 40 drawings a day*)
3 B (at least): restricts *art* to mean *his art*
4 C (whom): part of a relative clause referring to *street artists*

3 1 D (While): indicates contrast
2 C (are falling): Present Continuous for current situation (indicated by *have grown*)
3 A (must have decreased): a stipulation or condition for the 'vulnerable' classification
4 B (For this reason): preceded by a reason and followed by a consequence

4 1 B (collaborative): the faculty is working with museums, galleries and art organisations
2 D (active): adjective is needed to describe *mentors*
3 B (growth): noun is needed, collocation with *personal*
4 C (facilitate): verb needed, to agree with plural noun *studios*
5 B (opportunities): collocation with *travel*; the others don't create meaning in context

5 1 A (have been known): Present Perfect, Passive (others require *how* or are ungrammatical)
2 C (mates): the 'partners' of animals
3 D (take part): *simply* indicates the females do not do something themselves
4 B (still): to indicate a surprising fact – that something has continued long after it should have stopped

Test 2, Summarize spoken text (page 81)

1 (Model answer)
It is difficult to proofread your own work (*topic*), but it helps if you think about the problems you have had before (*point 1*). You have to remember to look for how the ideas flow (*point 2*) and to check the paragraphing and also the references (*point 3*). It might help if you read your essay aloud, and you should do this after a break so you will see the errors more easily (*point 4*).

2 (Model answer)
The lecture is reporting on research into local government that found there were three main issues (*overview*). Firstly, people need to be more involved as citizens and find out what they can do (*point 1*). Secondly, public servants need to be more customer-focused (*point 2*). Finally, the way the different levels of government interact with each other and with citizens needs to be looked at, because there are problems of over-centralization there (*point 3*).

Test 2, Multiple-choice, choose multiple answers (page 82)

1 B (Past students offer them help.): *the level of support that's available ... from ... alumni.*
E (A high percentage complete the degree and get jobs in their field.): *the college enjoys an excellent reputation for ... student employment after graduation.*

2 C (Rock art in both places depicted animals of interest to humans.): *Both feature outline images of human predators and prey, from bears and lions to stags, horses and bulls.*
E (It shows that people in widely separated places thought the same way.): *human beings are essentially the same in their thinking. So, whether it's the ancient people of Europe, or in Asia, ...*

ANSWER KEY

Test 2, Fill in the blanks (page 83)

❶ 1 mammals 2 adaptable 3 urban 4 native

❷ 1 searched 2 hostile 3 object 4 farms 5 tourist

Test 2, Highlight correct summary (pages 84–85)

❶ B *makes good business sense … Management needs to look at training, security and communication issues … equal access to resources and, of course, promotions … It's vital to screen employees carefully* (other options focus on just one part or have ideas not in the recording)

❷ D *you would think, that with all these consumer choices that people would be spending more money … when there were more varieties, more customers stopped to try … only about three percent of them actually … selected a product to buy … when there were just six varieties, fewer people stopped to try … but … 30 percent of them bought a jar of jam* (other options have ideas not mentioned)

Test 2, Multiple-choice, choose single answer (page 86)

❶ D (It has come back into favour in recent years.): *… seen as an unfortunate hangover from the 1960s, but … people's feelings about it have gone … to real appreciation now.*

❷ C (The main task should be divided into parts.): *To help overcome potential conflicts, the group can … break the larger group objective into smaller tasks.*

Test 2, Select missing word (page 87)

❶ A (from a number of angles): *People who study a breadth of topics, and who have a diverse range of interests, are actually better problem solvers* (ending suggests a reference to different ways of looking at a problem).

❷ C (were at stake): the text mentions the different ways people proved or achieved something by surfing, and collocation of *competition* and *at stake*

Test 2, Highlight incorrect words (page 88)

❶ Well, there are many factors that can cause one species to **diverge** (divide) into two. One of these is when populations get isolated from each other by something like a **lagoon** (lake) forming or forest being cleared. And there's another idea that as individuals adapt to their environment, this might have a knock-on **impact** (effect) on mate choice, a process called **sensitive** (sensory) drive speciation. Now this seems to occur in cichlid fish. They have shown that a female preference for either red or blue striped males only exists in **clean** (clear) water, where they are actually able to see.

❷ Social capital is a concept that was introduced by sociologists, many years ago. It's actually the networks and **reserves** (resources) that people use to deliver social outcomes. For instance, it might be holding a sporting event, running a community **fair** (fête), being part of a club.
It is difficult to measure social capital and one way of looking at it is the **amount** (extent) that people volunteer in their local community. So you can consider the volunteering rate as an **index** (indicator) for how healthy a community is. You can also look at something called a well-being index – the way people think about their lives and how **accepting** (trusting) they are of others, their general perception of the value of their life.

Test 2, Write from dictation (page 89)

See audio script on page 165.

Test 3, Read aloud (page 90)

See text on page 90.

Test 3, Repeat sentence (page 91)

See audio script on page 165.

Test 3, Describe image (pages 92–94)

❶ (Model answer)
The chart shows the population by age group for Australia (*overview*). The highest number of people are in the age groups 0–19, 20–39 and 40–59 (*point 1*) with slightly more males than females for each group (*point 2*). The two older age groups 60–79 and 80 plus are much smaller than the former three age groups (*point 3*), but the number of women in these age groups is higher than the number of men (*point 4*).

2. (Model answer)
The diagram shows the process of recycling cans (*overview*). First of all empty cans are put in a recycling bin (*stage 1*). A lorry then picks up the cans and takes them for recycling (*stage 2*). Next, the cans are broken down into small pieces (*stage 3*). Then, they are heated (*stage 4*) and made into new cans (*stage 5*). Finally, they are taken to the supermarket where the whole process starts again (*stage 6*).

3. (Model answer)
The bar chart shows the comparison of energy consumption by fuel type in the USA and China in 2010 (*overview*). With regard to the USA the majority of energy consumed came from three sources: oil, natural gas and coal (*point 1*) and less than 15 percent was from nuclear, hydro and non-hydro renewable energy (*point 2*). In the case of China the situation was different in that 70 percent of its energy came from only one source, coal (*point 3*). Oil was China's second main source of energy at about 35 percent, followed by hydro, then gas (*point 4*). Very little nuclear power was consumed and like the USA, China used very little non-hydro renewable energy (*point 5*).

4. (Model answer)
The diagram shows the features that whales and fish have in common and the features where they are different (*overview*). Both of them live in water and can swim (*point 1*). However, whales and fish are quite different in some things. Unlike fish, whales give birth to live young, they have horizontal tail fins and they are able to breathe air (*point 2*). Fish don't do any of these things. Instead of giving birth to live young they lay eggs, their tail fins are vertical, and they get oxygen from water not air (*point 3*).

5. (Model answer)
The pie chart shows the distribution of internet users around the world (*overview*). The highest number can be found in Asia where 38.7 percent of the world's internet users are located (*point 1*). Both Europe and North America have high numbers of internet users at 26.4 and 18 percent respectively (*point 2*), but in several areas the numbers of internet users are below 10 percent of the population, namely Latin America at 9.6 percent, Africa at 3.4 percent and the Middle East at 2.5 percent (*point 3*). The lowest number of users is in Oceania and Australia with only 1.5 percent (*point 4*).

6. (Model answer)
The diagram shows how solar panels work to make electricity in the home from the light of the sun (*overview*). First of all sunlight is caught by the solar panels which are situated on the roof of the house (*point 1*). When the sun shines, the solar panels create electricity as direct current which travels to the inverter which is inside the house, where the direct current is changed to alternating current (*point 2*). The electricity then travels to the fuse box (*point 3*). From the fuse box the electricity can power appliances in the home such as TVs and lights (*point 4*).

Test 3, Re-tell lecture (page 95)

1. (Model answer)
There is a new way of thinking about homework among educators (*overview*). Recent thinking and research suggests that homework is of little value especially to younger children (*point 1*). It also puts a lot of pressure on the parents because they are not able to help their children (*point 2*). Because of this, education officials are going to promote reading which they consider to be far more valuable than doing homework (*point 3*).

2. (Model answer)
The lecture is about the development of conflict theory as a subject (*overview*). It began as a means to better understand conflict in society (*point 1*). It was started by a group of academics who believed that studying conflict as a phenomenon using approaches from different disciplines would be useful (*point 2*). It was initially rejected by some academics (*point 3*) but it continued to thrive as a discipline and is now as important as other academic fields (*point 4*).

3. (Model answer)
The lecturer points out that the space within homes has become smaller (*point 1*) so we need to ask if there is any evidence that this is having effects on people's well-being (*point 2*). Research has shown that having smaller homes is having a negative effect on all the inhabitants of the home in terms of behaviour and even health (*point 3*). Therefore, it is vital for residents to have adequate private space within their home for their psychological health (*point 4*).

Test 3, Answer short question (page 96)

1. cheap
2. glasses/contact lenses
3. synthetic
4. fruit
5. twelve
6. west
7. water/liquid
8. honey
9. library
10. waiter/waitress

ANSWER KEY

Test 3, Summarize written text (pages 97–98)

1 (Model answer)
New research reveals that location, rather than class, is now the main factor in determining global inequality (*point 1*) and economic migration is the only solution for individuals from developing countries to improve their standard of living (*point 2*) until policy makers prioritize support for developing countries (*point 3*).

2 (Model answer)
Due to the widespread use of English in many fields, it is one of the most spoken languages (*point 1*) and this probably accounts for the fact that very few native speakers of English can speak another language (*point 2*), whereas in non-English-speaking countries in Europe over 50 percent of people are bilingual (*point 3*).

Test 3, Write essay (page 99)

1 (Model answer)
In the past it was more common for men to work than women but this situation has changed and nowadays both sexes work. However, it would seem that there are still some differences between the sexes as some professions seem to attract more men than women and vice versa (*introduction*).

It is quite common for men, rather than women, to be employed in jobs such as building and construction. This is probably due to the effort and strength needed for such kind of labour and many women may not have sufficient physical power for this (*point 1 regarding male suitability*). However, there are many other careers in which far more men work than women such as engineering. Additionally, there are far more senior male managers than female. This may have less to do with suitability and more to do with other factors such as education, expectations of family or social beliefs (*point 2 regarding male suitability*).

On the other hand there are other professions where mainly female employees can be found such as child care. This may be attributed to the fact that women are generally the child rearers at home and feel familiar and comfortable doing this type of work (*point 1 regarding female suitability*). Other jobs which have fewer males than females are caring professions such as teaching and nursing. It is believed that this could be due to the fact that women are seen to be good communicators with the ability to empathize (*point 2 regarding female suitability*).

In my opinion I believe that it is not a question of suitability based on sex but suitability based on personality. Each person should do the type of job they personally feel most suited to, regardless of their sex (*conclusion*).

1 (Model essay outline)
Some differences in jobs done by men and by women:

- Jobs suitable for men: strength
- Some jobs could be either but still more men
- Jobs dominated by women
- Women's characters determine jobs?

Opinion: Choice should be dependent on suitability not gender.

2 (Model answer)
It has become quite common for young people to leave home either for study or work purposes. This affords numerous advantages for those who do this but it is not without its difficulties either (*introduction*).

Living independently at a young age gives young people many opportunities to learn. For example learning how to budget money, manage time, complete paperwork or forms, work or live with new people and in some cases learn how to cook and look after a home (*point 1 advantage*). Without having parental guidance on every single issue or problem encountered young people can also learn about how to solve problems and make decisions independently (*point 2 advantage*).

However, living away from home is not without its drawbacks. For one thing youngsters may feel isolated, lonely and homesick living in a new place without their family for the first time (*point 1 disadvantage*). They may not be sufficiently mature to adapt and could fall into debt through not managing their money, or fail to keep up with their studies, or be late or absent from work due to lack of time management skills (*point 2 disadvantage*). In the worst scenario, without parental guidance, they may become friendly with, or influenced by, unsuitable people and get involved in criminal activities (*point 3 disadvantage*).

On the whole, however, I still believe it is a positive development for most young people to have independence at an early age, as long as they are made aware of the possible problems of living away from home. They should also be given advice prior to leaving home and continuing support, albeit from a distance, once they have left home (*conclusion*).

2 (Model essay outline)
Leaving home: advantages and disadvantages

Advantages:

- learn to manage money, cook, live independently
- solve problems, make decisions

Disadvantages:

- loneliness
- immaturity leading to problems
- get involved in crime

Opinion: positive outweighs negative but they need good advice

Test 3, Multiple-choice, choose single answer (page 100)

1 D (They assist in driving public issues.): *it is the figures that inform these issues.*

2 B (The number of species is constantly changing.): *new species are continually appearing, while at the same time existing species evolve and some become extinct.*

Test 3, Multiple-choice, choose multiple answers (pages 101–102)

1 A (Snow is formed from ice.): *tiny ice crystals collide … become snowflakes*

E (Dry snow falls in colder temperatures than wet snow.): *dry, cool air … This 'dry' snow … warmer than 0°C … This creates 'wet' snow …*

2 B (Industrial pollution can affect both underground and river water.): *industrial wastes … down old coal mine shafts. River water … industrial effluents*

C (There are numerous means by which water can become impure.): *… polluted surface water can enter the saturation zone of an aquifer … waste … River water can be affected by …*

Test 3, Re-order paragraphs (page 103)

1 D A result of not being connected to the electricity grid in rural areas of some countries means people light their homes using kerosene lamps (*a result* = first mention of topic).

B In addition to being fairly costly, these create smoke pollution and carbon emissions (*these* = kerosene lamps)

C Therefore, alternatives are being investigated (*alternatives to kerosene lamps*)

A One such example is a solar panel which could charge an LED lamp to create hours of light each day (*such example* = example of an *alternative* to *kerosene lamps*)

2 D Despite the financial stability a high salary brings, research has shown that the majority of top earners are not happy in their jobs (*earners* and *not happy* = first mention of topic)

C It seems that the lack of psychological reward is the reason for their dissatisfaction (*their* = top earners)

B However, most of these workers would not consider career alternatives (*these workers = top earners, However* indicates contrasting idea to *dissatisfaction*)

E Interestingly, it is not the risk of a decrease in salary which prevents this move (*this move* = career alternatives)

A The fear of criticism from colleagues, friends and family is the main factor that obstructs a change in their employment situation (*the fear of criticism* completes the idea in *it is not the risk of a decrease in salary*)

Test 3, Reading: Fill in the blanks (page 104)

1 1 option: collocation with *easy*

2 factors: the other words don't create meaning in context

3 requires: the other words don't create meaning in context

4 rate: collocation with *response*

2 1 interested: the other words don't create meaning in context

2 defined: definition follows

3 applied: must be used with *to*, and the other words don't create meaning in context

3 1 destination: collocation with *journey,* and the other words don't create meaning in context

2 purpose: collocation with *common,* and the other words don't create meaning in context

3 avoid: verb needed, and *experience* doesn't create meaning in context

4 1 positive: adjective needed, and *negative* doesn't create meaning in context

2 availability: noun needed, and the other words don't create meaning in context

3 gain: collocation with *experience and knowledge,* and *purchase* doesn't create meaning in context

Test 3, Reading & writing: Fill in the blanks (pages 105–107)

1 1 B (were): Past Simple Passive (finished time, *thousands of years ago*) third person plural (*some types*)

2 A (purpose): the other words don't create meaning in context, and *plan* would be followed by *for*

3 C (However): the other words don't create meaning in context

4 C (way): the other words don't create meaning in context

2 1 D (participants): the other words don't create meaning in context

2 D (basis): collocation with *regular,* and the other words don't create meaning in context

3 C (because): giving justification/reason for the link

4 A (which): relative pronoun introducing a defining relative clause

3 1 A (influenced): the other words don't create meaning in context

2 C (deliberate): the other words don't create meaning in context

3 C (are selected): Present Simple Passive

4 A (placement): the other words don't create meaning in context

4 1 C (other): the other words don't create meaning in context
2 A (will have improved): the only one that is grammatically correct
3 D (so): giving the result/effect of action (the others would indicate a contrasting action)
4 B (familiar): the other words don't create meaning in context

5 1 D (despite): fits grammatically (gerund *being*) and contextually
2 A (handled): the other words don't create meaning in context
3 D (factor): collocation with *distinguishes,* and the other words don't create meaning in context
4 D (If): conditional construction continued in *then*
5 A (become): refers to future possibility (so not *stay* or *remain*), and *involve* doesn't create meaning in context

Test 3, Summarize spoken text (page 108)

1 **(Model answer)**
Travel companies now market holidays as environmentally friendly under a variety of names such as eco-tourism (*point 1*). However, many of these increasingly popular holidays are actually often damaging to the environment and may also harm local cultures and economies (*point 2*). This presents an issue to those who are concerned about protecting and improving the environment and want a genuinely environmentally friendly holiday (*point 3*).

2 **(Model answer)**
In the last two hundred years the industrial revolution has led to the growth of industry worldwide (*point 1*). The result of this growth means that more and more harmful gases are released into the atmosphere (*point 2*). In the same period, sea and land temperatures have risen noticeably (*point 3*). Therefore, according to the speaker climate change is the result of human activity (*point 4*).

Test 3, Multiple-choice, choose multiple answers (page 109)

1 B (present different methods for grading writing): *talk to you about some of the ways written assignments or essays are marked.*
D (describe the findings of a research project): *The study showed that … a controversial result*

2 C (They reproduce more slowly than other fish do.): *sharks are not able to repopulate or reproduce themselves quickly and sharks are slow breeders.*
E (They are more likely to become extinct than other fish.): *This makes them much more vulnerable and in danger of dying out than many other fish species.*

Test 3, Fill in the blanks (page 110)

1 1 structured 2 valid 3 material 4 appreciate 5 assignments 6 excellent

2 1 genetic 2 intelligence 3 process 4 assessed

Test 3, Highlight correct summary (pages 111–112)

1 C *it was the domain of the wealthy and few people outside those circles were even aware that family ancestry could be recorded … But it was not until the mid twentieth century … became a more common activity among the general population.*

2 B *evidence that early humans used fire much longer ago than previously envisaged … One question … unanswered is why they were using fire.*

Test 3, Multiple-choice, choose single answer (page 113)

1 B (The subject area selected may not have sufficient focus.): *Another problem … topic … too broad and needs to be refined.*

2 D (It is suitable for less orally communicative patients.): *… this therapy is particularly successful with those who have difficulty expressing themselves verbally.*

Test 3, Select missing word (page 114)

1 B (could very possibly be fake): indicated by *sceptical about the authenticity, suspect*

2 D (current days): indicated by *it's been used … from … to* (must be a point in time)

ANSWER KEY

Test 3, Highlight incorrect words (page 115)

1. One of the most encouraging phenomena in recent years has been the development (growth) of lifelong learning in the education sector. Nowadays, students are embarking on courses at all ages. Higher education is no longer viewed (seen) as a place for the young. Mature students are appreciated and respected (valued). Recent research has also indicated that older students are dedicated (enthusiastic) learners, able to contribute a number of skills and talents (attributes) gained from work, family and other life experiences.

2. Conducting a video conference is now a popular method (means) of communication in the business world. This telecommunications technology allows two or more locations to communicate by simultaneous video and audio transmissions. It's designed to serve conferences or meetings in many (multiple) locations.
The advantages are obvious: no more lengthy phone calls or complicated (complex) correspondence with business contacts, partners or offices abroad (overseas). This relatively low cost, fast, effective communication method has made significant inroads in not just a business environment (context), but also education, medicine and media.

Test 3, Write from dictation (page 116)

See audio script on page 169.

Test 4, Read aloud (page 117)

See text on page 117.

Test 4, Repeat sentence (page 118)

See audio script on page 169.

Test 4, Describe image (pages 119–121)

1. **(Model answer)**
The map shows the continent of Antarctica (*overview*). It is roughly circular in shape with a diameter of approximately four thousand kilometres or two and a half thousand miles (*point 1*). Three different oceans touch its shores – the Atlantic, the Indian and the Pacific (*point 2*). The South Pole is more or less in the centre of Antarctica although the magnetic South Pole is several thousand kilometres away from that (*point 3*). There is a station there called the McMurdo Station and this is on the shores of the Ross Sea, near one of the two marked ice shelves, the Ross Ice Shelf (*point 4*).

2. **(Model answer)**
The graph shows the monthly temperatures in the southwest part of Tasmania and gives the average maximum and minimum daily temperatures for each month as well as showing what the recorded highest and lowest temperatures have been (*overview*). June and July are the coldest months and January and February the hottest (*point 1*). Temperatures in February can rise to as high as thirty degrees Celsius whereas those of July can fall to lower than minus ten (*point 2*). But overall, on average the temperatures are between two and 12 degrees Celsius in summer and minus five to two degrees in winter, so usually it is a cold area (*point 3*).

3. **(Model answer)**
The diagram shows the lifecycle of a plant, specifically a sunflower (*overview*). It shows someone digging the soil in order to sow the seed (*stage 1*). Then it shows how the roots grow under the ground and the stem begins to poke out of the earth (*stage 2*). Helped by rain and sunshine the stem grows taller and taller (*stage 3*). Eventually leaves sprout and then, when the plant is tall and strong enough, a flower comes out (*stage 4*). In the centre of the sunflower there are lots of small seeds and these then provide the potential for new plants (*stage 5*). And so the cycle begins again (*stage 6*).

4. **(Model answer)**
The table shows last year's export sales from Japan of motorcycles in terms of the region which imported the bikes (*overview*). North America was the largest customer and both it and Europe each accounted for slightly over one-third of sales (*point 1*). Asia, South America and Oceania were a long way behind, each taking approximately eight percent of the exported bikes (*point2*). Africa, Central America, and the Middle East took fewest bikes at under five percent of sales (*point 3*). The table also shows that sales to North, South and Central America all increased while all other regions have declined, especially Europe (*point 4*), but overall there was a 2.3 percent increase in exports of motorcycles from Japan last year (*point 5*).

5. **(Model answer)**
The pie chart shows the employment situation of Physics graduates one year after they graduate from university (*overview*). Many graduates continue to study, with the largest single group, 35 percent, in full-time education, and 15 percent combine part-time study with work (*point 1*). 30 percent of graduates are in full-time paid work and five percent are in part-time work, with another five percent doing unpaid work (*point 2*). The percentage of unemployed graduates was quite low at seven percent but another three percent said they were not available for work (*point 3*). So overall 90 percent of physics graduates were either working or still studying or both (*point 4*).

❻ (Model answer)
The bar chart shows how three different economic sectors contributed to the UK economy over the course of the twentieth century (*overview*). In 1900 agriculture was the largest sector contributing almost half, with manufacturing just behind at about 45 percent but the business and financial sector was far behind, contributing less than five percent (*point 1*). Agriculture continued to grow, reaching a peak of around 53 percent in 1950, but in the second half of the century, its importance fell very rapidly contributing only about two percent by the year 2000 (*point 2*). Manufacturing also declined but at a more regular pace (*point 3*). Business and finance, on the other hand, grew rapidly and steadily to the point where it was responsible for over one-third of the economy by 2000 (*point 4*).

Test 4, Re-tell lecture (page 122)

❶ (Model answer)
The lecturer is talking about the history of salt and its value (*overview*). In the ancient world salt was valuable because it was used to preserve food (*point 1*) and it also meant food could be carried over long distances without going bad (*point 2*). In fact the need to transport salt is possibly one reason why the Romans built roads (*addition to point 2*). Salt was so expensive because it was hard to produce (*point 3*) and it could be used to raise money by raising its price (*point 4*). In the ancient world salt was also important in other places such as Africa (*point 5*).

❷ (Model answer)
The speaker makes the point that children's literature has an important social role in that it helps to teach children the moral values of their society (*overview*). One of the ways it does this is through heroes, the characters who the young readers will want to be like (*point 1*). So these heroes have the qualities that society values – typically courage, honesty, consideration, a love of hard work and so on (*point 2*). All societies use children's literature in this way (*point 3*) but it can still be entertaining and enjoyable even though it also aims to be instructive (*point 4*).

❸ (Model answer)
Electric vehicles have been around since the beginning of the twentieth century (*point 1*), but petrol-driven cars became more important so electric power was only used in certain kinds of vehicle such as delivery vehicles and fork-lifts (*point 2*). However, in one area of transport electric power came to dominate, namely trains, especially in countries that had no oil or coal resources such as Switzerland (*point 3*). Today there is a lot of interest in electric cars for road travel because of the pollution caused by petrol-driven cars (*point 4*).

Test 4, Answer short question (page 123)

❶ triangle
❷ index
❸ source
❹ editor
❺ profit/profits
❻ agricultural (sector)/agriculture
❼ thesis/dissertation
❽ century
❾ graduation
❿ deadline/due date

Test 4, Summarize written text (pages 124–126)

❶ (Model answer)
A number of major internationally-recognized companies are encouraging staff to use meditation to become more 'mindful' (*point 1*) as they believe that this may have a very positive impact on performance and relationships at the workplace (*point 2*).

❷ (Model answer)
Academics have some standard answers to criticisms from politicians and business people that their research is frequently pointless and a waste of money (*point 1*) and the writer adds to these answers as a justification for this kind of academic research some evidence that it is impossible to know exactly how valuable a piece of research may ultimately turn out to be (*point 2*).

❸ (Model answer)
Although there is some research that suggests a correlation between physical activity and educational success (*point 1*), studies in this area are inconsistent (*point 2*) and have been criticized for various reasons including their research methodology (*point 3*) and a failure to establish whether sport leads to better academic performance or vice versa, or whether it depends on personality (*point 4*).

Test 4, Write essay (page 127)

1 (Model answer)

It is undoubtedly the case that computer technology has had a major impact on society. But the statement that this impact been mainly negative seems to me a gross exaggeration (*introduction*).

Of course, the widespread use of computers has had negative consequences. Children, for example, are more likely to sit indoors playing computer games than be outside running around in the open air. It has yet to be seen what the long-term impact on their health may be but it is clearly unlikely to be positive. Reliance on computers also opens us up to risks. If all our precious personal data is stored on computers – our diaries, photos, music – then we stand to lose a great deal that matters to us if our computer crashes or is stolen (*argument for negative impact*).

However, despite these serious issues, I maintain that computer technology has had more positive than negative effects. Computers have opened up access to knowledge to anyone regardless of where they are in the world, as long as they can get on the internet. Increasingly, for example, library and other resources are available on the web and you can do an online course in any subject whatever your geographical location or personal circumstances may be (*first counter argument*).

Computer technology has also made communication between people easier. I have kept in touch with friends much more than I would have done had I had to write letters, find stamps and wait days, even weeks, for responses. I'm in regular email contact with friends and relatives worldwide; indeed, we can even see each other when we talk on Skype. In this way relationships are not only maintained but also strengthened (*second counter argument*).

In conclusion, although the potentially negative impact that computers occasionally have must be taken seriously, I believe that computer technology has in many ways enormously enriched people's lives (*conclusion*).

1 (Model essay outline)

Impact of computer technology not entirely negative
Risks and dangers of computer technology:

- health
- losing data and records

Positive impact:

- access to knowledge
- distance education
- easy communication

Conclusion: computer technology has enriched our lives despite risks

Test 4, Multiple-choice, choose single answer (page 128)

1 C (Cathedral staff were reluctant to act too quickly.): *conservative nature … an idea that would need to prove its worth*

2 B (People have little motivation to develop a zebra that could be ridden.): *It would undoubtedly be possible to breed a zebra that would ride well but … there has not been much incentive to do so.*

Test 4, Multiple-choice, choose multiple answers (pages 129–130)

1 A (the nature of the climate there): *wood is not a very durable material in tropical conditions*

E (problems caused by insects): *may also have been destroyed by termites*

2 A (observing what happens during lessons): *we can study the curriculum in action … into the classroom itself*

D (considering what is taken into account when preparing the curriculum): first paragraph

F (reviewing actual learning compared to curriculum goals): final paragraph

Test 4, Re-order paragraphs (page 131)

1 E In the 1960s, the greatest obstacle for those who wanted to organize women was said to be women's conviction that they were actually inferior to men (introduction of topic *women's conviction that* … in standalone sentence).

B This acceptance that men were the superior gender had not developed by chance (*This acceptance that … = women's conviction that …*).

C It had been the view that had been socialized into them from the moment of their birth (*It = This acceptance = women's conviction; them, their = women* in Sentence 1).

D This will become clear if you look at any girls' magazine or popular film of the period (*This* = that the view of women's inferiority had been socialized into women from birth).

A There you will see how women are consistently portrayed as weak and in need of male protection (*There = any girls' magazine or popular film of the period*).

2 C Fishermen's knitted jerseys have always been recognizable in Britain by their colour and their shape (introduces topic in a standalone sentence; concepts of *colour* and *shape* are mentioned).

B Traditionally they are navy blue and they are basically square in shape, without a curved armhole or inset sleeve (*they = Fishermen's knitted jerseys; colour* and *shape* are both described).

E These navy jerseys are still a familiar sight on any quay or harbour in the land (*These navy jerseys* = those whose colour is described in sentence B).

D This continuing popularity cannot just be put down to a fondness for tradition (*This continuing popularity* = whole of sentence E).

A It is mainly due to the quality of the fabric which effectively resists salt water, direct sunshine and cold winds (*It = This continuing popularity*).

Test 4, Reading: Fill in the blanks (page 132)

1 1 skies: noun required (the other words don't create meaning in context)
2 principles: noun required (the other words don't create meaning in context)
3 describe: verb required (*models* can *describe* but not *confirm*)
4 fields: plural required (*fields* suggested by text describing two kinds of astronomy)
5 confirm: verb required (the other words don't create meaning in context)

2 1 kingdom: collocation with *ruled*
2 powerful: adjective required (suggested by *extremely*)
3 aid: collocation in the phrase *with the aid of*
4 strength: noun required (*strength* is a quality of a shark)
5 poet: suggested by *wrote songs*

3 1 team: collocation with *researchers*
2 participating: participle required (*involving* would require a direct object)
3 same: adjective required (suggested by *in all the universities*)
4 widely: adverb required; collocation with *read* (we don't say *read heavily*)
5 core: adjective required (suggested by *concentrate on a few*)

4 1 different: collocation with *many*
2 communicate: must match *with one another* (the other words don't create meaning in context)
3 sociable: suggested by *they live in groups*
4 range: suggested by comparison of numbers
5 capture: the other words don't create meaning in context

Test 4, Reading & writing: Fill in the blanks (pages 133–135)

1 1 A (from): collocation with *dates*
2 C (What): noun phrase as subject (not starting a relative clause)
3 A (showing): participle required
4 D (than): comparative with *earlier*
5 C (each): suggested by *take his turn* (*all of which* would be followed by *their turn*)

2 1 D (how): suggested by rest of passage and grammar
2 B (posted): past participle required
3 D (no): the other words don't make meaning in context
4 C (concerned): collocation with *as far as*
5 A (about): *knowledge* is usually followed by *of* or *about* + a topic

3 1 A (make): collocation with *music*
2 D (long): the other words don't make meaning in context
3 A (However): introduces an opposing idea (to the scientists' inability to explain the sound)
4 C (at): used with *a speed of*
5 C (as): collocation with *the same way*

4 1 B (has): Present Perfect Passive (for an event that began in the past and is still continuing)
2 B (more): modifier for *easily* (*too* does not make meaning in context)
3 D (can): Present Passive (for a present event)
4 C (so): to indicate effect
5 B (from): to indicate an effect while wearing the suit (not after)

5 1 B (which): relative clause introduced by *in which*
2 A (widely): adverb to modify the adjective *differing*
3 D (set): the other words don't create meaning in context
4 A (those): meaning *the ones*
5 A (in): collocation with *mind*

Test 4, Summarize spoken text (page 136)

1 **(Model answer)**
Allergies seem to be increasing these days (*point 1*) especially in more hygienic societies where children are less exposed to harmful situations at an early age (*point 2*). They are a result of the body's immune system reacting to something it believes is harmful and producing histamines to rid the body of this (*point 3*). Sufferers are advised to avoid the trigger for their allergy (*point 4*) and, when this is impossible, are prescribed anti-histamines (*point 5*).

2 **(Model answer)**
Europeans have always enjoyed reading about other countries (*point 1*), and particularly about travellers' experiences of America, (*point 2*) possibly due to the number of Europeans who emigrated to America (*point 3*). Two differing views about American society have emerged (*point 4*). One is that America is unique, different from anywhere else in the world, and cannot be imitated (*point 4a*). The other says simply that what America does today, the rest of the world does tomorrow (*point 4b*).

ANSWER KEY

Test 4, Multiple-choice, choose multiple answers (page 137)

1 B (Ask a native speaker if you are not sure of the meaning of something): *consult … someone whose mother tongue is the language you're translating from.*

D (Don't translate technical texts unless you are familiar with the subject): *You should refuse to do something if you don't know anything about the topic*

2 A (how attractive the building is to look at): *it's essential to consider the appearance of the building … should delight people and should raise their spirits.*

D (how long the building is likely to last): *the durability of the building … how well the building will stand up to the ravages of climate and time. Will it remain robust and in good condition?*

Test 4, Fill in the blanks (page 138)

1 1 overview 2 primary 3 developed 4 invaluable 5 details

2 1 issues 2 roles 3 events 4 Europe 5 decade

Test 4, Highlight correct summary (pages 139–140)

1 D *They can be careful and precise … they can also generate huge forces … How is it possible for our hands to be so incredibly flexible? … the extraordinary complexity of the bones, ligaments, nerves and muscles that lie beneath the skin* (the others include ideas not mentioned)

2 B *there are two distinct species … while sharks from the east side certainly travelled to the west side of the continent and vice versa, they always returned to their home areas to breed … sharks may be more susceptible to changes in local marine environments than had been previously thought* (the other summaries contain inaccurate information)

Test 4, Multiple-choice, choose single answer (page 141)

1 C (Whales may not survive in some situations where there is sound pollution.): *some whales, for example, died when they beached themselves after being exposed to excessive sonar*

2 B (make enough copies of their handouts): *don't forget to bring handouts for everyone. There won't be time to do photocopying that morning.*

Test 4, Select missing word (page 142)

1 A (they made an inappropriate choice of topic): must be a negative action to lose marks, and indicated by *be more prescriptive about what you focus on in your presentation.*

2 B (bringing the situation to the attention of the public): indicated by *Novelists have a major role to play in reflecting their time to their readers who may otherwise ignore social problems* (Dickens and Orwell are given as examples to show this)

Test 4, Highlight incorrect words (page 143)

1 English had barely established itself as a language in England when it began **spreading** (moving) to other countries to be used there as well. First it **passed** (headed) north to Scotland and then west to Wales. It then made its **path** (way) across the sea to Ireland. That was in the Middle Ages. Over the course of the following centuries it has put down roots all over the **earth** (world), from the USA to South Africa, from India to New Zealand. Of course, in all these **places** (countries) it has developed in special ways to suit the new **concepts** (contexts) in which it found itself.

2 Researchers at the University of California claim to have discovered that people who eat chocolate regularly tend to be lighter than those who **hardly** (rarely) eat it. The findings may seem **suspicious** (surprising) in that chocolate has a great many calories and, in general, the more calories people **contain** (consume), the more likely they are to put on weight. The recent studies **establish** (emphasize) that it is more the regularity with which people eat chocolate that is **important** (significant) rather than the amount they consume. Whether they eat a little or a lot seems to make no difference, whereas eating it **freely** (frequently) appears to reduce weight more than only having it occasionally.

Test 4, Write from dictation (page 144)

See audio script on page 172.

ANSWER KEY

STUDENT ANSWERS

Introduction

There are three sample student answers for each of the tasks with spoken or written answers in the Speaking and Writing, and Listening sections. Each answer has a comment from a PTE examiner explaining what is good about the answer and what the student could have done better. The answer itself is not scored, but you can see the student's overall score in the actual PTE Academic test.

Student answers for Test 1 are in the book, and for Tests 2–4 are on the CD-ROM. You'll find MP3 audio of all the student spoken answers on the CD-ROM.

Test 1, Speaking

Read aloud

TEST 1

STUDENT ANSWERS

❶ Topic: Market research

Student's overall PTE Academic score: 55

▶ 162 Market research is a vital part of the planning … of any business. However … experienced … you or your staff may be in particular field, if you are thinking of introducing a service to a new area. It is important to find out what the local population thinks about it first.

Examiner's comments: This student has read the whole text, but the pronunciation of the word 'particular' is very unclear. Fluency is also very poor because there are pauses between every word.

Student's overall PTE Academic score: 74

▶ 163 Market research is a vital part of the planning of any business. However experienced you and your staff may be in a particular field, if you are thinking of introducing a service to a new area, it is important to find out what the local population thinks about it first.

Examiner's comments: This student's response contains all but one word from the text and is delivered with good, though not native-like, fluency. However, the student suffers from many pronunciation problems, such as pronouncing 'of' like 'off'; 'of' should be pronounced with a 'v' sound at the end. The student would also lose points for saying 'and' rather than 'or'.

Student's overall PTE Academic score: 89

▶ 164 Market research is a vital part of the planning of any business. However experienced you or your staff may be in a particular field, if you are thinking of introducing a new service to a new area, it is important to find out what the local population thinks about it first.

Examiner's comments: This student has read the text completely, using natural pronunciation and fluency. The strong use of stress on the appropriate words would lead him to achieve a very high score.

❷ Topic: Transportation of goods by water

Student's overall PTE Academic score: 55

▶ 165 Not a lot– not a lot is known about how the transportation of goods by water first began. Large cargo boats were being used in some parts of the world up to five thousand years ago. However, sea trade become more widespread when large sailing boats travelled between port carrying speces, perfumes and objects made by hand.

Examiner's comments: Although this student says every word from the text, the score would be reduced because he has poor fluency and repeats 'Not a lot'. In addition, the pronunciation is weak; for example, the student pronounces 'goods' like 'goats'.

Student's overall PTE Academic score: 74

▶ 166 Not a lot is known about how the transportation of goods by water first began. Large cargo boats were being used in some parts of the world up to five thousand years ago. However, sea trade became more widespread when large sailing boats travelled between ports carrying, speces, perfumes and objects made by hand.

Examiner's comments: This student's fluency is quite natural, and every word from the text is included. However, the pronunciation is poor, and some words such as 'spices' are very hard for the listener to understand.

Student's overall PTE Academic score: 77

▶ 167 Not a lot is known about how the transportation of goods by water first began. Large cargo boats were being used in some parts of the world up to five thousand years ago. However, sea trade became more widespread when large sailing boats travelled between ports, carrying spices, perfumes and objects made by hand.

Examiner's comments: This student pronounces every word in a native-like way. Fluency is very natural, and pauses are suitably placed between each sentence of the text.

3 Topic: Young artist

Student's overall PTE Academic score: 55

▶ 168 When the young artist ha– was asked about his drawing, he explained, that he had started by– by taking a photograph of himself sitting by a window at home. He then drew his face from the photograph and replaced the buildings which were outside the window with trees. This gave the picture a softer, more artistic background.

Examiner's comments: This student's pronunciation is adequate and understandable but there are frequent unnatural pauses, such as between 'He then drew' and 'his face'. Every word from the text is included, but he would lose points because there are extra words, such as between 'When the young artist' and 'was asked'.

Student's overall PTE Academic score: 67

▶ 169 When the young artist was asked about his drawing, he explained that he had started by taking a photograph of himself sitting down a window at home. He then drew his face from the photograph and replaced the buildings which were outside the window with trees. This gave the picture a softer, more artistic background.

Examiner's comments: This student's pronunciation is clear and he pauses appropriately between sentences. However, his speech is slow and the use of the word 'down' instead of 'by' would reduce the score.

Student's overall PTE Academic score: 89

▶ 170 When the young artist was asked about his drawing, he explained that he had started by taking a photograph of himself sitting by a window at home. He then drew his face from the photograph and replaced the buildings which were outside the window with trees. This gave the picture a softer, more artistic background.

Examiner's comments: This student's speech is clear and each word is pronounced in a native-like way. Every word from the text has been included, there is no repetition and the speech would achieve the maximum score.

4 Topic: Energy and pollution

Student's overall PTE Academic score: 45

▶ 171 Humans need to use energy in order to exist. So it is unsurprising that the way people have been producing energy, is largely responsible for current environmental problems. Pollution comes in many forms, but those that are most concerning because of their impact of health, result from the combu– combustion of fills in power stations and cars.

Examiner's comments: This student's speech is staccato; in other words, there are pauses between different parts of words. For example, in the word 'unsurprising' there are three long, unnatural pauses ('un-sur-pris-ing'), and this would reduce the score for fluency and pronunciation.

Student's overall PTE Academic score: 74

▶ 172 Humans needs to use energy in order to exist. So it is unsurprising that the way people have been producing energy is largely responsible for current environmental problems. Pollution comes in many forms, but those that are most concerning because of their impact on health, result from the combustion of fuels in power stations and cars.

Examiner's comments: This student's speech is also staccato, and his fluency is very poor. Instead of reading 'Humans need', he says 'Humans needs', and this would reduce the score because the text has not been read accurately.

Student's overall PTE Academic score: 77

173 Humans need to use energy in order to exist. So it is unsurprising that the way people have been producing energy is largely responsible for current environmental problems. Pollution comes in many forms, but those that are most concerning, because of their impact on health, result from the combustion of fuels in power stations and cars.

Examiner's comments: This student reads every word from the text accurately, using appropriate stress and pronunciation.

5 Topic 5: Retirement

Student's overall PTE Academic score: 45

174 Clearly, times are changing and while many people are saving for theirs retirement, many more still need to do so. Most countries have a range of pensions shemes that are design-ed to provide individuals with an income once they stop working. People need to take advantage of this if they are to have sufficient money throughout their retirement years.

Examiner's comments: This student frequently mispronounces words, such as 'their', 'pension' and 'schemes', in a way that makes it impossible to understand what is being said. Although she reads every word from the text, her fluency is also very poor.

Student's overall PTE Academic score: 67

175 Clearly, times are changing and while many people are saving for their retirement, many, more still need to do so. Most countries have a range of pension schemes that are designed to provide individuals with an income once they stop working. People need to take advantage of these if they are, to have sufficient money throughout their retirement years.

Examiner's comments: This student's pronunciation is adequately clear and every word from the text is included. However, the speech would not score highly for fluency, as there are unnatural pauses within sentences, for example between 'many' and 'more'.

Student's overall PTE Academic score: 77

176 Clearly, times are changing and the while many people are saving for their retirement, many more still need to do so. Most countries have a range of pension schemes that are designed to provide individuals with an income once they stop working. People need to take advantage of this if they are to have sufficient money throughout their retirement years.

Examiner's comments: This student's speech is too slow for the first sentence, but her fluency becomes more natural later in the text. Her pronunciation is not native-like for some words, but it is always clear.

6 Topic: Good weather and mood

Student's overall PTE Academic score: 56

177 According to recent research, sunshine and warm weather have a positive effect on our moods. The British Journal of Psychology has published a report in which it claims that anxiety levels fall when temperature rise, while increased exposure to sunri– sunshine makes us think more positively about our lives.

Examiner's comments: This student mispronounces certain words in a way that makes the speech hard to understand; for example, he says 'worm', not 'warm'. He reads every word, but would lose points for saying 'sunri' which is not in the text.

Student's overall PTE Academic score: 74

178 According to recent research, sunshine and warm weather have a positive effect on our moods. The British Journal of Psychology has published a report, in which it claims that anxiety levels fall when temperatures rise, while increase exposure to sunshine make us think more positively about our lives.

Examiner's comments: This student mispronounces words such as 'warm' and 'of', but fluency is good throughout the response. He reads every word without hesitation or repetition.

Student's overall PTE Academic score: 89

179 According to recent research, sunshine and warm weather have a positive effect on our moods. The British Journal of Psychology has published a report in which it claims that axiety– anxiety levels fall when temperatures rise, while increase exposure to sunshine makes us think more positively about our lives.

Examiner's comments: This student's speech is naturally fluent and every word from the text is said in a native-like way, but his score would be reduced due to mistakenly saying 'axiety' before the word 'anxiety'.

Test 1, Speaking

Repeat sentence

❶ Topic: Design of a bridge

Student's overall PTE Academic score: 55

▶ 180 Factors [*unclear*] no.

Examiner's comments: This student only accurately repeats one word from the sentence. Three other words are incomprehensible due to poor pronunciation.

Student's overall PTE Academic score: 74

▶ 181 Factors such as cost and … influence the – the design of the building.

Examiner's comments: This student omits 'and function' from the sentence and there is a long hesitation in the middle of the response.

Student's overall PTE Academic score: 89

▶ 182 Factors such as cost and function influence the design of a bridge.

Examiner's comments: This student accurately repeats every word, with appropriate fluency and pronunciation.

❷ Topic: Waste disposal

Student's overall PTE Academic score: 45

▶ 183 It is important for humans … proper ways.

Examiner's comments: This student repeats less than 50 percent of the sentence; the response would receive a low score. It also lacks fluency due to a long pause in the middle.

Student's overall PTE Academic score: 74

▶ 184 It's important that … er … the humans dispose their waste in appropriate ways.

Examiner's comments: This student omits the word 'of' but otherwise repeats every word. Fluency is poor, but the pronunciation is adequate.

Student's overall PTE Academic score: 89

▶ 185 It's important that humans dispose of their waste … in appropriate ways.

Examiner's comments: This student accurately repeats every word, with appropriate fluency and pronunciation.

❸ Topic: Unable to complete

Student's overall PTE Academic score: 45

▶ 186 If you are not er … allowed to complete all the exams … er… me– noticed me by email.

Examiner's comments: This student replaces 'unable to' and 'the task' with 'not allowed to' and 'all the exams', and the response would lose points for these inaccuracies. In addition, the speech is too slow and hesitant.

Student's overall PTE Academic score: 74

▶ 187 If you're unable … to complete the task in time … please notify me by email.

Examiner's comments: This student repeats every word from the sentence, but his speech is slow and hesitant.

Student's overall PTE Academic score: 77

▶ 188 If you are unable to complete the task in time please contact me by email.

Examiner's comments: This student repeats most of the sentence accurately with good fluency and pronunciation. The response would not score maximum points because 'notify' is replaced with 'contact' and there is an unnaturally strong stress on the word 'me'.

4 Topic: Financial report

Student's overall PTE Academic score: 55

▶ 189 The financial report of the last quarter will be available this afternoon.

Examiner's comments: This student does not repeat the sentence accurately – 'for' is replaced with 'of'. In addition, pronunciation is poor and the word 'quarter' is incomprehensible.

Student's overall PTE Academic score: 74

▶ 190 The financial report for the last quarter will be an a– available this afternoon.

Examiner's comments: This student repeats every word, but would lose points for hesitations before the words 'will' and 'available'. His pronunciation is understandable but it is definitely not native-like.

Student's overall PTE Academic score: 89

▶ 191 The financial report for this last quarter will be available after noon– this afternoon.

Examiner's comments: This student accurately repeats most words, with appropriate fluency and pronunciation, but would lose points for saying 'this' rather than 'the', and for repeating the word 'afternoon'.

TEST 1 STUDENT ANSWERS

5 Topic: Extra seminars

Student's overall PTE Academic score: 45

▶ 192 Next year's schedules should be assisted by …

Examiner's comments: This student only repeats two words accurately and pronunciation and fluency are poor.

Student's overall PTE Academic score: 74

▶ 193 Extra seminars will be available to assist you in revision.

Examiner's comments: This student repeats every word apart from 'scheduled' and 'with', which are replaced with 'available' and 'in'. His pronunciation is of an intermediate level, but his fluency is relatively strong.

Student's overall PTE Academic score: 77

▶ 194 Extra seminar will be scheduled to assist you with revision.

Examiner's comments: This student speaks with appropriate fluency and good pronunciation, but she says 'seminar' not 'seminars' and, therefore, the response would not receive the maximum score.

6 Topic: Switch off electronic devices

Student's overall PTE Academic score: 56

▶ 195 Please switch off all electronic devices when you are attending the conferen– conference.

Examiner's comments: This student speaks with suitable fluency until the end of the sentence where the repetition of the word 'conference' and the omission of the word 'session' would reduce the response's score.

Student's overall PTE Academic score: 67

▶ 196 Please switch off all electronic devices when you are … attending a conference session.

Examiner's comments: This student repeats every word accurately and the pronunciation is adequate, but the hesitation before the word 'attending' is unnatural and this would reduce the score.

Student's overall PTE Academic score: 89

▶ 197 Please switch of all electronic devices while you are attending a conference session.

Examiner's comments: This student accurately repeats every word, with appropriate fluency and pronunciation.

❼ Topic: Team work

Student's overall PTE Academic score: 55

▶ 198 It is important that you work … as a team in this project.

Examiner's comments: This student accurately repeats every word, apart from saying 'in' instead of 'on'. However, his speech is too slow for a good fluency score and the pronunciation of the word 'project' is poor.

Student's overall PTE Academic score: 74

▶ 199 It is important that you work as a team in this project.

Examiner's comments: This student accurately repeats almost every word, with adequate fluency and pronunciation. The response would lose points because the student says 'in' rather than 'on'.

Student's overall PTE Academic score: 89

▶ 200 It's important that you work as a team on this project.

Examiner's comments: This student accurately repeats every word, with appropriate fluency and pronunciation.

❽ Topic: People's mood

Student's overall PTE Academic score: 55

▶ 201 The study by moods … are affected by …

Examiner's comments: This student only repeats four words from the sentence correctly, and therefore the response would receive a very low score. Pronunciation is unclear and fluency is very poor.

Student's overall PTE Academic score: 67

▶ 202 The study shows how people's move can be affected with weather change.

Examiner's comments: This student's speech has good fluency, but he would lose points for replacing words, such as 'that' with 'how', and for mispronouncing 'mood' as 'move'.

Student's overall PTE Academic score: 77

▶ 203 The study shows that people's mood can be affected by news and the weather.

Examiner's comments: This student would lose points for omitting the word 'reports', adding the word 'the', changing 'showed' to 'shows', and for mispronouncing 'mood'. However, pronunciation and fluency are generally good.

❾ Topic: Population growth

Student's overall PTE Academic score: 45

▶ 204 Details about population growth … will be attainding …

Examiner's comments: This student repeats less than 50 percent of the sentence, so the response would receive a relatively low score. Fluency is adequate, but the second vowel sound in the final word is mispronounced as 'attainding' rather than 'attending'.

Student's overall PTE Academic score: 67

▶ 205 Detail analysis of population growth has revealed some alarming … predictions.

Examiner's comments: This student accurately repeats every word, with adequate pronunciation. There is an unnaturally long pause before the word 'predictions', which would prevent the response from achieving a maximum score for fluency.

Student's overall PTE Academic score: 89

▶ 206 Detailed analysis of population growth has –vealed some alarming predictions.

Examiner's comments: This student accurately repeats most words, with appropriate fluency. However, he says 'revealed' in an unclear way so would not achieve a maximum score for pronunciation.

⑩ Topic: College laboratories

Student's overall PTE Academic score: 45

▸207 Please note that the laboratory will be closed next week.

Examiner's comments: This student repeats most of the sentence correctly and clearly. Her fluency is adequate but the omissions of the words 'college', 'for' and 'cleaning' would reduce the response's score.

Student's overall PTE Academic score: 74

▸208 Please note that the laboratories will be … closed during the cleaning.

Examiner's comments: This student replaces 'for cleaning next week' with 'during the cleaning', which would reduce the score. However, fluency is good and pronunciation is adequate.

Student's overall PTE Academic score: 89

▸209 Please note that the college laboratories will be closed for maintenance next week.

Examiner's comments: This student accurately repeats most words, with appropriate fluency and pronunciation. The student says 'maintenance' rather than 'cleaning' and therefore would not achieve a maximum score.

TEST 1

STUDENT ANSWERS

Test 1, Speaking

Describe image

❶ Topic: Percentage world population by region

Student's overall PTE Academic score: 55

▸210 The graph illustrate … the world population of Asia and Europe, since 1950 to 2000. Ah, so, Asia … have a population of 60 percent, and remains the same. Um Europe have a … slightly decrease from 20 percent to, little over 10 percent little under– under 10 percent.

Examiner's comments: This student's response does mention some key information, including the main topic of the graph and the continents featured. However, the response would receive a low score because a key feature is severely misrepresented when he says that the dates range from '1950 until 2000', as the data actually begins in 1750. The speech is hesitant and sometimes unclear, so the student would not achieve a high score for fluency or pronunciation.

Student's overall PTE Academic score: 67

▸211 The graph shows the percentage of world population by region, namely for um Asia and Europe from 1950 up to the year 2000. From the graph it can be seen that the world population … um for Asia has constantly, decreased from 19– from 1750 to 1850. And then as from 1950 up to 2000– the year 2000 it has increased. For Europe there has been a constant increase from 1750 to 1900, and then its shows a slight decrease. Um … [*cut*]

Examiner's comments: This student misreads the data and says '1950' rather than '1750'. This misrepresentation of a key feature would significantly reduce the score. In addition, by merely reading the graph's title 'World population by region', he does not demonstrate complete understanding of the data. The score would have been improved by paraphrasing the graph's title. Despite problems with the description, the student's fluency is relatively good, and the pronunciation is clear.

Student's overall PTE Academic score: 89

▸212 Er the graph shows the world population by region. When you look at Europe, um up until the late 1800s, the world population, er I mean the European population was on the rise. From 1900 till about 2000 it's been steadily declining. However, when you look at Asia, the percentage of the world population is much, much larger, and, even though it is on the decline it's not as rapid as, the European population.

Examiner's comments: This student describes all key features of the graph, and also refers to implications when he says 'until the 1800s the European population was on the rise'. The student shows a strong understanding of the relationships between the graph's different elements through the comparison between Asian and European populations. In addition, the speech is natural and native-like in terms of fluency and pronunciation.

❷ Topic: Reasons for no longer attending school

Student's overall PTE Academic score: 45

> ▶213 This graph illustrates, the ... the amount of employment between er two groups, male and female and it can be see that er female complete study five percent more than male. And the ... personal of– or family is the the 30 percentage er, about female, the second is of– about obtain employment.

Examiner's comments: Most elements of the data are described in this response. However, because the student only reads the different labels, an understanding of the charts is not clearly demonstrated. No implications of the data or the relationship between the two charts are mentioned. In addition, the student's mispronunciation of the word 'female' sometimes makes the description impossible to understand. The student's speech is hesitant and lacks natural stress and intonation, so it would receive a low score for fluency.

Student's overall PTE Academic score: 74

> ▶214 This two charts compare a both a female and male, in er terms of the studies er economic studies, and probably in terms of the, University studies and you can see that while 65 percent of female has completed the studies, only 60 percent of male did it, however, more men, 25 percent obtain employment compare to 12 percent of er female that obtain that employment.

Examiner's comments: This student describes most key features of the charts and effectively contrasts some elements; for example, he says 'and you can see that, while 65 percent of female has completed their studies, only 60 percent of male did it'. His pronunciation is not native-like, but it is generally clear. However, fluency is poor, due to the slow speed of the speech. This slow speed prevents the student from describing all key features of the data within the time limit.

Student's overall PTE Academic score: 77

> ▶215 The graphic shows the comparison of er male and female, in terms of er, the status I think. We can see the percentage of completed study is quite similar between male and female, while male, 60 percent of the male complete their study and 65 percent of the female complete their study. However, when we look at obtain employment, the percentage of male reach as high as 25 percent while the percentage of obtain employment for female, is er quite low at 12 percent only, and the, if we look at the percentage of personal ... [*cut*]

Examiner's comments: This response would receive a good score because it describes differences and similarities between the two charts accurately. The student intelligently selects the most important features of the data – the difference between rates of 'completed study' and 'obtained employment' for males and females. However, the speech is slow and she does not have time to talk about all key features. Despite relatively poor fluency, pronunciation is quite native-like so this response would receive a good score for this.

❸ Topic: US citizens over 65 years

Student's overall PTE Academic score: 56

> ▶216 The graph showing a prediction of how US citizen, will be over the next 65 years, and we can see the growth is um, very slight, from 2010 to 2035 and we can see, there will be only um, seven percent peep– um population, more than now in 65 years, so we can see how they will control the birth.

Examiner's comments: This student misrepresents the key feature of the chart. He incorrectly says the chart shows 'a prediction of how US citizens will be *over the next 65 years*', whereas the chart actually shows a prediction of how many US citizens *who are over 65 years old* there will be within a 25-year period. The student also says 'the growth is very slight' but actually it is significant (over 60 percent). Despite poor fluency, his pronunciation is adequate.

Student's overall PTE Academic score: 67

> ▶217 The graph shows the percentage of US citizens over 65 years from the year 2010 until 2035. Basically it is a prediction, um as from the year 2012 and it can be seen that, the um population of over 65 is gonna constantly increase over the years. In the US.

Examiner's comments: This student mentions one key element of the data which is that the population of US citizens over 65 'will constantly increase'. However, there is no mention of any figures. The score would have been higher if the student had said 'will constantly increase from 12.5 percent to 20 percent of the population'. In addition, he misrepresents a key feature when he says '2012', as this year is not included in the data. Fluency and pronunciation are of an intermediate level, but the answer is too short.

Student's overall PTE Academic score: 77

> ▸218 The graphic shows the percentage of US citizens aged over 65 years old, across the year 2010 to 2035, so it's an estimative, number I think. We see that the percentage of citizens over 65 years old, er will be expected to grow steadily over the years, in 2010 it reach about 13 percent, while in 2035 is expected to reach as high as 20 percent.

Examiner's comments: This student clearly states all of the key features of the chart. There is statistical information in the response and it shows that she understands that the figures are predictions. Although the answer would receive a good score, it would not get maximum points as the student fails to develop the answer by mentioning possible causes for the changes in population. Fluency and pronunciation are both strong.

4 Topic: Revenue growth

Student's overall PTE Academic score: 56

> ▸219 The graph showing the revenue will generate by two companies X and Y and as you can see, both of the company will start from 0 and in 18 years, the position that Y company will exit X revenue. From the beginning to the end X company's revenue was growing slowly as er Y, but from 2018, Y company has got boom in their revenue.

Examiner's comments: This student mentions some key features, such as the speed of growth, and compares the two companies. However, the comparison is limited to the speed of growth, and the amount of revenue is not mentioned. In addition, there is a misrepresentation of some basic features of the graph; for example, the student says 'both companies will start from 0', whereas, in fact, Company X starts with $300 million revenue. His pronunciation is of an intermediate level, but his fluency is relatively poor.

Student's overall PTE Academic score: 67

> ▸220 The graph shows the revenue growth in terms of millions for two companies, namely company X and company Y, from the year 2006 until 2024. It can be seen that company X has a more steady growth over the years when compared to company Y. … Although both of them seem to attain the same amount of growth, um by the year 2024.

Examiner's comments: This student clearly describes some key features of the graph and compares Company X's and Company Y's growth and revenue accurately. However, the description does not mention the amount of revenue in millions of dollars, which is another key feature. The speed of speech is usually very good, but the student would fail to achieve a maximum fluency score because of a long pause between 'Company Y' and 'although both of them'.

Student's overall PTE Academic score: 89

> ▸221 Um this graph shows the revenue growth for two different companies. Company Y starting in about 2006 – it's starting at the bottom, so that's probably a new company, and it, well it rises quite a lot up until 2024, where it's at 2,000 million dollars. Company X started about 300 million dollars and rises to 1,800 million dollars. However Company Y, it seems to rise exponentially and Company X is a bit more constant.

Examiner's comments: This student would receive a maximum score for his answer. Every key feature of the graph is mentioned, and implications of the data, such as saying Company Y 'is probably a new company' because of its low revenue at the start of the period, are also clearly described. The student's speech is native-like in terms of fluency and pronunciation.

5 Topic: Reading achievement

Student's overall PTE Academic score: 45

> ▸222 This graph illustrates the … reading achievement through the Grade 1 to Grade 3. Er … this success– successful readers, the highest point is 120, and, that– that means that er … they– they know 120 words per minute. This is about the oral reading fluency, and … [*cut*]

Examiner's comments: This student does not mention many key features of the graph, such as the struggling readers and Grades 1 to 3. In addition, this response would receive a low score because the student misrepresents another key point by saying that successful readers 'know' 120 words per minute. In fact, successful readers 'can read' 120 words per minute. Her answer is slow and she frequently pauses in a way which is not native-like. Pronunciation is adequate.

Student's overall PTE Academic score: 67

▶ 223 The graph shows the reading achievement for three different Grades, over three different seasons, namely Grade 1 2 3 over fall, winter and spring. It can be sure– it can be seen that, struggling the– Grades for struggling rea– readers has um, been quite um constant, whereas the Grade for successful readers has increased constantly.

Examiner's comments: This student describes some but not all the key features of the graph. The number of words per minute that struggling and successful readers can read is not mentioned, so the difference between these two groups is not shown. However, the response does successfully describe the changes in these groups' ability from Grade 1 to 2. The student's fluency is poor and pronunciation is clear, but it is not native-like.

Student's overall PTE Academic score: 89

▶ 224 And this graph shows the oral reading fluency in words per minute for successful readers and struggling readers. Starting with the successful readers, they can read 20 words per minute in Grade 1, and then two years later they can read up to 120 words a minute, which is about six times as much. Struggling readers can only read about seven to eight words a minute when they start and two years later they are stuck on about 40 words per minute.

Examiner's comments: This student describes all key features of the graph, with native-like fluency and pronunciation. This answer would receive a very high score, but not a maximum score because it does not develop beyond description. In order to obtain a maximum score, some implications of the data on the graph should be mentioned, such as reasons why successful Grade 1 readers improve more rapidly.

TEST 1

6 Topic: Shadouf

Student's overall PTE Academic score: 45

▶ 225 OK just, er flow chart illustrates the ... er method of water collection. At the beginning of the process, the operator moves er, the ... pivot up and down and the other person, collect the water, and ... the level rise and dow, to collect the water, and ... so it can be see that, needs two– two... [*unclear*]

Examiner's comments: This student would receive a high score for describing most key features of the diagram. However, poor pronunciation of important words, such as 'operator', sometimes makes the description difficult to understand. This would reduce the score for pronunciation and the overall score. As the student frequently hesitates at unnatural times, the score for fluency would also be low.

STUDENT ANSWERS

Student's overall PTE Academic score: 67

▶ 226 The graph shows a method of water collection. The operator moves up and down um the– moves up the walk way so as to pivot the walkway and ... and make the level fall, and ... following which the bucket um drops into the water, with the suspending rope ... Once the water is collected the operator moves down and the bucket comes up and, the um other operator at the other end of the rope ... [*cut*]

Examiner's comments: This student's speech has many hesitations and repetitions, which would reduce the score for fluency. In addition, he mispronounces many key words such as 'pivot', which makes the description of the diagram's features unclear at times. However, the answer does successfully mention most basic features of the diagram.

Student's overall PTE Academic score: 89

▶ 227 The diagram shows a method of water collection called, I think, shadouf. Um there's a climbing post with notches which you climb up on, and then there's a walkway with stairs on it. As the operator moves up and down the stairs, a lever rises and falls, causing a bucket to drop in the water or to rise from the water. Someone else erm, can just get the bucket and the water on the other side.

Examiner's comments: This student describes all key features of the graph, with native-like fluency and pronunciation. The answer would receive a very high score, but not a maximum score because it does not develop beyond description. In order to obtain a maximum score, the student should comment on the implications of the diagram; for example, they could say the diagram shows that shadouf was a simple and effective way to get water.

Test 1, Speaking

Re-tell lecture

❶ Topic: Air pollution

Student's overall PTE Academic score: 56

▶ 228 The speaker was talking about er, the change in air pollution and he was talking a 99, 1950s, there was air pollution called Black Fog, which normally called by the factories, and caused to the, lots of health problem which leads, to 4,000 deaths in London. In 1956, they, made a legislation, to clean the air, but most, still it is a big issue, to the environment, but now the difference is we can't see the pollution, um we use lots of cars and lorries and which … [*cut*]

Examiner's comments: This student's description of the first half of the lecture is very good. However, because his speech is slow and hesitant, he does not complete the description and fails to mention many key points from the second half of the lecture. Pronunciation is relatively good, but the score for fluency and the overall score would be low.

Student's overall PTE Academic score: 74

▶ 229 Er the issue for air pollution is analysed by the speaker and he mentioned that it was an issue since 1950. Er at the time in the 50s, pollution was too many too factories, and those factories were actually causing severe health problems er in– in Britain. The– the Clean Act was introduced to resolve these problems. Today it is still and issue, however, we cannot see the pollution, the pollution is not visible. Still has … [*cut*]

Examiner's comments: This student effectively describes most key points of the lecture. However, the answer fails to mention examples, such as 4,000 deaths in 1952, so it would not achieve a maximum score for content. The student's pronunciation and fluency are both slightly above intermediate level.

Student's overall PTE Academic score: 77

▶ 230 Um this, this lecture compares the changes of air pollution in 1950s and the twenty-first century. In about 1950s, er the air pollution was visible; people could see a black fogs or a clouds in the sky. And the sources of air pollution come, majorly come from the factories and it caused the severe er health problem, and they caused something like 4,000 death in London. And in 1950, there is a Clean Air Act introduced to the UK and it improved the conditions, however nowadays … [*cut*]

Examiner's comments: This student mentions some key points from the lecture, but fails to describe the situation nowadays, so the overall score would be relatively low. In addition, she does not develop her answer or mention any implications or conclusions of the lecture. However, the student would receive a good score for fluency and pronunciation.

❷ Topic: Focus groups

Student's overall PTE Academic score: 45

▶ 231 The speaker talk about the researcher and how do the focus group, how, er find out the, the information that you need with er, through focus group. So, the first, er important information is how large is the group, the ideal is, er six to seven people. And bigger than, bigger than seven could be break the conversation and change the focus. The second erm … [*cut*]

Examiner's comments: This lecture contains three main points about focus groups, and this student only mentions one of them, namely the importance of the size of the focus group. For this reason, the overall score would be very low. The student's speech is slow and there are frequent pauses in a way which is not native-like. In order to improve the score, the test taker should give an overview of all the key points of the lecture at the start of the response.

Student's overall PTE Academic score: 67

▶ 232 The lecture is about tips or how to use a focus group. It is mainly about what the focus group is about, how large er the focus group should be and also the minimum number of people in the focus group. Um also the focus group needs to have a moderator, so as to ensure that um, everybody in the focus group is actually participating and that nobody is actually going away from the subject matter of the lecture.

Examiner's comments: This student's response mentions some but not all of the lecture's main points. Although the response mentions the importance of size and moderators for focus groups, it does not mention the lecturer's third point regarding materials, such as photos and diagrams. Therefore, the answer would not achieve a high score for content. However, pronunciation is clear and the speech contains very few long hesitations.

Student's overall PTE Academic score: 74

▶ 233 This er lecture talks about, what, a focus group is and what major areas need to be pay attention to when you are planning to use a focus group, so first of all what is the perfect size of a ... focus group. Ideally it should be somewhere between six and seven. If it's too small, then you may not be able to get all the er, opinions you like. If the group is too large then the people might start to have some side conversation. And the second, key point is you need to have a moderator to facilitate and guide the discussion, and to make sure that the discussion is, well on– on the track.

Examiner's comments: This student gives a good overview of the first two of the lecture's three main points, the size of the focus groups, and the role of the moderator. Speech is very fluent and the answer would therefore receive a good score for this and for pronunciation. However, the answer does not mention the lecture's third main point, the need for materials such as photos and diagrams, and it does not develop further, so it would not receive maximum points.

❸ Topic: Setting up a website

Student's overall PTE Academic score: 45

▶ 234 So it is important if you want to, err start a website, err to understand the really value to, to do this. So the first one is, who is your target and what, what he need, and the second is accessibility, and the third one is retention. About accessibility, make sure that your site, should be finded in the last one [*unclear word*], make sure that information's exactly what the people need.

Examiner's comments: This student presents a good overview of the lecture's three main points about setting up a website – target audience, accessibility, and retention. However, the student does not fluently develop the answer and does not mention the implications of the lecture. In addition, pronunciation is very poor and it is often very difficult to understand what it is being said; for example, the student says that websites must be 'finded', instead of correctly saying 'found'.

Student's overall PTE Academic score: 67

▶ 235 The lecture is about setting up a website, and the, um, author is giving three main points that people need to focus about. First being who the target audience is, that is, um, group the people by what the people need, second being the accessibility of the website, that is, to make sure that the website can be found either by, links via other websites or the social media. And the third point would be, um retention. That is, to make sure that the target audience returns to the website and this can be achieved by um, keeping the website up-to-date, and having more interesting news so as ... [*cut*]

Examiner's comments: This student's response effectively describes all three main points of the lecture, and gives details about the first two main points. It would not receive a maximum score for content because it does not describe details about 'retention', the lecturer's third main point. Pronunciation and fluency are good, but the speech is clearly not native-like, so the student would not score maximum points for either skill.

Student's overall PTE Academic score: 77

▶ 236 This er lecture talks about how to set out, a website and, add value to your website. So the most important thing is you need to know who your target audience is, what information that your audience might want to find on your website and the design, the content of the website need to be based on their needs. And the second thing need to consider, you need to consider is the accessibility. How your website can be found. Maybe the, the, you can provide links on other website or you can use a social media. And the third point is the retention, how you make sure that the, your user will be re– returning to your website.

Examiner's comments: This answer would receive a high score because it clearly describes the key points of the lecture, and provides details about each point – target audience, accessibility, and retention. Although all the key points are included accurately, it does not describe the implications of the lecture; for example, it does not mention that setting up a website requires lots of time. For this reason, the response would not achieve a maximum score. However, fluency and pronunciation are both very strong.

Test 1, Writing

Summarize written text

❶ Topic: Tea

Student's overall PTE Academic score: 55

> The second most popular drink in the world after water is tea which mostly came from Asia because it requieres particular weather factors to grown up such as temperature, rainfall, diferent altitudes, and other kind of tress and vegetation around necessaries to give the tea the best quiality.

Examiner's comments: Appropriately, this answer is one sentence and this student's response provides a fair summary of the passage's content. However, it does not include one key aspect – the fact that, after being originally grown in three countries, tea is now a major export for over 50 countries. In addition, this student's response has poor grammar ('to grown up') and spelling ('requieres', 'diferent', 'tress', and 'quiality'), which would reduce their score.

Student's overall PTE Academic score: 74

> Producing a good quality tea that is highly demanded by world's consumers requires certain growing conditions, such as a suitable weather environment and specific geographical features.

Examiner's comments: This response does not include one key aspect – the fact that, after being originally grown in three countries, tea is now a major export for over 50 countries. Although the answer is appropriately one sentence in length, it does not contain sufficient information to be an effective summary. On the other hand, the student has used a correct grammatical structure and a suitable choice of words.

Student's overall PTE Academic score: 89

> Having originally been grown in three countries, Tea is now produced in over fifty and behind only water it is one of the most popular drinks in the world, as it is used in social settings and appeals to a wide variety of tastes.

Examiner's comments: This student's summary of the passage has the appropriate length and contains accurate grammatical structure. The response also has appropriate choice of words and provides a strong summary of the passage's main points.

❷ Topic: Over-fishing

Student's overall PTE Academic score: 55

> Currently people are trying to help the environment in order to preserve a balance in the ecosystem, and fishing is an activity that is every day is increasing since the demand of healthy meat rise around the world.

Examiner's comments: This answer's good points are its length (just one sentence), and the fact that it provides a fair summary of the passage. However, the summary does not make the link between fishing and protecting the earth clear. In addition, the student has made grammatical errors ('is every day is' and 'the demand of healthy meat rise') which could make his response difficult to understand. As there are no spelling mistakes, this student would receive the maximum spelling score.

Student's overall PTE Academic score: 67

> Along with preserving the planet, we should also be preserving fish as nowadays it considered as healthy compared to meat and its consumption has increased which can result to extinction because of overfishing and hence a negative effect on the ecosystems.

Examiner's comments: This answer provides a good summary of the passage's main points in one sentence and it makes the link between preserving fish and the environment reasonably clear. However, there are grammatical errors ('nowadays it considered') and mistakes with word choice ('can result to extinction') which would reduce the student's score.

Student's overall PTE Academic score: 89

> The consumption of fish has skyrocketed in the developed world, leading to overfishing and ultimately extinction and destruction of entire ecosystems.

Examiner's comments: This student's response provides a good summary of the main points of the passage in one sentence. In addition, it contains no grammatical errors or mistakes with vocabulary.

Test 1, Writing

Write essay

❶ Topic: Increasing life expectancy

Student's overall PTE Academic score: 45

> Can you imagine a world without any desease? In large part of the world the life expectancy are becoming increasingly concern and tought. Some people believe that the advances in medical care are the solution of the problems with ageing for men and women. In stark contrast, othesbelieve that it is just a excuse to make money as well as could bring some unkowndemagde to body. I firmly believe that the increase of life expentancy is a positive develop of human being. This issue warrants further discussion.
>
> An obvious starting point is that with more years to live, all people will have more chance and time to do what they really what to do in their lifes. This is particularly relevant when you consider that is to unfair when in the past young people died before fulfill their dreams. A clear example of this is case of people who died just because the medicine do not know how to solve their desease.
>
> It is often cited that if people live more, people just will suffer for more years. Whist, if all human being could live longer, they could take care more properly of health and do …

Examiner's comments: This student's essay is incomplete and, therefore, would receive a low score for development, structure and coherence. As the last paragraph in the body of the essay is not finished, the student's last point is not easy to understand. There are frequent grammatical errors, such as 'the life expectancy are becoming' and 'when you consider that is to unfair when …', and these errors prevent effective communication. The student would also lose points for frequent spelling mistakes and for the inadequate length of the essay (198 words).

Student's overall PTE Academic score: 67

> Nowadays, medical science is well advanced and this has eventually led to the average life expectancy of human beings to increase. This of course has both its advantages and disadvantages. Let's talk about the latter.
>
> The first disadvantage with an ageing population is that the society has to provide more for the old people in terms of benefits. Secondly the young people of nowadays can find it as a burden to look after the aged ones; and the longer they live, the longer they will have to be looked after. Also aged people tend to have health issues and as a matter of fact, that means that they need to be looked after. In the busy world that we live nowadays, this might not be always possible. Therefore aged people will end up being sent to homes and they might not like it. Also, more hospitals will be needed.
>
> One personal example is my grandfather who passed away when I was a kid. He was quite old and due to a mixture of diseases he was suffering from, he needed someone to look after him all the time. He was quite fortunate to have someone by his side all the time.
>
> As a conclusion, I would like to say that there is no point in increasing the life expectancy of human beings if they will end up suffering. I'd rather people die younger without having to suffer rather than living donkey years and having to suffer.

Examiner's comments: This student has dealt with the question quite well. The response clearly describes some disadvantages of an increasing life expectancy, and supports this point of view well with reasons and examples. However, the response does not deal directly with the question 'Do you think most people will see this as a positive development?' Although the essay mentions that young people find looking after old people a burden, this part of the essay could have been improved by stating that 'Most people think that this development is (not) a positive one'.

The student's choice of vocabulary is sufficient to provide a clear description, but the term 'donkey years' is inappropriately casual and vague. In order to achieve a maximum vocabulary score, the test taker would need to use more precise language. The essay has appropriate development, structure and cohesion. With 246 words, it has appropriate length.

Student's overall PTE Academic score: 89

The average life expectancy has gone up, due to medical advances. This brings many issues with it, mostly financial and will continue to do so for the foreseeable future.

As birth rates all over the world have gone up and death rates have been steadily declining, an imbalance has been created, leaving the world overpopulated. Many ailments that simply didn't exist in the last century have now suddenly cropped up due to our increased lifespan. Contributions towards social health care will have to increase to accommodate this phenomenon. I've noticed over the past 10 years that mediction for more and more ilnesses aren't included in the "free" part of the public health system any more, and personal contributions have gone up.

In addition, the stereotype is that the elderly can't work, and this thinking will almost certainly be perpetuated in the workplace; this has (and will) put an enormous strain on benefits systems, as the work force will once again have to pay up. This has made the current recession very difficult to manage, as the majority of people have little disposable income left, and cannot afford to contribute more to the welfare state, myself included.

Lastly, housing will become an even bigger problem than it is, as younger people generally don't mind living in shared accomodation, whereas the elderly prefer not to. The only exception is when they live in care homes, due to physical restraints. This has effected me personally: when I wanted my own space, it was almost ompossible to receive a house from the council as most of them were earmarked for the retired.

In conclusion, the increased life expectancy is creating massive problems globally.

Examiner's comments: The essay answers the questions effectively and supports the student's opinion with strong explanations and a wide variety of examples. There is good development and a logical structure. The essay also shows consistent control of complex language. The student's range of vocabulary is good enough to clearly express arguments and points of view. With 277 words, the essay is appropriate in length. However, the student would lose points for spelling mistakes ('effected' and 'accomodation') and a typing error ('ompossible').

TEST 1

STUDENT ANSWERS

2 Topic: Preparation for university or work

Student's overall PTE Academic score: 45

In Brazil you bargaing for this common statement: "Is better have your own business instead of do nothing at university". Some believe that it is extremely impportant that schools prepared pupils for university. I am of the opinion that it is relevant teach students how university works but also more impportant is prepare young people for a real life, for work. What are the consequences of take this instance?

In some countries it is often cited that is better to prepare young people for academic life rather than for professional life when they were just at school. However, it is extremaly relevant consider that student needs to know about work to be more prepared for the university as well. A clear illustration of this is students who do not know what they whant to do for the rest of their lifes as well as spend years to finally find what they really like and are happy doing it.

On the other hand, it is not correct the student start in the university withou any preparation.

Examiner's comments: This student's response contains defective choices of words and spelling mistakes which make the response very difficult to understand from the first sentence onwards. The essay has no conclusion and, therefore, the student would receive a low score for development, structure and coherence. In addition, the essay is only 175 words, so it would not receive full points for length, which should be between 200 and 300 words.

Student's overall PTE Academic score: 67

The following statement 'schools should prepare students for university, rather than for work' can be argued both ways. I personally think that schools should actually prepare students for both university and work.

The reasons why I believe that schools should prepare students for university are as follows. First of all, university is the next level after school and therefore, there is every reason for its preparation. As there is a big gap between school level and university level, the preparation will help to breach that gap. Also, at university level, there is less spoon feeding and more self study. So, if school children are prepared for that, it will help and this can lead to better results.

Schools should on the other hand, also prepare students for work. The gap between school and work is even bigger than the gap between school and university. As a matter of fact, preparing children for work at school level will help to shorten the gap between university and work. If students are at a young age being inbuilt with work values, this will help to develop better and more responsible students.

In a nutshell, I would say that school should be encouraged to prepare students for both university and work. This will have a positive impact on the individuals, thus helping them for the future.

Examiner's comments: This is a good essay which clearly shows the student's opinion and supports it with reasons and examples. The answer is appropriately divided into paragraphs and the introduction and conclusion are both written in a suitable style. With 222 words, the essay is also appropriate in length. The student has also used a wide range of language and grammatical structures, yet one or two points are slightly unclear, particularly in the second paragraph.

Student's overall PTE Academic score: 89

I think that schools should prepare for work, rather than university as they are two completely different worlds, and often mutually exclusive.

School is meant to give you a solid grounding in life, from where you can flourish, whether it be further studies or work. It is a fact that most people will only spend a small part of their lives in university, and a larger proportion in the workforce. For instance, I spent roughly 6 years in university, and have spent many more years as a worker. Surely it makes more sense to pour resources into what will effect people for greater periods of time?

Also, a university does not guarantee a job; I know many people with impressive degrees, who simply cannot find any work due to lack of work experience. A lot of employers are also struggling due to what I call the "bitesize culture": Schools create unrealistic expectations for students because everything is being spoon fed. Managers simply have neither the time, nor the patience to spoon feed new recruits. This is especially noticably when it comes to spelling and appropriate social behaviour

University is but one way to nurturing a successful life, and should be treated as such; in the current recession we see a lot less young people opting for university

Examiner's comments: This essay answers the questions effectively and supports the student's opinion with strong explanations and a wide variety of examples. There is good development and a logical structure. The essay also shows consistent control of complex language. The student's range of vocabulary is good enough to clearly express arguments and points of view. With 217 words, the essay is appropriate in length. However, the student would lose points for spelling mistakes ('will effect' and 'noticably') and a grammar error ('one way to nurturing').

Test 1, Listening

Summarize spoken text

1 Topic: Technological nature

Student's overall PTE Academic score: 45

Nature's picture is real view of life. People who appretiate pictures of nature recover of stress. Exist two groups of people and both groups agree that nature picture is recovering.

Examiner's comments: This student's response is too short (only 30 words) and it omits the main aspect of the short lecture; it does not mention the comparison between real nature and a virtual picture of nature. The answer does mention one relevant aspect, the fact that the two groups agreed, but it contains very poor choices of vocabulary, such as 'recovering', which prevent effective communication. In addition, there is a spelling mistake, 'appretiate'. Therefore, this response would receive a very low score.

Student's overall PTE Academic score: 74

The speaker talks about technological nature, which is used to produce a picture that seems real using computer graphics. A scene of nature for example could be beneficial for an ill person. However, when doing an experiment with two groups (one with a real view and another one with a virtual view), it is demonstrated that the recovery from stress is faster with the real view.

Examiner's comments: The student's response contains all of the main points from the short lecture and it is of appropriate length (66 words). However, some of the word choices are poor and unnatural; for example, the meaning of 'technological nature' could be explained more effectively. The answer contains appropriate grammatical structure.

Student's overall PTE Academic score: 77

This lecture describes new technology using computer graphics to create virtual natural scenes and discusses to what extent such virtual images would have the same beneficial impact as the real natural scene. One study shows that the group with an authentic natural garden scene recovers much faster than the other group presented with a virtual one, which concludes that the virtual image cannot re-create the same effect as the real nature.

Examiner's comments: This student has summarised all the key points from the lecture. The grammatical structure used is appropriate and does not lead to problems in communication. The student has also selected suitable vocabulary for the summary. With 71 words, it is appropriate in length, and there are no spelling mistakes.

❷ Topic: Memories in criminal trials

Student's overall PTE Academic score: 55

> In criminals crimes there are various ways to investigate and look for details about the crime. Researchers found that if different people watch a video of the situation everybody describes different things and see other type of evidence. These is useful to obtain more details and information on a crime with the aim of solving it faster developing the process.

Examiner's comments: This student's answer provides a fair summary of the lecture. It correctly mentions that people who watch a video describe different things, but because of poor choice of vocabulary, it does not make the link of this fact to memory clear. The summary is also weak because it does not describe the importance of memory to criminal trials, which is one of the lecturer's main points. The length of the response is suitable, but it would also lose points for grammatical errors which hinder communication, such as 'These is useful'.

Student's overall PTE Academic score: 74

> In criminal trials, memory becomes an important factor, as witnesses are often used to prove evidence. However, memory can be unreliable if witnesses need to recall events that happen some time in the past. It has been demonstrated that when retelling events, witnesses may include objects that were never there in real. They may therefore distort reality.

Examiner's comments: This student's answer contains all the key points from the lecture, however, some mistakes with vocabulary would reduce the score. For example, the summary says that witnesses 'prove' evidence, whereas actually witnesses 'provide' evidence. It also says 'events that happen some time in the past', but this should be written in the past tense as 'happened'. With 57 words, the answer is a suitable length, and the choice of vocabulary is also appropriate.

Student's overall PTE Academic score: 77

> In criminal courts, the prosecution or the defence usually have witnesses to testify for them. However, research has shown that human's memories are not as reliable as expected when new information is added. For example, the subjects are asked to re-tell what they see in a video, and they would describe something that is never included in the video when new idea or object is presented.

Examiner's comments: This student's summary has an appropriate number of words (66) and it describes all the main points from the short lecture, including the importance of memory in criminal courts and the results of the research. The choice of vocabulary and the use of grammar are both accurate, and the summary has no spelling mistakes.